The Essential
Ernest Holmes

Also by Ernest Holmes

The Essential
Ernest Holmes

Edited by the
Reverend Jesse Jennings

Jeremy P. Tarcher/Putnam
a member of Penguin Putnam Inc.
New York

Most Tarcher/Putnam books are available at special quantity discounts for bulk purchase for sales promotions, premiums, fund-raising, and educational needs. Special books or book excerpts also can be created to fit specific needs. For details, write Putnam Special Markets, 375 Hudson Street, New York, NY 10014.

Jeremy P. Tarcher/Putnam
a member of
Penguin Putnam Inc.
375 Hudson Street
New York, NY 10014
www.penguinputnam.com

Library of Congress Cataloging-in-Publication Data

Holmes, Ernest, 1887–1960.
[Selections. 2002]
The essential Ernest Holmes / edited by Jesse Jennings.
p. cm.
Includes bibliographical references and index.
ISBN 1-58542-181-2
1. United Church of Religious Science—Doctrines.
I. Jennings, Jesse.   II. Title.
BP605.U53 H625   2002   2002025698
299'.93—dc21

Printed in the United States of America
1   3   5   7   9   10   8   6   4   2

Book design by Meighan Cavanaugh

For my grandparents,

Merrill and Nita Katherman

Acknowledgments

I am grateful to the United Church of Religious Science for asking me to create this book, for the rich relationship I've enjoyed with them all of my adult life, and for continuing to bring Ernest Holmes's life-changing message to the world. My thanks go to the editorial staff of *Science of Mind* magazine, especially Jim Shea; Rev. Lee Hite, who gifted me with a rare copy of Ernest's out-of-print *The Bible in the Light of Religious Science*; the archives staff of the *Los Angeles Times*; Rev. Marilyn Leo and her late husband, Dr. Richard Leo, who inaugurated the UCRS Home Office archives work; the community of Creative Life Spiritual Center, which both employs me and cheers me on in new endeavors; and most of all my tremendously thoughtful and supportive wife, Jaye Barrow.

Contents

Part III
The Veil Is Thin Between

You may be sure of this: there is an integrity to your soul such as you will find nowhere else in the Universe. Here you will meet life; here you will decide; and here you may neutralize the thought patterns of the ages by simply denying them—and saying something greater than that (and I believe in it): "There is a Power greater than I am, and I accept It." And no matter what the mistakes are, the Universe holds nothing against us, ever.

—ERNEST HOLMES

Happy is he who knows the causes of things.

—VIRGIL

Foreword

Selecting the core of Ernest Holmes's writings has been a joyful exercise and a highly subjective one. To me, everything he expressed is worth hearing. We may run across the same ideas stated numerous different ways from book to book, but they are extraordinary ideas, and the more we hear them the more likely we are to let them reshape our beliefs about the world and how it works. When we encounter them, at the least, we're a little more peaceful, a little more happy; at most, our lives are completely transformed.

Some of the writings included here are from the "textbook" of the institution he founded, and his masterwork—*The Science of Mind*—a hugely worthwhile study in both the standard 1938 version and the 1926 original. Excerpts deal with Ernest's occasionally overlooked insights on sexuality and psychic phenomena. Also featured are selections from *This Thing Called Life* and *This Thing Called You*, which, when read completely, help to personalize Ernest's freeing message. Selections from *The Voice Celestial*, an astonishing book-length epic poem that Ernest wrote with his brother Fenwicke, begin each chapter here, but the whole work warrants devouring. And I'm very taken with the three books compiled, mostly from Ernest's class lectures to practitioners, by the late George Bendall—*The Anatomy of Healing Prayer, Ideas of Power,* and *The Philosophy of Ernest Holmes.* As presented here, they reveal a chatty, relaxed individual in his perfect element: teaching.

In assembling this material, I refer to the man by his given name as was the practice among all who knew him, and I have altered as little as reasonably possible in his words. Ellipses are mostly mine, sometimes his. Where mine, I've skipped either his brief restatements of a preceding thought, or a favorite verse of poetry or Bible passage he used to punctuate a point. Also, Ernest wrote as energetically as he spoke, so in the same sentence he might emphasize a statement in a noisy mixture of italics or all capitals. I have put both in italics for sheer ease of reading. I kept his vagaries of initial capitalization of such words as *life, reality, truth* and *universe;* and would point out to anyone new to his work that over the course of his writing life he used several terms for Deity interchangeably: chiefly God or Father ("He"), and Presence, Spirit, or Father/Mother God ("That" or "It")—and Life, Reality, Truth and Universe were synonyms for It.

As to his exclusive use of male pronouns in generic situations—which may be a little jarring to the modern ear of either gender—the whole gist of his teaching makes clear he meant neither offense nor exclusion in wording things as he did. These terms have been left as Ernest rendered them.

Introduction

An obituary article in the April 8, 1960, *Los Angeles Times* called him "one of America's leading churchmen-philosophers . . . the active leader of a denomination of more than 100,000 members in 62 churches throughout the United States . . . [whose] writings have been followed by many famous religious thinkers and authors, including Dr. Norman Vincent Peale."

Ernest Shurtleff Holmes had passed away at age seventy-two, leaving behind a legacy that only now is beginning really to flourish in the world. Being a spiritual genius just naturally puts you ahead of your time.

Ernest was a butcher's apprentice, scoutmaster, purchasing agent and self-taught lecturer whose steel-trap intellect and personal charisma eventually led people by the thousands to his lectures in a succession of ever-larger venues across greater Los Angeles, and periodically elsewhere. He published his first book, *Creative Mind*, in 1918 at the age of thirty-one. He married a widowed opera singer, Hazel Foster, fairly late in life, had no children, and loved company and conversation, often dining with entertainers one day and university department heads the next. He started a magazine, *Uplift*, which in 1927 became *Science of Mind* and is still published monthly. His lectures caused some to seek him out for in-depth mentoring, which grew into the Institute of Religious Science and Philosophy, where men and women could be trained as practitioners of the art of spiritual mind treatment, the particular form of affirmative prayer he was developing.

Recollections by his longtime friend and colleague Reginald Armor and others indicate that Ernest was genuinely surprised at the massive turnouts for his public talks, and took it not to mean that he was anyone special, but as a sign that people were hungering for someone, anyone, to offer them consistent, logical spiritual nourishment. He especially liked that his audiences came from all walks of life, and encouraged them to take what they learned from him back into their own houses of worship to enhance their experience of the spiritual paths they were already on. Still, it was inevitable that sooner or later, having tried this, some would return to him and complain how their original affiliations just didn't fit for them anymore—and would he please start a church?

His initial alarm at this idea is chronicled in several places (see chapter 8), and it's a credit to the church he did start that his reaction still gets brought up among Religious Science clergy and congregants in the form of "Are we doing the right thing?" As a Religious Science minister, I've heard committee deliberations on everything from writing a new mission statement to improving ministerial training fall back to the same question: "Are we really a church?"

What evidently swayed him into going the religious route was a combination of practicality—it was what the people wanted—and ingenuity—a church organization would be cobbled together that could model the essence of the Science of Mind teaching: democratic, equitable, and honoring of the direct spiritual experience of everybody alike, rather than enforcing one person's divine revelation handed down through the generations as stale but rigid dogma.

Whereas the practicality may have suffered somewhat over time—there are not today millions of card-carrying Religious Scientists, nor churches in every neighborhood (except in Los Angeles, where it all started)—the ingenuity lingers on, particularly in its sense of human equity. For example, while Ernest was in many respects a man of his era, his denomination was among the first of any stripe in America to license and ordain women to its ministry.

The equitable aspect wasn't always seamless. The third branch church to be organized and chartered was in East Los Angeles, led by Rev. J. Arthur Twyne, an African-American, with a congregation both black and white. When some complaints were murmured about this (resulting in the June 1945 issue of *Science of Mind* magazine dropping East Side from first to last in the hitherto alphabetical listing of metropolitan L.A. branches—and tacking on the designation "Colored"), Ernest arranged with his friend Rev. Twyne to go there and speak. To a hushed, packed house, he began, "I have been told that too many non-Caucasians attend these lectures. True, there are Caucasians and non-Caucasians in this congregation. But this we must affirm: We are all children of One Living God—One Life that permeates all, without exception—One Intelligence that governs all—and, most important, every man and woman who abides in the universe is a significant entity in the One Universal Consciousness. Our doors will forever be open to all. Whoever you are, be proud—you are a Divine Idea in the Mind of God."

The magazine immediately reverted to the way it had been. Somebody had briefly bowed to the segregationist conventions of the day, only to be reminded that Ernest's teachings were anything but conventional—or exclusive.

Profound influences on Ernest's thinking included Ralph Waldo Emerson, whose transcendentalist essays he had read growing up in rural Maine; the Christian Science doctrine of Mary Baker Eddy, which he encountered in Boston; and the mental science ideas of British judge Thomas Troward. He called himself (and, later, his organization) Christian but defined true Christianity as adherence to the specific teachings of Jesus on forgiveness, loving one another, prayer "in faith believing" and God as a loving Father rather than cruel disciplinarian. He rejected all notions of duality, whether of opposing good and evil forces wrestling over the world's soul, or obstinate humankind and its grieving Creator, or real mind versus illusory matter. Everything, he said, could be reconciled into one Thing, Itself: something infinite, eternal, ever fully present and creative and utterly begging of description, so that all we have left to call it is God.

Getting to know Ernest Holmes through his work, I find someone who was modest about his own abilities and relentless in his elevation of everybody else's. He felt he knew what made people tick, yet throughout his life he seems never to have met a person who didn't intrigue him with his newness, always remaining willing to be astonished by what he found in human actions and reactions. Similarly, while setting forth a series of spiritual laws that describe the universe as a whole system, he rejoiced in the likelihood that new laws of Spirit and matter would sometime be found to encompass what was already known, in the same way that laws governing flight build upon the law of gravity. He insisted that his teachings remain forever "open at the top" when entrusted to the structures he left behind.

Even if Religious Science as such should become a huge presence in the world (or "the next great spiritual impulsion," as he styled it), the light Ernest Holmes cast will always outpace the groups and writings that travel under his name. The obituary mentions Dr. Peale's acquaintance with Ernest's work, but cannot enumerate the countless number of leaders in every field who at some point crossed paths then and since with the ideas Ernest espoused. Human potential and self-help books dominate the publishing industry today. Fundamentalist firebrands who would turn and run from Ernest's overall theology nevertheless teach positive thinking and "praying the answer instead of the problem." Medical schools produce guided-imagery tapes, while corporations offer stress-reduction classes and meditation periods to executives. The new consciousness in our world doesn't come from any one person or theory. It's a synthesis of ancient wisdom and modern discovery, from medieval labyrinths to quantum physics. Ernest was a masterful synthesizer.

What it all boils down to, though, is this: All is One. Thoughts and feelings mesh into creative beliefs, which then "outpicture" as qualities of personal experience. Mind and body are a unified whole. Earth and her inhabitants interrelate in ways we had not imagined. And the bottom of it all is not some tiny originating "stuff," as at the bottom of a cup of tea, but pure and intelligent energy that layers itself as patterns on into infinity—Universal Mind.

Introduction

From the very first time I encountered the ideas of Ernest Holmes, they have felt like the exquisitely exact words to the music already inside me. I resist the urge to gush about his being the greatest this or the most illumined that; it's a little like betting that Jesus could outheal Buddha. Ernest did not invent the concept of wholeness and oneness—he called his work a "correlation" and in fact paid so much homage to his predecessors that one almost wishes he would have stopped to take more bows himself along the way. His gift was to state the wisdom of the ages fluently, persuasively, engagingly—with nary a pompous moment. And his dream was simply to have us all be well and happy knowing what we know and being who we are, while graciously extending this awareness of the fullness and majesty of life to all the world's peoples, "that the living Spirit shall through us walk anew into Its own creation and a new glory come with a new dawn."

Part I

The Law of Mind

Brother Fenwicke had been an ordained a minister, and in 1910, seeking a warmer climate for reasons of health, had settled in the Los Angeles suburb of Venice, where he became a home missionary and built a small, thriving church.

Fenwicke's letters had spoken glowingly of Los Angeles' constant good weather and the rich scenery. In 1912 Ernest, then twenty-five and fresh from his Chautauqua experience, thought that it might be worthwhile to make an exploratory visit to California to do dramatic readings in churches.

He found Los Angeles an exciting place, a growing city of progressive people in a ferment of expanding their horizons, not only physically but mentally and spiritually. It was a community of stimulating intellectuals. Anything that anyone might want to study was taught there. And he did study! He read and studied everything he could get ahold of—no one single thing. From the beginning, as he later put it, "I didn't take one bondage away from myself only to create another. I have always been very careful about that."

Especially of interest, though, was what went by the name of New Thought . . . It was looser, more open, and based as much as possible on *results* rather than on the additional element of somebody's theology and revelation.

His early reading had convinced him that no one of the Truth Movement leaders or doctrines contained the whole truth. Perhaps the whole truth was too much for one person. He early began toying with the idea of *synthesis.*

—REGINALD ARMOR

I.

There Is One Life

THE FARER:
I know that poets, seers and those they call
The avatars—embodiments of gods—
Declare they know by other means
That there exists another world beyond.
They say it was revealed to them or to
Another who stood behind another whom they knew.
The mystery, they say, has been unsealed
Unto a "chosen few."

But I would like to know what I myself can know.
I crave to know the meaning of great words;
I ask that *life* may be defined, and what
Is *love.* Perchance I, too, can grasp a key
That opens up the door and for myself
Unveil the Mysteries. Or I may hear
A voice beyond earth's hearing, or see
A *Presence* which shall *reveal to me!*

I know in part, at least, the sayings of
Old faiths, religions great and small—and creeds,
And creeds and creeds! I shudder here
Within my lonely room. Complex and dread,
How often they affirm damnation each to each!
From them no answer comes to me unless
A Something stirs within me, and I hear
A Voice from out the Void, if such there be.

THE SCRIBE:
His mind was spinning like a whirling wheel
That comes to rest by chance yet never moves
Beyond its orbit to a higher plane.
He seemed himself to be upon the wheel,
Bound there by dread necessity and fate.

He knew the wheel had spun and once again
Had come to rest upon the same old shibboleth,
A form to hide the emptiness that lies
In ancient, mystic abracadabra.
"Though folly pass from age to age and through
Ten thousand years of tonsured heads, it still
Is folly at the end. 'Tis so with Truth
But how am I to know, though true or false?"

He laughed at this, a bitter laugh. "How now,
O Timeless Sphinx," he said, "thou face inscrutable,
Cold, calculating, cruel question mark
Who dost bestride the ages like a god,
Will Delphic speech break from thy sandstone lips
To shatter all the silence of the ages?"

THE FARER:

Perhaps I am myself the Sphinx, the dumb
Unblinking stone that broods but does not think.
O God, if God there be, O soul of souls,
I cannot bear the hollowness and pain
That fills my heart with loneliness and grief;
How can I bear the emptiness of ignorance?
I want to know and know I know.[1]

—FROM *THE VOICE CELESTIA*

The whole Science of Mind teaching is positioned around the idea of oneness. Here Ernest explains that idea in some pivotal material from his better-known works:

There is a Universal Wholeness seeking expression through everything. We are calling it simply *Life.* The religionist calls it *God.* The philosopher calls it *Reality.* Life is infinite energy coupled with limitless creative imagination. It is the invisible essence and substance of every visible form. Its nature is goodness, truth, wisdom and beauty, as well as energy and imagination. Our highest satisfaction comes from a sense of conscious union with this invisible Life. All human endeavor is an attempt to get back to first principles, to find such an inward wholeness that all sense of fear, doubt and uncertainty vanishes.[2]

Could we but comprehend the fact that there is a Power that makes things directly out of Itself—by simply becoming the thing It makes—could we but grasp this greatest truth about life; and realize that we are dealing with a Principle, scientifically correct and eternally present, *we could accomplish whatever it is possible for us to conceive.* Life externalizes at the level of our thought.[3]

Building on this idea, he offers the "Science of Mind" as

- the study of Life and the nature of the laws of thought; the conception that we live in a spiritual Universe; that God is in, through, around and for us. There is nothing supernatural anywhere, on any plane; that which today seems to us supernatural, after it is understood will be found spontaneously natural.[4]

- based entirely upon the supposition that we are surrounded by a Universal Mind, into which we think. This Mind, in Its original state, fills all space. It fills the space that man uses in the Universe. It is *in* man, as well as outside him. As he thinks into this Universal Mind, he sets a law in motion, which is creative, and which contains within Itself a limitless possibility.[5]

- not necessarily creat[ing] a new religion or sect, for it may be added to any spiritual system of thought since it is a complement to all.[6]

- not a personal opinion, nor . . . a special revelation. It is a result of the best thought of the ages. It borrows much of its light from others but, in so doing, robs no one, for Truth is universal.[7]

Later, in material furnished with the **Extension Course,** *he expands on this in terms of Religious Science, the edifice constructed to deliver the Science of Mind teaching:*

Religious Science is the outcome of what has gone before and, we believe, a forerunner of what is to come. Religious Science is not a personal opinion nor is it a special revelation. It is a result of the best thought of the ages. It borrows much of its light from others, but in so doing robs no one, for Truth is universal.

Taking the best from all sources, Religious Science has access to the highest enlightenment of the ages. Shorn of dogmatism, freed from superstition, and always ready for greater illumination, Religious Science offers the student of life the best that the world has discovered.

In its practice and teachings, Religious Science endeavors to include the whole life. It is not a dreamy, mystical cult, but the exponent of a vigorous philosophy applicable to the everyday needs of life, and this accounts for its rapid growth. Men and women find in it a message that fits in with their daily needs.

The conventional idea of a future life, with its teachings of reward and punishment, is not stressed; the gospel is the good news for the *here and now.* Religion, if it means anything, means right living, and right living and right thinking wait upon no future but bestow their rewards in this life—in better health, happier homes, and all that makes for a well-balanced, normal life.[8]

Especially in smaller group gatherings where his audience was more well-versed in this worldview, Ernest would discuss primary reality in more lofty, poetic ways, as in these two selections.

We believe that for every visible object there is a divine pattern of that object in the invisible to which the object is related. This applies to a bed, the grass or an archangel, if such a creature exists and I suppose he does! There must be beings beyond us as we are beyond tadpoles, but it will be time enough to consider this when we arrive at that next state of consciousness. We really wouldn't know how to be an archangel right now! I can conceive in my imagination a beauty so splendid that should I perceive it now it would shatter even my physical being. There must be such beauty because now we do see only in part and beyond that which we do see is more and more. Always there is something locked behind the border, something yet to learn. We always find it so, and the search and seeking are eternal. The Spirit will be true to Itself at every level of expression but it will never be completed. If it were ever to be completed, then we should have to add the assumption of completion, continuation and eternal boredom, and then even God would become tired of Himself! God is doing something to and through every one of us all the time. As Emerson said, "The ancient of days is in the latest invention."[9]

Here we have the Spirit or the Absolute, and we have this medium, or the Law of Mind in action (the psychic world), and we have the body—manifestation, or effect. The divine spark falls, we will say, to the lowest arc of the material, to the lowest objective manifestation of the "mundane clod." In all sacred literature you read references to this. It is that spark which impregnates everything and is buried in everything. It is the spark which Browning said we can desecrate but never quite lose. It is there, and it contains within itself the upward push of all evolution.

The evolutionary process that impels things upward and onward from lower to higher forms of intelligence is occasioned because everything is impregnated with intelligence as unconscious memory, not as an intellectual conception. The *logic* of Spirit is in the intellect, but the Spirit is in the heart. The logic of faith may be in the intellect as a mathematical equation; the Spirit is something that cannot be analyzed or dissected. You can kill the nightingale, but you cannot capture its song. Here is the spark that causes all evolution.

Since everything is an individualization of the Universal, every spark is alike in that it is divine. It is made of the same Cosmic stuff, but no two sparks are identical. The process in Nature is the multiplication of an infinite variation of unified identities, no one of which is identical with the other, even though each and all are in the same field.

Unity and uniformity are not the same thing. No two blades of grass are alike. What does it mean, spiritually? It means that incarnated within each one of us is not only a divine Spark, not only an incarnation of the living Spirit of the Cosmos, but a unique presentation of the Cosmic Whole, if we can judge the Unknown by the known. We have nothing to disprove and everything to prove that this individualization of the Spirit in each one of us, rooted in common soil, having the characteristics and potentialities of its common background, contains what the ancients called the microcosm.

We have every reason to suppose that there is, back of and within and around every individual, the divine representation of himself as the Son of God, forever expanding. The Universe is alive and awake and aware. It's an interesting thing that all the great intuitions of the ages are gradually being verified by the investigations of modern science. The nature of the physical universe has been known intuitively from time immemorial; but that which anciently was conceived by intuition, which went in the front door of the Spirit by a natural and logical affinity, is, in our day and generation, gradually being reproven by the inductive method of science, which goes in the back door of the Spirit, but which, when it gets into the living room, sees the same furniture.[10]

The four brief introductory sections of The Science of Mind *(1938) lay out Ernest's key ideas. Religious Science ministers traditionally base their first four sermons of each new year on these. Here is the first of them. Note his opening remarks about science and religion. It was his contention that human spirituality is simultaneously scientifically provable and spontaneously mystical.*

The Thing Itself

We all look forward to the day when science and religion shall walk hand in hand through the visible to the invisible. Science knows nothing of opinion, but recognizes a government of law whose principles are universal. Yet any scientist who refuses to accept intangible values has no adequate basis for the values which he has already discovered. Revelation must keep faith with reason, and religion with law—while intuition is ever spreading its wings for greater flights—and science must justify faith in the invisible.

To suppose that the Creative Intelligence of the Universe would create man in bondage and leave him bound, would be to dishonor the Creative Power which we call God. To suppose that God could make man as an individual, without leaving him to discover himself, would be to suppose an impossibility. Individuality must be spontaneous; it can never be automatic. The seed of freedom must be planted in the innermost being of man, but, like the Prodigal Son, man must make the great discovery for himself.

We see abundance in the Universe. We cannot count the grains of sand on a single beach. The earth contains untold riches, and the very air is vibrant with power. Why, then, is man weak, poor and afraid? The Science of Mind deals with these questions. The Divine Plan is one of Freedom; bondage is not God-ordained. Freedom is the birthright of every living soul. All instinctively feel this. The Truth points to freedom, under Law. Thus the inherent nature of man is forever seeking to express itself in terms of freedom. We do well to listen to this Inner Voice, for it tells us of a life wonderful in its scope; of a love beyond our fondest dreams; of a freedom which the soul craves.

But the great Love of the Universe must be One with the great law of Its Own Being, and we approach Love through the Law. This, then, is our teaching: Love and Law. As the love of God is perfect, so the law of God also is perfect. We must understand both.

Whatever the nature of any principle may be—in so far as it is understood by anyone—it may be understood by all who take the time to investigate. This does not require an unusual degree of intelligence, but, rather, a practical application of what we now know in order that we may increase our knowledge. The study of the Science of Mind is a study of First Cause, Spirit, Mind or that invisible Essence, that ultimate Stuff and Intelligence from which everything comes, the Power back of creation—the Thing Itself.

We accept this "Thing" and believe in It. What we desire is to know more about It, and how to use It. From proof alone, we know we are dealing with a definite principle. If one (through the conscious use of his knowledge) can produce a certain result, he must know with what he is dealing.

It may seem as though, in dealing with metaphysics, we are dealing with something that is too abstract. But what is tangible other than results? Principles are forever hidden from our eyes. We accept the deductions of science insofar as they are proved, and we recognize that they are built upon immutable, but invisible, principles.

We are so used to the thought that if we mix certain colors we get certain other colors, that we do not realize we are dealing with a principle. We know that *whoever* blends these particular colors will get the same result, but we do not know why; *the wisest man living does not know why!* We do not have to stretch our credulity any more in metaphysics.

We think of metaphysics, perhaps, as something that only the most profound thinkers have known about, but we should remember that we also are thinkers. The profound thought of all ages has stood in awe of Life itself, realizing that here is a power and potentiality, the highest possibilities of which the human intellect cannot fathom.

Universal principles are never respecters of persons; the Universe has no favorites. Therefore, it is written, "And let him that is athirst come. And whosoever will, let him take the water of life freely." (Rev. 22:17)

Let us approach the Science of Mind—the Science of Spiritual Psychology—with awe, but not with fear; with truly a humble thought, but not with a sense that we are unworthy. Let us approach it normally, happily, willing to accept, glad to experiment, hoping and believing that as the result of our efforts we shall each derive a great good—a sound understanding of the natural laws of Life, as they apply to the individual and his relationship to the whole universal scheme of things.

This is the simple meaning of true metaphysical teaching, the study of Life and the nature of the Law, governed and directed by thought; always conscious that we live in a spiritual Universe; that God is in, through, around and for us. There is nothing supernatural about the study of Life from the metaphysical viewpoint. That which today seems to us supernatural, after it is thoroughly understood, will be found spontaneously natural.

We all know that many have been healed of physical disease through prayer. Let us analyze this. Why are some healed through prayer while others are not? Can we believe that there is a God who picks out some man and says, "I will honor your prayer, but I do not think so much of Mr. So and So"? It is superstitious to believe that God will answer the prayer of one above another. Jesus said that God "maketh His sun to rise on the evil and on the good, and sendeth rain on the just and on the unjust" (Matt. 5:45).

Since some people have been healed through prayer, while others have not, the answer is *not* that God has responded to some and not to others. Their prayer (their thought) has responded by corresponding. The answer to prayer is in the prayer. But what is a prayer? A prayer is a movement of thought, within the mind of the one praying, along a definite line of meditation; that is, for a specific purpose.

21

What is the mind? No man living knows. We know a great deal about the mind, *but not what it is.* By mind, we mean consciousness. We are now using it. We cannot locate mind in the body, for, while the body is a necessary vehicle for consciousness while we are here, it is not consciousness. We cannot isolate mind. All we know about it is not what it is, but *what it does,* and the greatest philosopher who ever lived knows no more than this . . . except that he may tell us more of how it works.

Mind—the Thing, Spirit, Causation—is beyond, and yet not beyond, our grasp. *Beyond,* in that It is so big; *within,* in that wherever we grasp at It, *we are It to the extent that we grasp It;* but, since It is Infinite, we can never encompass It. *We shall never encompass God, and yet we shall always be in God and of God!*

Mind comes under two classifications. There are not two minds, but rather two names employed in describing states of consciousness: the *objective,* or conscious, and the *subjective,* or unconscious. We think of the conscious state as our conscious use of mind. The subconscious (or subjective) state of mind—sometimes called the unconscious state—is that part of mind which is set in motion as a creative thing by the conscious state . . .

Marvelous as the concept may be, it is none the less true that man has at his disposal—in what he calls *his* Subjective Mind—a power that seems to be Limitless. *This is because he is one with the whole on the subjective side of life!* Man's thought, falling into his subjective mind, merges with the Universal Subjective Mind, and becomes the law of his life, through the one great law of all life.

There are not two subjective minds. There is but one Subjective Mind, and what we call *our subjective mind* is really the use we are making of the One Law. Each individual maintains his identity in Law, through his personal use of It. And each is drawing from Life what he thinks into It!

To learn how to think is to learn how to live, for our thoughts go into a medium that is Infinite in Its ability to do and to be. Man, by thinking, can bring into his experience whatsoever he desires—if he thinks correctly, and becomes a living embodiment of his thoughts. This is not done by *holding thoughts* but by knowing the Truth.

Within us, then, there is a creative field, which we call the subjective mind; around us there is a creative field which we call Subjective. One is universal and the other is individual, but in reality they are one. *There is one mental law in the universe, and where we use it, it becomes our law because we have individualized it.* It is impossible to plumb the depths of the individual mind, *because the individual mind is really not individual but is individualized.* Behind the individual is the Universal, which has no limits. In this concept alone lies the possibility of eternal and endless expansion. Everyone is Universal on the subjective side of life, and individual only at the point of conscious perception. The riddle is solved, and we all use the creative power of the Universal Mind *every time we use our own mind.*

Since this is true, it follows that we cannot say that one thought is creative while another is not. We must say that all thought is creative, according to the nature, impulse, emotion or conviction behind the thought. Thought creates a mold in the Subjective, in which the idea is accepted and poured, and sets power in motion in accordance with the thought. Ignorance of this excuses no one from its effects, for we are dealing with Law and not with whimsical fancy.

The conscious mind is superior to the subjective and may *consciously* use it. Great as the subconscious is, its tendency is set in motion by the conscious thought, and in this possibility lies the path to freedom. The Karmic Law is not Kismet. It is not fate but cause and effect. It is a taskmaster to the unwise; a servant to the wise.

Experience has taught us that the subjective tendency of this intelligent Law of creative force may consciously be directed and definitely used. *This is the greatest discovery of all time.* There is no mystery here, but a profound fact and a demonstrable one. The road to freedom lies, not through mysteries or occult performances, but through the intelligent use of Nature's forces and laws. The Law of Mind is a natural law in the spiritual world.

But what do we mean by the *spiritual world?* We mean the world of conscious intelligence. The Subjective is a world of Law and of mechanical order; in our lives, it is largely a reaction, an effect, a way. *It is never a person though it often appears to act as though it were one.* Right here, many are completely misled, mistaking subjective impulses for actual personalities. This, however, is a field of investigation not fully to be considered here.

The simplest way to state the proposition is to say that we have a conscious mind that operates within a subjective field, which is creative. The conscious mind is Spirit, the subjective mind is Law. One is a complement of the other and no real individuality could be expressed without a combination of both.

No man has ever plumbed the depths of either the conscious or the subjective life. In both directions, we reach out to Infinity, and since we cannot encompass Infinity, we shall always be expanding and always enlarging our capacity to know and to experience.

We need not ask *why* these things are so. There can be no reasons given as to why the Truth is true. We do not create laws and principles, but discover and make use of them. Let us accept this position relative to the laws of Mind and Spirit, and see what we can do with them—rather than how we may contradict the inevitable. Our mind and spirit is our echo of the "Eternal Thing" Itself, and the sooner we discover this fact, the sooner we shall be made free and happy. The Universe is filled with Spirit and filled with Law. One reacts to the other. We are Spirit and we are Law. The Law of our life reacts to our spiritual or material concepts, and builds and rebuilds according to our beliefs and faith.

All men seek some relationship to the Universal Mind, the Over-Soul, or the Eternal Spirit, which we call God. And Life reveals itself to whoever is receptive to it. That we are living in a spiritual Universe, which includes the material or physical universe, has been a conclusion of the deepest thinkers of every age. That this spiritual Universe must be one of pure Intelligence and perfect Life, dominated by Love, by Reason and by the power to create, seems an inevitable conclusion.

There is a Power in the Universe that honors our faith in It; there is a Law in the Universe which exacts the "uttermost farthing." We all wish to feel that the power behind everything is good, as well as creative, an Eternal and Changeless Intelligence, in which man lives and moves and has his being. Intuitively, we sense that every man, in his native state, is some part or manifestation of this Eternal Principle; and that the entire problem of limitation, evil, suffering and uncertainty is not God-ordained, but is the result of ignorance. It has been written that the Truth shall make us free, provided we know the Truth, and we note that the evolution of man's consciousness brings with it the acquisition of new powers and higher possibilities.

We find ourselves torn by confusion, by conflict, by affirmation and denial, by emotion congested by fear, congealed by pride. We are afraid of the Universe in which we live, suspicious of people around us, uncertain of the salvation of our own souls. All these things negatively react and cause physical disorders.

Nature seems to await our comprehension of her and, since she is governed by immutable laws—the ignorance of which excuses no man from their effects—the bondage of humanity must be a result of our ignorance of the true nature of Reality. The storehouse of Nature may be filled with good, but this good is locked to the ignorant. The key to this door is held in the mind of Intelligence, working in accordance with Universal Law. Through experience, man learns what is really good and satisfying, what is truly worthwhile. As his intelligence increases, and his capacity to understand the subtle laws of Nature grows, he will gradually be set free. As he learns the Truth, the Truth will automatically free him.

When we learn to trust the Universe, we shall be happy, prosperous and well. We must learn to come under that Divine Government, and accept the fact that nature's table is ever filled. Never was there a Cosmic famine. "The finite alone has wrought and suffered, the Infinite lies stretched in smiling repose" [Emerson] God is always God. No matter what our emotional storm, or what our objective situation, may be, there is always a something hidden in the inner being that has never been violated. We may stumble, but always there is that Eternal Voice, forever whispering within our ear, that thing which causes the eternal quest, that thing which forever sings and sings.

This is The Thing Itself. Briefly, let us recapitulate. There is that within every individual which partakes of the nature of the Universal Wholeness and—in so far as it operates—is God. That is the meaning of the word *Emmanuel*, the meaning of the word *Christ*. There is that within us which partakes of the nature of the Divine Being, and *since it partakes of the nature of the Divine Being, we are divine.* It reacts to us according to our belief in It; and it is an immutable Law, subject to the use of the least among us; no respecter of persons, It cannot be bound. Our Soul will never change or violate its own nature; all the denying of it will never change it; all the affirming of it will never make it any more than it is. But since it is what it is, and works in the way that it works, it appears to each through his belief. It is done unto each one of us as we believe.

We will say, then, that in spirit, man is One with God. But what of the great Law of the Universe? If we are really One with the Whole, we must be One with the Law of the Whole, as well as One with the Spirit of the Whole.

If we try to find something difficult to grasp, then we shall never grasp it, because we shall always think of It as being incomprehensible. The mind which we discover within us *is the Mind which governs everything.* This is The Thing Itself, and we should recognize its simplicity.[11]

These next four passages build on oneness: It's in us as well as around us; it's constantly in motion; and its vehicle for motion is **thought.**

We must learn to live by inspiration. That means that we should let the spiritual depths of our being flow through our conversation and into our acts. Living by inspiration does not mean living chaotically. Our whole purpose is to make the intellect an instrument for the Spirit. This is exactly what an artist does. We must all become artists in living. To live by inspiration means to sense the divine touch in everything; to enter into the spirit of things; to enter into the joy of living.

In our ignorance we try to find our center outside the self. This can never be. The ancients said that God's center is everywhere and His circumference nowhere. We are like the upward thrust of a wave. We look about seeing other waves, apparently dissociated from us, but underneath is the One Ocean pushing all waves upward. There is One Mover in every movement, one undulating passion for self-expression.[12]

The universe is not a static thing forever reproducing itself in exactly the same way. Neither is it something that was wound up, left to its own devices and is now running down. It is, rather, a vast and infinite potential which, while it must ever remain true to the laws of its nature, will always be manifesting itself in infinite variations.[13]

Taking as the starting point the idea that the essence of man's life is God, it follows that he uses the same creative process. Everything originates in the One, comes from the same Source and returns again to It. As God's thought makes worlds, and peoples them with living things, so our thought makes our world and peoples it with our experiences. By the activity of our thought, things come into our life and we are limited only because we have not known the Truth. We have thought that outside things controlled us, when all the time we have had that within which could have changed everything and given us freedom from bondage.

Everyone automatically attracts to himself just what he is, and we may set it down that wherever we are, however intolerable the situation may be, we are just where we belong. There is no power in the universe but ourselves that can free us . . . Man must bring himself to the place in mind where there is no misfortune, no calamity, no accident, no trouble, no confusion; where there is nothing but plenty, peace, power, Life and Truth. He should definitely, daily (using his own name) declare the Truth about himself, realizing that he is reflecting his statements into Consciousness and that they will be operated upon by It.

This is called, in mysticism, High Invocation; invoking the Divine Mind, implanting within It, seeds of thought relative to oneself.[14]

There is one ultimate Thinker, yet this Thinker thinks through all of us. That is why our thought is creative. That is why we think at all. The universal Mind is incarnated in everyone. Every man has access to It; every man uses It, either in ignorance or in conscious knowledge. In other words, the mind of each one of us is the Mind of God functioning at the level of perception of life. Consciously using It, we bring into our experience today something we did not appear to have yesterday—a better environment, a happier circumstance, more friendships, more joy. These manifestations are of the nature of Reality.[15]

In the 1927 inaugural issue of Science of Mind *magazine, Ernest wrote "What I Believe," which has become known as the "Declaration of Principles," or the closest thing Religious Science has to a formal creed. You can find it in most issues of the magazine. The following material by the same title, an expansion on his earlier essay, comes from a republishing of one of his 1934 lectures at the Ebell Theater.*

What I Believe

First, I believe that God is Universal Spirit, and by Spirit I mean the Life Essence of all that is—that subtle and intelligent Power which permeates all things and which, in each individual, is conscious mind. I believe that God is Universal Spirit, present in every place, conscious in every part, the Intelligence and mind of all that is.

I believe that humankind is the direct representative of this Divine Presence on this plane of existence. I believe that the relationship between God and the individual is a direct one and that the avenue through which the Spirit expresses Itself to us is through our mind. Our ability to think, to know and to act are direct channels through which the Universal Spirit flows.

It does not seem necessary, to me, that we approach God through any formula or intermediary, but rather that the Spirit of God, the Eternal Mind, is the power by which we think and know. It is self-evident that the only God we can know is the God our consciousness perceives.

But some will say that while it is true that we cannot think outside ourselves, we can know of that which is outside the self. This is true, as is the fact that we have a City Hall, but it would have no reality to me unless I was first aware of its existence. This is true of everything, and while the possibility of knowledge may and must expand, we are ignorant of that which we do not perceive.

Therefore, I believe that God is to each one what that person is to God. The Divine Nature must be Infinite, but we know only as much of this Nature as we embody; in no other way can God be known to us. I believe the relationship between God and humankind is hidden within, and when we discover a new truth, or have a better understanding about an old truth, it is really more of this Infinite Mind revealing Itself through us.

I believe in a direct communication between the Spirit and the individual—the Universal Spirit personifying Itself through each and all; this is a beautiful, a logical and an unavoidable conclusion. This makes of the human a Divine being, a personification of the Spirit; but if we are Divine Beings why is it that we are so limited and forlorn, so poor, miserable and unhappy? The answer is that we are ignorant of our own nature, and ignorance of the Law excuses no one from its effects.

I believe that all things are governed by immutable and exact laws. These laws cannot be changed or violated; our ignorance of them will offer no excuse for their infringement and we are made to suffer, not because God wills it, but because we are ignorant of the truth of our being. We are individuals and have free will and self-choice. We shall learn by experience, things mental and physical. There is no other way to learn, and God Himself could not provide any other way without contradicting His own nature. The Spirit is subject to the law of Its own nature, and so are we . . .

I do not believe in hell, devil or damnation, in any future state of punishment, or any of the strange ideas which have been conceived in the minds of morbid people. God does not punish people . . . It is one thing to believe in hell and damnation and quite another proposition to believe in a law of just retribution.

I am sure that full and complete salvation will come at last alike to all. Heaven and hell are states of consciousness in which we now live according to our own state of being. We need worry neither about reward nor punishment, for both are certain. Eventually all will be saved from themselves through their own experiences; this is the only salvation necessary and the only one that could be intelligent.

I believe in every religion that exists, for it is an avenue through which people worship God. I believe in my own religion more than that of anyone else, because this is the avenue through which I worship God.

I do not believe that there is anything in the universe which is against us but ourselves. Everything is and must be for us. The only God who exists, the "Ancient of days," wishes us well, knows us only as being perfect and complete. When we shall all learn to know as God knows, we shall be saved from all mistakes and trouble. This is heaven . . .

I believe that we are surrounded by an intelligent law which receives the impress of our thought and acts upon it. This is the law of our life and we may use it consciously and for definite purposes. I am not superstitious about this law any more than I would be about the law of electricity or any other natural law, for nature is always natural.

I believe in a religion of happiness and joy. There is too much depression and sorrow in the world. These things were never meant to be and have no real place in the world of reality. Religion should be like the morning sun sending forth its rays of light; it should be like the falling dew covering the land with fragrance and sweetness; like the cool of evening and the repose of night. It should be a spontaneous song of joy and not a funeral dirge. From the fullness of a joyous heart the mouth should speak.

I believe in the brotherhood of humanity, the Parenthood of God and a unity binding all together in one perfect whole. I believe the Spirit is in the wind and wave, and manifests Its presence throughout all Nature. But most completely, through our own minds and in our hearts, It proclaims our livingness and Its lovingness.[16]

Often Ernest used anecdotes or conversational exchanges to deliver his message. A definite extrovert, he would talk with anybody about anything.

I was explaining to a young fellow this morning—young producer at one of the studios. He was working so hard, and I said, "Larry, you don't force anything, you don't coerce anything, you don't hold any thoughts, you don't put in anything—you always take it out. Always. It is already in there." His mind was all burdened with things he has to do. He has a great responsibility, and he was making it a personal thing—he had to make things happen. Now is the time to relax, I told him; we take everything out. And he said, "Then what makes it happen?" I said, "It is like you put the acorn in the ground, that is your part. Now there is an idea involved in that; and nothing can happen to the idea but that it will grow, and nothing can stop it but its own law. It is its own evidence; the oak tree is already there. You put an idea into your mind, and it will work exactly the same way, because the Universe is one system."[17]

His lectures and classes always began and ended with affirmative prayer, and his books are filled with affirmations for the reader's use. So I'll close this and all subsequent chapters with one, and invite you to make it personal to you, feeling the words as you read them.

The Law of Good is continuously operative in my life. I am always equal to any task set before me. I am confident of my ability to meet every situation. I can solve every problem, overcome every difficulty. Realizing that Spirit knows no obstruction, I have implicit confidence in Its ability to operate through me always, and under every situation.[18]

II.

What We Are Looking For,
We Are Looking At
and With

THE FARER:
"The brazen gates of doubt are riven to show
The wonder of the Whole!" . . . Would I could know
The meaning of the *part* . . . I who in pain
Have searched the wisdom of the world in vain!

THE PRESENCE:
O foolish soul, O child of ignorance,
Who knows so much and knowing, does not know,
I come to thee as I to Moses came,
Unstopped his eyes and showed the Holy Land.
To know too much is not to know at all;
The vessel full, too full, to hold
The waters drawn from deeper wells,
Cannot contain the draughts more newly drawn;
For how can Wisdom gain from Knowledge,
If knowledge be of that which is untrue?
A thousand falsehoods never make a fact.

Turn then from thy half-truths, thy mortal mind
And go with me. Nay, not to distant stars
The way of Truth is never out but in.[1]

If all is One, Ernest reasoned, then that Oneness is right where each of us is, and Its ways are our ways. The part of us that seeks God is the Presence of God at our level of awareness, seeking to consciously, deliberately reconnect with Itself. These excerpts from his chapter on "Mental Equivalents" in The Science of Mind *discuss our oneness in God, how we may have come to believe in separation from God as our source . . . and what to do about it.*

We walk by falling forward; water falls by its own weight; the planets are eternally falling through space; everything sustains itself in nature. The only reason man is limited is that he has not allowed the Divine within him to more completely express. Man's Divine Individuality compels Infinity to appear in his experience as duality *because he has believed in duality.*

Prayer does something to the mind of the one praying. It does not do anything to God. The Eternal Gift is always made. The Gift of God is the Nature of God, the Eternal Givingness. God cannot help making the gift, because *God is the gift.* We do not have to pray God to be God. God is God.

. . . Faith, then, touches a Principle which responds, we may be certain of this. We should have more faith than we do rather than less, nor is it foolish to cultivate faith. *All prayers will be answered when we pray aright.* The first necessity is faith. Faith! But someone may exclaim, "This is what has always been taught, this is nothing new!" Correct, we have nothing new. We simply have a new approach to an old truth, a more intelligent, a more systematic way of consciously arriving at faith. This is what that treatment is for.

Why is it that Jesus could say to the paralyzed man, "Take up thy bed and walk?" Because Jesus *knew* when he said this that the man *would* get up and walk. *He not only believed that there was something to respond to him but he had an equivalent of its response,* which is just as necessary.

The Law is Infinite and Perfect but in order to make a demonstration *we must have a mental equivalent of the thing we desire.* A demonstration, like anything else in the objective life, is born out of a mental concept. The mind is the fashioning factor, and according to its range, vision and positiveness, will be the circumstance or experience. For example: if one sees only unloveliness in others, it is because unloveliness is a strong element in himself. The light he throws on others is generated in his own soul and he sees them as he chooses to see them. He holds constantly in his mind a mental equivalent of unloveliness and creates unlovely reactions toward himself. He is getting back what he is sending out. If a man believes himself to be a failure and that it is useless for him to try to be anything else, he carries with him the mental equivalent of failure. So he *succeeds* in being a *failure* according to law. This is his demonstration. Having a strong picture or mental concept, and holding to that equivalent regardless of circumstances or conditions, we must sooner or later manifest according to the concept.

It follows, then, that the range of our possibilities at the present time does not extend far beyond the range of our present concepts. As we bring ourselves to a greater vision, we induce a greater concept and thereby demonstrate more in our experience. In this way there is a continuous growth and unfoldment taking place. We do not expect to give a treatment today, for prosperity, and have a million dollars tomorrow. But little by little we can unfold our consciousness, through the acquisition of greater and still greater mental equivalents, until at last we shall be made free.

The way to proceed is to begin right where we are. It is not scientific to attempt to begin somewhere else. One who understands the systematic use of the Law will understand that *he is where he is because of what he is,* but he will *not* say, "I must remain where I am, because of what I am." Instead he will begin to disclaim what he appears to be. As his statements release wrong subjective tendencies, providing in their place a correct concept of life and Reality, he will automatically be lifted out of his condition; impelling forces sweeping everything before them, will set him free, if he trusts in Spirit and the working of the Law.

Stay with the One and never deviate from It, never leave it for a moment. Nothing else can equal this attitude. *To desert the Truth in the hour of need is to prove that we do not know the Truth.* When things look the worst, that is the supreme moment to demonstrate, to ourselves, that there are no obstructions to the operation of Truth. When things look the worst is the best time to work, the most satisfying time. The person who can throw himself with a complete abandon into the Limitless Sea of Receptivity, having cut loose from all apparent moorings, is the one who will always receive the greatest reward.[2]

Since, as he says, "all prayers will be answered when we pray aright," exactly what does he suggest? The core of his teaching being the oneness of all life in God, the type of prayer he advocates is one where the mind of the one praying moves to a place of acceptance. God, being all there is, need not be begged to provide. It's simply a matter of faith—the faith of God. The name given this type of prayer is spiritual mind treatment, *the essential spiritual tool in his whole philosophy, that you'll encounter again and again, by reference or allusion, in all the rest of his writings. Here he takes us through it, step by step.*

What are requisites for the constructive use of our thought? Experience has shown that usually an effective prayer or spiritual mind treatment in some way incorporates within it these four elements: Recognition, Identification, Declaration and Acceptance.

But before we discuss these four steps we need to remember that they are but suggestions. They are not hard-and-fast rules that must be followed. One or all four may be used. There is no formula involved, no ritual to repeat. There is only an easy, consistent flow of thought that is convinced of the truth of the content involved . . .

The manner in which each will be able to use and direct his thought in constructive and beneficial channels will have to be worked out individually. The results forthcoming will verify the rightness of how each uses the creative power of his thought.

There is no time, no place, no condition or situation that is more appropriate than another for the use of thought as affirmative prayer. Prayer has had immediate manifestation, the answer, in the midst of confusion and disaster. It has also had results that came from moments of peace and quiet. Most people have found it helpful to be alone, to be quiet, to be removed from distracting surroundings, to have the mind free of a sense of pressure, worry and tension.

Let us now consider the four elements that are usually contained in prayer that works, in thought that is creative.

I. *Recognition.* We know that there is One Life, that Life Is God. There is One Creator, one creation. One Law. One Intelligence. One Ultimate Reality. It is good, whole, perfect, complete, harmonious.

2. *Identification.* We identify ourselves with God. "I am that which Thou art. Thou art that which I am." The Father and I are one. There needs to be a conscious, intelligent sensing and feeling of the Divine Presence within and as what we are. We are a creation of God and we are expressing God. There is no separation between us and God. We are one.

3. *Declaration.* There is a definite and specific action and movement of intelligence through thought, word or idea for some definite purpose or person. Not supplication, wishing, hoping or begging, but a concrete declaration of fact, a specializing of universal Good in some way. There is definitely established in thought, the spiritual level of cause and creativity, a complete idea. An idea to which we may mentally point and know its reality as though we were pointing to the sun and saying, "There is the sun." We know that such a declaration of an idea is God speaking His word in us, God being an active agent in His own creation.

4. *Acceptance.* We accept our declaration, the word we have spoken, as being manifest now. No delay is involved between this cause and its appearance as effect. We accept that our word, the declaration we have made, is the supreme Intelligence speaking through us, and that according to the nature of the way It works, through Law, our word automatically manifests in accord with Law. And in our acceptance of the reality of this good as a tangible effect in our experience we give thanks that it is so, that as we now believe it is done unto us.[3]

Ernest was attracted to a spiritual method that delivered results in the here and now, instead of promises of the hereafter. He used the term "demonstration" to mean results, as had Mary Baker Eddy before him, in the sense that what is intangibly known and felt then demonstrates—or shows itself—in tangible form.

In the language of metaphysics, a "demonstration" is made when the thing is accomplished which the one treating desires to achieve . . . whether it be health, happiness or abundance. A demonstration is a manifestation. It is prayer answered. When the word of a practitioner takes form, this is a demonstration. When desire is given a subjective mold and then becomes objectified in the life of the one for whom the practitioner is working, this is demonstration . . .

We cannot demonstrate beyond our ability to mentally embody an idea. The argument is between our experience, what the world believes, and what we are convinced is the Truth . . .

The possibility of demonstrating does not depend upon environment, condition, location, personality or opportunity. It depends solely upon our belief and our acceptance, and our willingness to comply with the Law through which all good comes. The Universe will never deny us anything, unless we conceive that it is possible for us to think of something that is impossible for the Universe to produce! Everyone who asks receives, according to his belief.[4]

Here are some additional thoughts of his on the nature of effective prayer:

Every day and every hour we are meeting the eternal realities of life, and in such degree as we cooperate with these eternal realities in love, in peace, in wisdom and in joy—believing and receiving—we are automatically blessed. Our prayer is answered before it is uttered.[5]

Prayer in its truest sense is not a petition, not a supplication, not a wail of despair; it is rather an alignment, a unifying process which takes place in the mind as it reaches to its Divine Self and to that Power which is greater than human understanding. In the act of such prayerful and reverent communion with God one senses the Unity of Good, the completeness of Life and at times the veil of doubt is lifted and the face of Reality appears. This consciousness, which has been referred to as the Secret Place of the Most

High, is an experience rising out of the conviction that God is all there is, beside Whom there is none else.

Prayer, then, is communion, and this communion pronounces life to be Good. Prayerful communion ascends to that place where unity has not yet become variety, where the unformed One is ready to take any specific shape. In this act of communion the individual becomes copartner with the Eternal and gives birth to time, space and conditions.[6]

All manifestation of Life is from an invisible to a visible plane, through a silent, effortless process of spiritual realization. We must unify in our own mentalities with pure Spirit. To each of us, individually, God or Spirit is the Supreme Personality of the Universe—the Supreme Personality of that which we, ourselves, are. It is only as the relationship of the individual to the Deity becomes enlarged that one has a consciousness of power.

In treatment there should always be a recognition of the absolute Unity of God and man: the Oneness, Inseparability, Indivisibility, Changelessness. God as the big circle and man as the little circle. Man is in God and God is man, just as a drop of water is in the ocean, while the ocean is the drop of water.[7]

But what is fear? *Nothing more or less than the negative use of faith* . . . faith misplaced; a belief in two powers instead of One; a belief that there can be a Power—opposed to God—whose influence and ability *may* bring us to evil.[8]

We do not say that man cannot sin; what we say is, that he does sin—or make mistakes—and he is thereby automatically punished *as long as he continues to make mistakes* . . . We are not punished *for* our sins but *by* them. Sin is its own punishment and righteousness is its own reward![9]

In giving mental and spiritual treatments, it is better not to dwell too much on the negative, since we are liable to give it undue importance. To affirm the presence of God is better than to deny the presence of evil.[10]

When Jesus explained to his disciples that they had failed to heal because of lack of faith, they protested that they did have faith *in* God. Jesus explained to them that this was insufficient; they must have the faith of God. The *faith of God* is very different from *a faith in God*. The faith of God *is* God.[11]

Therefore, it is imperative that we turn from the relative, because *to view limitation is to impress it upon the mind,* and accentuate the state of consciousness which produced it.[12]

He even offers suggestions on how often to "treat."

Never let go of the mental image until it becomes manifested. Daily bring up the clear picture of what is wanted and impress it on the mind as an accomplished fact. This impressing on our minds the thought of what we wish to realize will cause our own minds to impress the same thought on Universal Mind. In this way we shall be praying without ceasing. We do not have to hold continually the thought of something we want in order to get it, but the thought that we may inwardly become the thing we want. Fifteen minutes, twice each day, is time enough to spend in order to demonstrate anything, but the rest of the time ought to be spent constructively. That is, we must stop all negative thinking and give over all wrong thought, holding fast to the realization that it is now done unto us. We must know that we are dealing with the only power there is in the Universe; that there is none other beside it, and that we are in it partaking of its nature and its laws.

Life will become one grand song, when we realize that since God is for us, none can be against us. We shall cease merely to exist; we shall *live.*[13]

Changing one's experience of life comes easy once the viewpoint is shifted to an acceptance of greater good. Here he expands on the idea, "to have a friend, be a friend."

When we find that we are without friends, the thing to do is at once send our thought out to the whole world—send it full of love and affection. Know that this thought will meet the desires of some other person who is wanting the same thing, and in some way the two will be drawn together. Get over thinking that people are queer. That kind of thought will only produce misunderstanding and cause us to lose the friends that we now have.

Think of the whole world as your friend; but you must also be the friend of the whole world. In this way and with this simple practice you will draw to you so many friends that the time will be too short to enjoy them all. Refuse to see the negative side of anyone. Refuse to let yourself misunderstand or be misunderstood. Do not be morbid. Know that everyone wants you to have the best; affirm this wherever you go and then you will find things just as you wish them to be.[14]

In this, the first of several excerpts from his magazine articles, Ernest speaks of the universal availability of God—and good.

Most people who believe in God, believe in prayer. It is natural that each one who prays shall feel his way of praying is the only way to pray, and that it is the right way. We are all more or less familiar with different religious beliefs and approaches to Reality, each prescribing a way to pray. And each is right for him who believes in it. I believe every man's prayer is good; but I believe that all men's prayers, insofar as they are effective, are effective because they embody certain universal principles, which, if we understood, we could consciously use, and that power which is obtained by a few would be as easily used by all.

If spiritual things be true, it is not enough simply to declare they are so; we have to understand how they work and why—the laws governing them. Then we shall be able to say: "Here it is; this is the way it works. You can use it and I can use it." There is no special dispensation of Providence; there is no God who cares more for the Jews than He does for the Gentiles, or cares more for the Gentiles than He does for the Jews. As intelligent observers, we must realize that God is a Universal Presence—a neutral force, an impersonal observer, a divine and impartial giver—forever pouring Himself upon His Creation.

God is an indwelling Presence. I do not believe in lost souls, but I do believe that every living soul is in search of himself and his relationship to what Reality is. We have to come to believe there is a Reality which we sense in our own being, giving birth to a direct relationship to the Infinite—all the magnificence and the beauty and the power and the peace which is commensurate with the estimation of the meaning of the Infinite—God.[15]

———

We have been discussing perfect Intelligence, perfect Law, and perfect Life. But a practical question which might arise is: "How much can apparently imperfect man expect to demonstrate?" Should we expect absolute physical perfection, limitless wealth or flawless happiness?

Of course there must be a sensible and logical answer to such questions. We do not say that because a man thinks *about* a million dollars he will *have* a million dollars. What we do say is this: While it is true that, so far as Principle is concerned, we can have what good we desire according to the Law of Cause and Effect, it is also true that no matter what we may desire we shall only have what we are *able to accept.* Since this accepting is mental, we shall only experience what we are able to embody in our thought. In other words, each one will automatically attract good into his experience in accord with his acceptance of Life. This is one of the principal ideas of the Science of Mind and is called the Law of Mental Equivalents.

What would fill the needs for one person might not do it for another. What one person might regard as normal, possibly would stagger the imagination of another by its very bigness. Our standard of *expectancy depends entirely upon ourselves.* Every demonstration is made at the exact level of the expectancy, the expectancy embodied in thought. Since no one can step out of or away from himself, it would be impossible for anyone to escape the logic of his own thought.

There is a very nice song entitled "Wishing Will Make It So." It sounds encouraging, but it is not true. The world is full of "wishers" who are not "getters." We never get that for which we *merely wish.* A wish means nothing until it becomes a definite declaration that we now possess the good we need, a declaration backed by conviction of the quality and quantity of good which we expect to experience.

At this point we must understand that we have to rise above much of the world's confused thought. The world has dropped its eyes to the ground. Hungry for much, it is satisfied with little. Therefore we must strike out for the heights, away from the mists and fogs of man's doubts, and must see things *through the eyes of Spirit.* Spirit is the only Reality, but most of man's thinking is colored by the relative. If one has a little better health than his neighbor, he is content. If his business is a little better than the average, he is pleased. If he finds a fuller measure of happiness than that of the general run of mankind, he feels that he is blessed.

He is making the mistake of measuring his experience by an imperfect standard. Instead of establishing his expectancy in accord with the limited experience of mankind generally, he needs to base it on something better and bigger. The standards of the race are always in a state of flux, changing from generation to generation, from day to day, and from individual to individual. But the standard of Spirit is ageless, changeless, unvarying. *It is perfection, nothing less.*

When the level of the individual's thinking is divorced from that of the world and raised to that of the Spirit, his standard changes from that of imperfection to perfection. And this is the true norm. Regardless of his present experience, man has access to perfection for the minutest detail of his life.

Spirit could not possibly have any idea which is less than perfection. Anything less than this implies an imperfect Spirit, or something opposed to God, which cannot be. Spirit knows only the perfect, and knows nothing of the imperfect. Every step of the great creative activity of Spirit has been characterized by perfection. The tiniest organism adheres to a perfect pattern and functions according to a perfect law.

The blade of grass is a thing of perfection, functioning perfectly in its particular sphere. All its atoms are things of perfection, acting and reacting according to perfect law. The same perfection is true regarding man. But with this exception, man can think and he has gradually built mental concepts of imperfection, has gazed upon them, then has fallen down and worshipped them. Instead of knowing a God of Perfection, man in his imagination has created many gods of imperfection, and they are all creatures of his own imagination—*they have no basis in reality.*[16]

The idea of our being at choice in our lives leads to large questions about why things happen as they do. Did we choose them? Did we choose by **not** *choosing? Or is our choice limited and situational? Ernest believed in perfection-as-inclusivity, meaning that everything happens for a reason (which may not be the reason we first imagine) and is* *either an expression of our wholeness, or an opportunity to heal. Here he discuses accidents from this standpoint.*

Who would stand in front of an automobile and let it run over him just for the fun of it? Or jump off a roof and break a leg merely to take a rest cure in the hospital?

It is said that eighty percent of all accidents are unconsciously invited. "Unconsciously invited" is not such an innocent term as it seems to be, because it deals with the fact that nine-tenths of our thinking is not even conscious. We do not consciously think of driving our cars, or walking down the street, or having our food digest or making our hearts beat.

Just as there are automatic reactions in our physical body, so there are deeper automatic reactions in our mind. Our mind is really the creative thing within us. But what has this to do with accidents? Well, let us see! It is now known that when we unconsciously look forward to more trouble than pleasure from some particular incident, we unconsciously try to avoid that situation.

For instance, a person starts down the street on an important mission but perhaps he feels it is a situation that he fears he cannot quite handle. He is not willing to admit this because then he would be calling himself a coward and we all need self-esteem. But his subconscious reaction, without the consent of his intellect or conscious awareness, causes him to fall down and break his arm, his leg or his nose.

His emotional, unconscious desire has won over his intellect. It has seen to it that he need not meet a situation which he is unconsciously afraid of. One of the axioms of [Émile] Coué was that when the will and imagination are in conflict, the imagination and not the will always wins. Such is our nature. It is well known that this can be carried so far that perhaps instead of meeting with an accident he might be seized with a physical ailment.

This mind of ours is a pretty terrific thing. If it can produce eighty percent of our accidents, what else can it do to us? There is no question but that it governs the unconscious functioning of the body, all these silent forces that conspire to maintain our physical well-being.

The Bible says: "As [a man] thinketh in his heart, so is he." And Jesus, the most enlightened of all men, said that it is done unto us as we believe.

But Jesus did not explain to his followers that ninety percent of their belief was unconscious. It has taken the world two thousand years to discover this. But does this mean that we are to be afraid of the unconscious workings of our mind? Of course not. Because the very fact that the mind is creative shows that we are persons in our own right. If we were not creative we merely would be mental automatons, robots, nonentities. We would not be persons at all; we would be like cogs in a wheel or bolts in a piece of machinery, and this is not what Life has intended for us at all.

When Life created us It gave us the two great endowments of God, the two highest gifts of heaven: love and creativity. Love, so that we may have confidence in life, a sense of security and peace and joy in living; creativity, so that we can really live as persons and express ourselves individually. Life has done very well by us. Would it be too much to say that God has given us the best He has and then let us alone to discover ourselves?

We are somebody. I am glad that we are. I would rather have this creative Thing within me, even though It does produce a pain now and then, or break a toe or two, than to be without It. After all, It is the Thing that painted all the madonnas and built all the cathedrals. It is the Thing that made all the inventions and wrote all the books. We should not be afraid of this creative Thing in us for It is the greatest gift of Life.

God never makes mistakes and there are no accidents in the Divine Life. Everything is so ordained that when we learn to make a right use of the laws of Life, freedom, love, beauty, happiness and wholeness must follow, because Life Itself is neither weak, unhappy nor inadequate.[17]

The second of his introductory essays presents a discussion of the Law of Mind—the creative process by which thoughts becomes things.

The Way It Works

The Science of Mind is not a special revelation of any individual; it is, rather, the culmination of all revelations. We take the good wherever we find it, making it our own in so far as we understand it. The realization that Good is

Universal, and that as much good as any individual is able to incorporate in his life is his to use, is what constitutes the Science of Mind and Spirit.

We have discussed the nature of The Thing as being Universal Energy, Mind, Intelligence, Spirit—finding conscious and individualized centers of expression through us—and that man's intelligence is this Universal Mind, functioning at the level of man's concept of It. This is the essence of the whole teaching.

There is a Universal Mind, Spirit, Intelligence, that is the origin of everything: It is First Cause. It is God. This Universal Life and Energy finds an outlet in and through all that is energized, and through everything that lives. There is One Energy back of all that is energized. This Energy is in everything. There is One Spirit back of all expression. That is the meaning of the mystical saying: "In Him we live, and move, and have our being" (Acts 17:28).

The life which we live is the Universal Life expressing through us, else how could we live? Our thought and emotion is the use we make—consciously or unconsciously—of this original creative Thing that is the Cause of everything. Therefore, we shall say that the mind, spirit and intelligence which we find in ourselves is as much of this original, creative God as we understand. That this is not robbing God is a self-evident fact. Since we are, then we are real and actual and have existence; and since we can reduce all that is to a fundamental unit, we find that we have this proposition:

There is Spirit—or this Invisible Cause—and nothing, out of which all things are to be made. Now, Spirit plus nothing leaves Spirit only. Hence there is One Original Cause and nothing, out of which we are made. In other words, we are made from this Thing. That is why we are called the "son of God."

We now know that this is what we are—because we could not be anything else—but we do not know how much of this we are! When we see It as It is, then, we shall see ourselves as we are. We can only see It by looking at It through our own eyes. Hence, we shall find a better God when we have arrived at a higher standard for man. If God is to interpret Himself to man, He must interpret Himself *through* man. And the Spirit can make no gift that we do not accept.

This Original Life is Infinite. It is good. It is filled with peace. It is of the essence of purity. It is the ultimate of intelligence. It is power. It is Law. It is Life. It is in us. In that inner sanctuary of our own nature, hidden perhaps from objective gaze, "nestles the seed, perfection."

In our ignorance of the truth, we have misused the highest power we possess. And so great is this power—so complete is our freedom in it, so absolute the domain of law through it—that the misuse of this power has brought upon us the very conditions from which we suffer. We are bound because we are first free; the power which appears to bind us is the only power in the universe which can free us. This is why Jesus summed up His whole philosophy in this simple statement: "It is done unto you as you believe." The great Teacher looked so deeply into Nature, that She revealed Her fundamental simplicity to him. That "believe" and that "as" symbolize heaven and hell. And so we suffer, not because suffering is imposed upon us, but because we are ignorant of our true nature.

The Thing, then, works for us by working through us and is us, always. It cannot work for us in any other way. It spreads Itself over the whole universe and shouts at us from every angle, but It can become power to us *only when we recognize It as power.*

We cannot recognize that It is, while we are believing that It is not. Hence, it is written: "they . . . entered not in because of unbelief" (Heb. 4:6). We may enter in because of our belief, but we cannot enter while there is unbelief. Here we come to a house divided against itself. If we say we can only experience a little good, then we shall experience but a little good. But, if we say, with Emerson, "There is no great and no small to the soul that maketh all," then we may experience a greater good because we have conceived it.

Therefore, our belief sets the limit to our demonstration of a Principle which, of Itself, is without limit. It is ready to fill everything, because It is Infinite. So, it is not a question of Its willingness, or of Its ability. It is entirely a question of our own receptivity.

That we must go the way of the Law is a fundamental tenet of this Science, because Nature obeys us as we first obey It, and our obedience to It is our acceptance of It. How much can we believe? *As much as we can believe* will be done unto us.

When the consciousness speaks, the law receives and executes. When a farmer plants a seed, he invokes the law. That which follows is done by the mechanical side of Nature, which has no volition of Its own. Involution is the cause and evolution is the effect. When a practitioner thinks, or gives a treatment, or makes a prayer, he is dealing with involution—the first step of the creative order. This is what the Bible calls the Word. That which follows is evolution, or the unfoldment of the word or concept, into objective existence.

We are thinking, willing, knowing, conscious centers of Life. We are surrounded by, immersed in and there is flowing through us, a creative Something . . . call It what you will. The sum total of all our thought, will, purpose and belief creates a tendency in this Law that causes It to react to us according to the sum total of that belief.

Ignorance of the law excuses no one from its effects. If, then, certain specific ways of thought and belief have produced limitations, other beliefs will change them. We must learn to believe. The approach should be direct, and it should be specific.

Suppose one is laboring under the idea of limitation. His whole thought is a picture of limitation. Where is he placing himself in Mind? Is he not, in substance, saying, "I *cannot* have and enjoy good things"? And he is demonstrating that he cannot have, or accomplish, good. It may take time to reshape the basis of his thought; he must commence by saying, "I perceive that because I am what I am—because of this Infinite Thing that overshadows eternity and finds Its abiding place in me, I know that good is now mine—all good." There is no mental coercion in this. We do not will things to be done; things are brought into being, not by will, but by the power of self-assertive Truth.

How much can one demonstrate? Just what one can believe. How much can we see, how much can we accept, how much can we find in our consciousness that is no longer repudiated by our own denials? Whatever that is, *that much can we have.*

The gardener goes forth in faith to sow his seeds. He has learned that as he sows, so shall he reap; that the law works for all alike. We must accustom ourselves to the concept of the impersonalness of the law, the availability of the law, and the mechanical accuracy of the law. If we can conceive only a little good, that is as much as we can experience.

We must instill into the mind the fundamental proposition that good is without bounds. Only good and loving-kindness shall "follow me all the days of my life" (Psalms 23). We must get this concept, rather than continuing to think there is a power of evil as opposed to the power of Good. We experience good and evil because we perceive a presence of duality rather than unity.

Then, knowing that The Thing can work for us only through us, let us begin to accept today more good than we experienced yesterday, and to know that we shall reap a harvest of fulfilled desires. The time must come when we shall have left the apparent evil behind; when it shall be rolled up like a scroll and numbered with the things which were once thought to be.

Let us realize and work with this sound knowledge and perfect faith: That as high as we shall make our mark in Mind and Spirit, so high shall be Its outward manifestation in our material world.[18]

His affirmation for you:

I expect everything I do to prosper. I enthusiastically expect success. I let good flow into my experience. I am seeking good in every direction I look. I am looking forward to more good. I am entering into a deeper understanding of life. I am recognizing my union with all people and all events.[19]

III.

What Mind Can Conceive

THE PRESENCE:
In simple words the Truth can be defined:
That good shall come if you in it believe
While forms of fear accursed will fall on him
Whose mind envisions fear and doubt and grief.

Faith is the thought which Truth will bring to form,
Though faith may be in evil or in good;
But Truth itself stands clear, remote from ill.
Truth is the prototype immaculate,
The pattern of perfection never lost,
The Cosmic mould in the Creator's mind.
And flesh is counterpart to symbolize
That which exists above, hid from your eyes—
A crystal mould of unimagined grace
By which Life's Sculptor shapes the human face.
So flesh is soul while soul and flesh are one:
This is the Truth by which a new effect is won.

And he who dares to turn to Truth and Truth
Alone and say, "Thy will be done," will ope
The door to Paradise . . .
He who denies the Truth must live without
The good that Truth might bring from Heav'n to him
But Truth itself will suffer no defeat
And like a tree upon the desert's edge,
Wind-blown, sand-scoured and buffeted by age,
Can stand alone against the ravages
Of time and still hold life within itself.
So is the man upheld by Truth. His roots
Run deep and drink their fill from hidden springs.
Yet few there be who claim this heritage,
Discard tradition's blight and choose to live
Free souls! For *one* with Truth is better than
Ten thousand bowing to a golden calf
Within the wilderness of ignorance.[1]

How much grace, peace, love and wonder can we accept? **That** *much, we can have.*

We believe in an absolute, unconditioned first Cause, operating spontaneously, through self-proclamation, and answering only unto Itself out of an immutable law that is contained within Itself. Because this Mind is self-existent, self-creating, self-perpetuating, self-animating and self-expressing, it possesses everything necessary to create anything that is ever going to be, or ever was or ever shall be. This is what we believe, and these are the two great realities with which we deal. We know that the consciousness of the Presence, the motivation of love and the feeling of the desire to give, which partakes of the nature of the original giving, brings back into wholeness that which seemed to be sheared off. We know that everything seeks this wholeness as the river seeks the ocean. We know this, but a scientific spiritual mind practitioner is one who, understanding it, realizes that he often has to resort to a method or a technique. This, most of us have to do most of the time![2]

Because . . .

No matter how often they are told, many people do not understand the significance of spiritual mind healing nor what it is nor what it is based on. Most people think we are materializing spirit or spiritualizing matter or that we are influencing lower planes by a higher plane—and there is no such thing—or that we have suddenly gotten so spiritual that God sits up and takes notice. There is no such God, and there are no such people. I wish there were such people but know there couldn't be such a God.[3]

And . . .

Lessons on *prosperity* and mental control of conditions are sometimes dangerous because of the misunderstanding of this subject. Science of Mind is not a "get-rich-quick" scheme . . . We do not teach that you can get what you want. If we could all get what we want, it might be disastrous, for it is certain that most of us would want things that would interfere with the well-being of someone else . . . Consequently, this Science of Mind does not promise something for nothing. It does, however, tell us that if we comply with the Law, the Law complies with us.[4]

Because . . .

What we demonstrate today, tomorrow and the next day is not as important as the *tendency which our thought is taking* . . . the dominant attitude of our mind. If every day things are a little better, a little happier, a little more harmonious, a little more health-giving and joyous; if each day we are expressing more life, we are going in the right direction.[5]

Here are some more evocative pieces on why affirmative prayer works as it does, our conscious connection with the Infinite and the subconscious mind—the seat of all our creative beliefs.

It is held in our philosophy that there is no such thing as *your* subjective mind and *my* subjective mind, meaning two, for this would be duality. *But there is such a thing as the subjective state of my thought and of your thought in Mind.*[6]

The unfoldment of personality is a projection of the eternal, creative Spirit, which is the essence of all personality and the background of all individuality.[7]

Man's consciousness of God constitutes his real and immortal self. There is really only one man viewed from the Universal sense, but in this one, or "grand man" as it has been called, there are innumerable persons. Each is in direct relationship to the Whole. Each is an image of God but God is not lessened by being represented in innumerable forms and through limitless numbers of mentalities any more than the figure five would become exhausted by being used by innumerable mathematicians.[8]

It is impossible to plumb the depths of the individual mind, because the individual mind is really not individual but is individualized. Behind the individual is the Universal, which has no limits. In this concept alone lies the possibility of eternal and endless expansion. Everyone is Universal on the subjective side of life, and individual only at the point of conscious perception. The riddle is solved, and we all use the creative power of the Universal Mind *every time we use our own mind.*[9]

The artist knows that even though he has created something beautiful, it can be destroyed. His real and innermost satisfaction is not in the object, but in the subject; that thing within him which penetrates the mystic splendor of Beauty itself. So it is with all our temporary creations. Empires may rise and fall. Chance and change, the vicissitudes of fortune, the comings and goings of human events, the isolated dramas of our own experiences, the temporary or more or less permanent friendships in our lives inevitably must give way to something bigger. You are greater than the sum total of all the experiences you have had.[10]

Meeting privately with people who requested spiritual mind treatment from him for solutions to personal challenges, Ernest would usually treat silently, since he maintained that the exact form of the treatment, or the eloquent words in it, made no difference to the outcome. What only mattered was the feeling of yes in the mind and heart of the person doing the treatment.

A treatment is an active statement expressed inaudibly as thinking or audibly as words; it does not matter which so long as it is definite. The treatment is for the purpose of convincing the one giving it, and it operates at whatever level of awareness one reaches during that particular treatment. At times we have a greater level of awareness than at others, but the treatment is always an affirmation of our inner conviction.

There must be faith and conviction and acceptance through the treatment. Here is where our consciousness has attached itself to a greater possibility, must not limit what *may* happen by what *has* happened. The time track is past. "... let the dead bury their dead." Something new and dynamic is being born, right now. The Law, acting on the treatment, is bringing new situations, new people, new ideas and new activities; it cannot fail to operate at the level of our consciousness.

It might be asked about John, the one whom we are treating, "Can he be helped unless he also believes?"

If we cannot help a person unless he also believes, we will not be able to help many people. His belief has nothing to do with it. It is our belief that has to be transcended, and the transcendence of our belief will neutralize the negativity of his, and do it right where we are and in such degree as the activity of our affirmation takes place at a high level.

In treatment we may have to deny something, and we should not be afraid of it. An affirmation and a denial are the same thing because the human mind can only affirm, but it can do so positively or negatively. So we should not worry whether we are affirming or denying. We are arguing to convince ourselves that God is all there is, that there is a power greater than we are operating right where we are; all the confusion of thought or ignorance of this truth cannot change one bit of it. When we use a principle there is no whimsical response either of the Almighty or the less mighty. It is an absolute Law of action and reaction activated by consciousness, and a high degree of awareness inevitably produces a greater reaction.[11]

People live in a world of space and time, and decide that things are important or trivial, permanent or fleeting. On the other hand . . .

God is not conscious of matter as we know it. God is conscious of form, but not of size. God is conscious of manifestation but not of space. God is conscious of outline but not of limitation. God is conscious in many forms, *but not as division.*[12]

So far as the Law is concerned, It does not know anything about big and little . . . God cannot know anything which is contradictory to the Divine Being. It is impossible for the Infinite to know that which is finite. The superlative cannot be the comparative.

This does not mean that God cannot know the mountain and the molehill. We have tried to make it plain that God knows form but not size. He knows both the mountain and the molehill, but not as big and little. The Infinite knows experience but not duration. *Anything that Spirit knows, is!*[13]

Never look at that which you do not wish to experience. No matter what the false condition may be, it must be refuted. The proper kind of denial is based upon the recognition that, *in reality*, there is no limitation, for Mind can as easily make a planet as an acorn. The Infinite knows no difference between a million dollars and a penny. It only knows that *It is.*[14]

How often should we treat? And does repeating a treatment negate the power of the first one? Again, it's done unto us as we believe. It's only negated if we call it so! Here he discusses treating for someone else, called the "patient," another term from Christian

Science. Later this became "client," to distinguish mental treatment, which affects spiritual causation, from medical or similar treatment, which addresses physical effects.

Always come to a complete conclusion when giving a treatment. Always feel that it is done, complete and perfect, and give thanks for the answer, as if it were already objectified. In the interval between treatments, do not carry the thought of the patient around with you. To do so is to doubt, and this mental attitude must be completely overcome. Each treatment should be a complete statement of the Reality of Being.[15]

It would not be correct practice to spend one's whole time contemplating or meditating. There should be a balance between the inner and the outer states; from an inner communion of the soul with the Spirit there comes inspiration and guidance; but this inner state would remain an idle dream unless heaven were brought to earth, and spiritual perception woven into the fabric of everyday experience.[16]

More on treatment, our inner acceptance and using the spiritual power inherent in us (our "divine pedigree") toward positive ends:

Nothing is real to us unless we make it real. Nothing can touch us unless we let it touch us. Refuse to have the feelings hurt. Refuse to receive anyone's condemnation. In the independence of your own mentality, believe and feel that you are wonderful. This is not conceit. It is the truth.[17]

Repeat: "God is All. There is but One Power, Intelligence and Consciousness in the Universe, but One Presence. This One Presence cannot change. There is nothing for It to change into but Itself. It is Changeless, *and It is my life now, It is in me now.*" Claim that no form of race-suggestion, belief in limitation, subjective idea of limitation, thought of karma, fatalism, theology or hell, horoscope or any other false belief has power. Accept none of them. If you have ever believed in them, if you have ever believed that the stars govern you, or that your environment governs you, or that your opportunities govern you, recognize this as an hypnotic condition into which you have fallen, and deny every one of them until there is no longer anything in you that believes in them.[18]

To assert our individuality is to rise above the law of averages into that more highly specialized use of the Law which brings freedom rather than bondage, joy in the place of grief and wholeness instead of sickness. We cannot do this unless we are first willing to "judge not according to appearances." In this judging "not according to appearances" we are impressing the Law with a new idea of ourselves . . . a less limited idea; and we are learning to think independently of any existing circumstances. This is what is meant by entering the Absolute.[19]

Know—without a shadow of doubt—that as a result of your treatment, some action takes place in Infinite Mind. Infinite Mind is the actor and you are the announcer. If you have a vague, subtle, unconscious fear, be quiet and ask yourself, "Who am I?" "What am I?" "Who is speaking?" "What is my life?" In this manner think right back to Principle, until your thought becomes perfectly clear again. Such is the power of right thinking, that it cancels and erases everything unlike itself. It answers every question, solves all problems, is the solution to every difficulty. It is like the sunlight of Eternal Truth, bursting through the clouds of obscurity and bathing all life in glory. It is the Absolute with which you are dealing. *All there really is, is God!*[20]

To daily meditate on the Perfect Life, and to daily embody the Great Ideal, is a royal road to freedom, to that "peace which passeth understanding," and is happiness to the soul of man. Let us learn to see as God must, with a Perfect Vision. Let us seek the good and the true and believe in them with our whole heart, even though every man we meet is filled with suffering, and limitation appears at all sides. We cannot afford to believe in imperfection for a single second, to do so is to doubt God; it is to believe in a Power apart from God, to believe in another Creator. Let us daily say to ourselves: "Perfect God *within* me, Perfect Life *within* me, which is God, come forth into expression through me as that which I am; lead me ever into the paths of perfection and cause me to see only the Good." By this practice, the soul will become illumined and will acquaint itself with God and be at peace.[21]

In Universal Mind is contained the essence of everything that ever was, is or shall be. The seen and the unseen are in It and governed by It. It is the sole and only Creative Agency in the universe and all other apparent agencies are *It* working in different ways. Things exist in the Universal Mind as ideas. Ideas take form and become things in the concrete or the visible world. Thought calls things forth from the universal into expression.[22]

A good practice is to sit and realize that you are a center of Divine attraction, that all things are coming to you, that the power within is going out and drawing back all that you will ever need. Don't argue about it, just do it, and when you have finished leave it all to the Law, knowing that it will be done. Declare that all life, all love and power are now in your life. Declare that you are now in the midst of plenty. Stick to it even though you may not as yet see the result. It will work and those who believe the most always get the most. Think of the Law as your friend, always looking out for your interest. Trust completely in it and it will bring your good to you.[23]

Negative forces operating in our lives will die a natural death if we practice the habit of being disinterested in them. All outward forms of behavior are automatic results of inner mental picturings, be these pictures conscious or unconscious.

We are continuously being drawn into situations or circumstances, sometimes against our objective will, but seldom against our unconscious willing. Most of our mental imagery is unconscious. It comes either from previous experiences or the experiences of the race. There is much in the subconscious of which the intellect is not aware, but one thing is certain, our subjective or unconscious thought patterns can be changed. We have created them and we can change them . . .

We cannot live without God. Every attempt to do this has failed. No fear can remain where faith holds sway. Faith reunites us with the original, creative Spirit, the Divine Mind, which already exists at the center of our being. This kingdom of heaven, which is the kingdom of wholeness, is within.

You must have a faith in something greater than your previous experiences. You must bind yourself back in faith to the God Principle within you. If we come daily to the supreme Source of all life; if we let the dead bury their dead; if we forget the impositions placed upon us by our own imaginations, or the dictatorial attempts of life to replace the joy which belongs to everyone, we shall soon plunge into the ocean of our being where wholeness and peace abide forever.[24]

What we put into the treatment will come out of it. *More* than we appear to put into it can come out of it, but not a *different* type. If I plant a watermelon seed, I will get watermelons, but I will get a number of melons, and they will have a lot of seeds which can produce more melons, so the thought is *multiplicity* but never *division.*[25]

The way to give a treatment is first of all to absolutely believe that you can; believe that your word goes forth into a real Creative Power, which at once takes it up, and begins to operate upon it; feel that to this Power all things are possible. It knows nothing but Its own power to do that which It wishes to do. It receives the impress of your thought and acts upon it.[26]

The third of the four textbook introductory pieces sums it up beautifully:

What It Does

We should approach the study of this Science rationally, never expecting to derive any benefits from it that its Principle does not contain. For while it is true that we are immersed in an Infinite Intelligence, a Mind that knows all things, it is also true that this Intelligence can acquaint us with Its ideas only as we are able and willing to receive them. The Divine Mind is Infinite. It contains all knowledge and wisdom, but, before It can reveal Its secrets, It must have an outlet. This outlet we shall be compelled to supply through our own receptive mentalities.

All invention, art, literature, government, law and wisdom that has come to the race has been given to it through those who have deeply penetrated the secrets of nature and the mind of God.

Perhaps the simplest way to state the proposition is to say that we are surrounded by a Mind, or Intelligence, that knows everything; that the potential knowledge of all things exists in this Mind; that the abstract essence of beauty, truth and wisdom coexists in the Mind of the Universe; that we also exist in It and may draw from It. *But what we draw from It we must draw through the channel of our own minds.* A unity must be established, and a conscious connection must be made, before we can derive the benefits which the greater Mind is willing to reveal or impart to us.

The Spirit can give us only what we can take; it imparts of Itself only as we partake of Its nature. It can tell us only what we can understand. The Infinite Knowingness becomes our wisdom only in such degree as we embody Its Intelligence. It has been said that we can know God only in so far as we can become God. This is a far-reaching thought and should be carefully scrutinized. It is to be taken figuratively and not too literally, for we cannot really become God, but we can and do partake of the Divine Nature, and the Universal does personify Itself through man in varying degrees, according to man's receptivity to It.

The Universe is impersonal. It gives alike to all. It is no respecter of persons. It values each alike. Its nature is to impart, ours to receive. When we stand in the light, we cast a shadow across the pathway of our own experience. Emerson advises that we get our *bloated nothingness* out of the way of the divine circuits.

It is a beautiful and true thought to realize that every man stands in the shadow of a mighty Mind, a pure Intelligence and a Divine givingness! Not alone unto the great comes the soft tread of the Unseen Guest. The arrogant have not perceived the simplicity of faith, but the pure in heart see God. The farmer has seen the Heavenly Host in his fields. The child has frolicked with Him at play. The mother has clasped Him to her breast and the fond lover has seen Him in the eyes of his beloved. We look too far away for Reality.

The intelligence by and through which we perceive that there is a Spiritual Presence and an Infinite Mind in the Universe constitutes our receptivity to It, and decides Its flow through us. We have made a riddle out of simplicity; therefore, we have not read the sermons written in stones, nor interpreted the light of love running through life.

To return to a sane simplicity is one of the first and most important things to do. All men receive *some* light, and this light is always the same light. There is one nature diffused throughout all nature; One God incarnated in all peoples.

The Divine Incarnation is inherent in our nature. We are immersed in an Infinite Knowingness. The question is, how much of this Reality are we going to express in our own lives? The direct approach is always the best and the most effective. In so far as any man has spoken the truth, he has proclaimed God—it matters not what his particular approach may have been. The scientist and the philosopher, the priest and the professor, the humanitarian and the empire builder, all have caught some gleam of the eternal glory and each has spoken, in his own tongue, that language which is of itself Universal.

Let us do away with a ponderosity of thought and approach the thing simply and quietly. It is the nature of the Universe to give us what we are able to take. It cannot give us more. It has given all, we have not yet accepted the greater gift.

Spiritual wisdom says that God manifests through everything and is incarnated in all men; that all is Divinity and that Nature herself is the body of God. The mechanical laws of nature are set and immutable, but the spontaneous recognition of these laws gives us the power to bring them into practical use in everyday life and experience.

Here we have a dual unity; law and order, spontaneous choice, volition, conscious action and automatic reaction. The laws of the universe are to be trusted but we must come to understand them before we can use them. Once understood, any law is available and is impersonally responsive to each and all alike.

In an intelligent study of the teachings of the Science of Mind, we come to understand that all is Love and yet all is Law. Love rules through Law. Love is the Divine Givingness; Love is the Way. Love is spontaneous;

Law is impersonal. We should study the nature of Reality with this in mind, and in this way we shall avoid two grave mistakes: either viewing life as made up only of mechanical laws, or viewing it as made up only of spontaneous actions, irrespective of law and order.

As we gain the broader viewpoint, we shall see that Life must contain two fundamental characteristics. We shall see that there is an Infinite Spirit, operating through an Infinite and Immutable Law. In this, Cosmos, and not chaos, finds an eternal existence in Reality. Love points the way and Law makes the way possible.

If we observe any scientific discovery, we shall see that this is the way it works. Some man's mind discovers the law, or principle, governing the science; this is the way of Love, of personal volition, of choice—this is the spontaneous element in the universe. Following this knowledge of the way the principle works—having discovered the operation of the Law—the spontaneous element now rests its case on immutable reactions inherent in the Law. All science is based upon proven principles.

But we should not overlook the significant fact that it is the *Mind* which discovers and makes use of the mechanical law! Is not this mind the Spirit in us? We can never completely fathom the Infinite Mind: we shall always be discovering new lands. Consequently, evolution is an eternal unfoldment of the more yet to be.

Since it is the mind which must first come to see, know and understand—and since all future possibility for the race must first find an avenue of outlet through someone's mind—we shall do well to look to the mind for the answer to all our problems.

Undoubtedly we are surrounded by, and immersed in, a perfect Life: a complete, normal, happy, sane, harmonious and peaceful existence. But *only as much of this Life as we embody will really become ours to use.* As much of this Life as we understand and embody will react as immutable law—the reaction of the mechanical to the volitional. The concept is wonderful and fraught with tremendous significance. In it are bound up our hopes and fears, our expectations and our future and present realizations.

Since an understanding of any law must pass first through our conscious mind before we can make use of it, it follows that with all our getting, we should get understanding. Should we wish to know a certain truth, we should state that this truth is already known in Mind and this statement will be true, but the Over-Mind must be accepted into our mind before we can understand It. How, then, are we to accomplish the desired result? By stating and feeling that *our mind* knows the truth about the thing we desire to know. In this way we draw the Infinite Mind into our mentalities, for definite knowledge of some particular good.

The Universal Mind contains all knowledge. It is the potential ultimate of all things. To It, all things are possible. To us, as much is possible as we can conceive, according to law. Should all the wisdom of the universe be poured over us, we should yet receive only that which we are ready to understand. This is why some draw one type of knowledge and some another, and all from the same source—the Source of all knowledge. The scientist discovers the principles of his science, the artist embodies the spirit of his art, the saint draws Christ into his being—all because they have courted the particular presence of some definite concept. Each state of consciousness taps the same source, but has a different receptivity. Each receives what he asks for, according to his ability to embody. The Universal is Infinite; the possibility of differentiating is limitless.

Life always becomes to us the particular thing we need *when we believe that it becomes to us that particular thing*. The understanding of this is the essence of simplicity. As all numbers proceed from the fundamental unit, as all material forms are but different manifestations of one formless stuff, so all things proceed from that which is neither person, place or thing, but is of the essence of all things.

Our thought and conscious receptivity differentiate this Universal Possibility, by drawing It through our minds and causing It to flow into particular channels, through the conscious receptivity of our different faiths. One state of consciousness will differentiate one kind of a result, another mental state a different manifestation.

Mental work is definite. Each state of thought taps the same Principle, each uses the same Law, is inspired by the same Spirit, but each draws forth a different result. Here is multiplicity proceeding from Unity. This is what Emerson meant when he said that Unity passes into variety.

But, someone will ask, can we bring out both good and evil from the One Source? Of course not. The First Principle is goodness, and only in so far as our thought and action tend toward a constructive program, will it eventually succeed.

We cannot fight the Universe. It refuses to be budged from Its course. We can only go with It.

But there is ample latitude for personal expression. How then, are we going to know what is right and what is wrong? We are not going to know; we already do know. Every man knows right from wrong, in its broadest sense.

It should be considered right to love and to enjoy living. To be well, happy and to express freedom is to be in accord with Divine Law and Wisdom. Here is latitude enough for the most expectant, and the most enthusiastic.

Let us restate our Principle. We are surrounded by an Infinite Possibility. It is Goodness, Life, Law and Reason. In expressing Itself through us, It becomes more fully conscious of Its own being. Therefore, It wishes to express through us. As It passes into our being, It automatically becomes the law of our lives. It can pass into expression through us only as we consciously allow It to do so. Therefore, we should have faith in It, and Its desires and Its ability to do for us *all that we shall ever need to have done.* Since It must pass through our consciousness to operate for us, we must be conscious that It is doing so.

The one who wishes to demonstrate some particular good must become conscious of this particular good, if he wishes to experience it. Therefore, he must make his mind receptive to it and he must do this consciously. There is no hocus-pocus in a mental treatment. It is always definite, conscious, concrete and explicit. We are dealing with Intelligence, and should deal with It intelligently.

There is no occult trick in giving scientific treatments. It is just the reverse. Simplicity should mark our every effort and positivity should accompany all statements that we make into the law of Good.

A treatment is a statement in the Law, embodying the concrete idea of our desires and accompanied by an unqualified faith that the Law works *for* us, as we work with It. Let us waste no further time looking for the secret of success or the key to happiness. Already the door is open and whosoever will may enter.

Undoubtedly, each of us is now demonstrating his concept of life, but *trained* thought is far more powerful than *untrained*, and the one who gives conscious power to his thought should be more careful what he thinks than the one who does not. The more power one gives to his thought—the more completely he believes that his thought has power—the more power will it have.

A treatment is an active thing. When one gives a treatment, he is not sitting around, hoping that something may happen. He is definitely, constructively, actively stating, sensing, knowing some specific good. This is in accord with the Principle which we seek to demonstrate. If we give treatments without a definite motive in mind, the most we can accomplish will be to promote a salutary atmosphere. A *passive* meditation will never produce an active demonstration, any more than an artist can paint a picture by sitting down with his paints but never using them.

The mind must conceive before the Creative Energy can produce; we must supply the avenue through which It can work. It is ready and willing. It is Its nature to spring into being through our thought and action.

In an iron foundry, the pig iron is thrown into a great furnace and melted. That which was solid becomes liquid, and is then poured into molds which are fashioned in different shapes. The iron itself neither knows nor cares what particular form it takes, it is formless, ready to take any form supplied. If we did not place it in the proper molds, the liquid would assume no particular form.

This is the way it is in dealing with the subtle energy of Spirit, but the molds are made in our own subjective minds, through conscious and specific thought, purpose and direction. We should be very careful not to think that because we make the mold, we must create the substance. It already exists; it is part of the Life in which we live, a part of the Universal Energy. Definite molds or concepts decide the shape which is to be created from the general liquid. This should prove to us that there is a specific technique in mental treatment which we should not overlook. If we wish a *certain* good, we must instill into our own minds a realization of this specific good and then—as this idea is the mold we place in mind—it will be filled by the substance necessary for the complete manifestation of this good in our lives.

Therefore, if a man is seeking to demonstrate, he must tell himself that he has faith in his power, in his ability, in the Principle and in the certainty of the demonstration for which he works. Faith, being a mental attitude, is according to law; and even though one doubts, he can overcome his doubts and create the desired faith, definitely. If this were not so, only those who by nature have faith in God could ever hope to understand the Principle of the Science of Mind and Spirit, which is subject to certain, definite, immutable and impersonal laws. However, even though faith is a necessary attitude, it is something that can always be established by explaining the theory and proving the Principle.

Faith in a certain specific statement has power consciously to oppose, neutralize, erase and obliterate the opposite mental attitude. It is because of this fact that this study is a science that can definitely be used, and we must accept it as such. The mystery with which most people surround the search for Truth, relative to this Principle, is not read out of It, but is read into It.

It stands to reason that if thought and faith, prayer, hope and appreciation are anything at all, they are definite; and if they are definite, they must be specific; if they are specific, then they unquestionably must accomplish their desire.

Many people correctly begin their treatment in this manner: "I know that the Principle of Intelligence within me will direct me, etc.," then they complete it with the thought: "Well, I certainly hope it does." This is entirely forgetting any definite statement, and is simply wondering if possibly some good will come along. This is not a correct treatment, and is not the scientific use of this Principle.

Hope is good; it is better than despair, but it is a subtle illusion and is an unconscious compromise, and has no part in an effective mental treatment. We should say to doubt: "Where did you come from, who is your father, etc. . . . . You have no place in my mind. Get out! I know that the faith within me now neutralizes all doubt." This is the scientific use of a mental statement. There must be no compromise with the consciousness.

We have discovered what the Principle is and How It Works, and now this is What It Does. Specifically turn to that thought which tells us we do not know how to use It, and repudiate the falsehood. The Principle that we have to demonstrate is perfect, and—in so far as we can compel the mind to perceive this perfection—so far it will automatically demonstrate. Experience has proved this to be true.

We waste much time in arguing over things that cannot be answered. When we have arrived at the ultimate, *that is the ultimate.* It is the way the Thing works. Therefore, we have a right to say that there is a law involved, and that this Law executes the word. We discover laws, find out how they work and then begin to use them. Therefore, this question is answered, when we say it is the nature of thought of the Creative Energy, and the nature of Being *to be this way.* We would say that Law is an attribute of God. God did not make Law; it coexists with the Eternal. The Infinite Law and the Infinite Intelligence are but two sides of the Infinite Unity. One balances the other and they are the great personal and impersonal principles in the universe. Evolution is the out-working of the mechanical, and involution is the in-working of the conscious and the volitional.

When we think, something happens to thought. The field through which thought operates is Infinite. There is no reason to doubt it. No matter how it is approached, to thought there can be no limit, so we will say that it is the nature of Being to react in this way. Here and now, we are surrounded by, and immersed in, an Infinite Good. How much of this Infinite Good is ours? *All of it!* And how much of It may we have to use? *As much of it as we can embody.*[27]

Here's a powerful thought to declare to yourself:

I carefully guard my thought. I refuse to permit anything antagonistic or unlovely to enter my consciousness. I am learning to live in joy, in peace and in calm confidence. I am putting my whole trust, faith and confidence in the good. I think with clarity, move with ease and accomplish without strain.[28]

IV.

The Power Responds
to All Alike

THE FARER:

O you who have been bound, as I have been,
In bonds of superstition and of doubt,
I cry to you: ye bear false witness to
The power of that which nonexistent is;
Ye have but made a *law* of accident
And chance, of fallen man and angry gods
Who send offending souls to purgatory
Or buy them back again. How strange the story!

THE PRESENCE:

The God whom I proclaim is not such God,
But Being Absolute, from Whom outflows
A ceaseless stream of wisdom bathed in love:
For *being* is both essence and a state
Of consciousness or mind in action which
At all times has harmony within itself
And cannot know the feeling of revenge
For sin, because it knows no sin; for sin

Is but a name for states of consciousness
Of those who fail to harmonize with law.
The river will not make you drink though you
Should die of thirst; it does not leap the banks
To lave the parching fields nor force the roots
To drink, yet rushes joyously to fill
The channel or the reservoir when once
The gate swings wide to let it give itself . . .

Say not, "I search, how can I enter in?
I know no way to free myself from sin."
From what you seek you are so swiftly fleeing,
When deep within, you are, *already, being!*
No more of *Being* can there ever be
Than that which is this moment in the Me.
From this deduce the truth—*none else* can view
Or state the terms by which Love comes to you,
Nor can he give the verdict "No" or "Yes"
For entrance into cosmic consciousness;
And love alone reveals such unity
And soul by soul it wakens in the Me.

Most wisely do you speak and wise the soul
Who heeds; for consciousness of God alone
Provides a way for mind to unify
And synthesize all fields of knowledge in
A comprehensive whole, where opposites
Converge to form a perfect round and where
All faiths will be dissolved into a flux
Of direct knowing. Frictions disappear
Where harmony is found—and love is key.
No one can doubt that in the Over-Soul
No conflicts can exist between the fields
Of knowledge nor the laws of things or thoughts

Or of religious faiths. The truths in each
Are true in all and in the cosmic mind;
Untruth cannot exist.

The Over-Soul
And lesser self are one, and he in whom
The union is complete must share with God
In freedom from the conflicts that divide
Mankind and rend their hearts and lives.
Once more I say to you, you need not wait
For heaven, for heaven waits for you, and it
Is Now. Immortal life is *here* and he
Who has through love found life within the Me
Resolves all doubts and solves life's mystery.[1]

Taking what we know, and living it, is the subject of the final introductory material in **The Science of Mind.** *It reveals Ernest at his most powerful.*

How to Use It

One of the great difficulties in the new order of thought is that we are likely to indulge in too much theory and too little practice. As a matter of fact, we only know as much as we can prove by actual demonstration. That which we cannot prove may, or may not, be true but that which we can prove certainly must be, and is, the truth.

Of course, the theory of any scientific principle goes beyond its application, at any given stage of the unfoldment of that principle, and the evolution of its accomplishments. If this were not true, there would be no progress in any science. The sciences are objectively real to us only in so far as we demonstrate them, and until demonstrated they are suppositional, so far as practical results are concerned. If there is *any* field of research where the practical application is necessary, it is in the metaphysical field, the reason being that the principle of metaphysics seems less tangible to the average person than does the principle of other sciences. As a matter of fact, *all principles are as intangible,* but the world at large has not yet come to consider the Principle of mental practice in the same light that it considers other given principles of life and action. *Its apparent intangibility is lessened whenever and wherever anyone actually demonstrates the supremacy of spiritual thought force over apparent material resistance.*

It is easy enough to rush about shouting there are no sick people, but this will never heal those who appear to be sick. It is easy to proclaim that there are no needy. Anyone can *say* this, whether he be wise or otherwise. If we are to prove such statements to be facts in our experience, we shall be compelled to do more than *announce a principle,* no matter how true it may be.

There is no doubt about the immutability and the availability of the Law. The Law is Infinite. It is right where we happen to be at any given time. It occupies all space and fills every form with differentiations of Itself. The Law also flows through us, because It flows through everything, and since we exist, It must be in and through us. This is the crux of the whole matter. Infinite and immutable as the Law is—ever-present and available as It must be, the potential possibility of all human probability—It must flow *through* us in order to manifest *for* us.

It has been proved that by thinking correctly and by a conscious mental use of the law of Mind, we can cause It to do definite things for us, through us. By conscious thinking, we give conscious direction to It, and It, consciously or unconsciously, responds to our advance along the line of our conscious, or subjective, direction.

It must and will respond to everyone, because It is Law and law is no respecter of persons. We are surrounded by an intelligent force and substance, from which all things come—the ultimate Essence, in the invisible and subjective world, of all visible and objective forms and conditions. It is around us in its original state, ready and willing to take form through the impulse of our creative belief. *It works for us by flowing through us.* This law we did not create; this law we cannot change. We can use It correctly only as we understand and use It according to Its nature.

Hence, it follows that if we believe that It will not work, It really works by appearing to "not work." When we believe that It cannot and will not, then, according to the principle, It *does not.* But when It does not, It still does—only It does according to our belief that It will not. This is our own punishment through the law of cause and effect; we do not enter in because of our doubts and fears. It is not a punishment imposed upon us by the Spirit of God, but an automatic result of failing constructively to use the Law of God.

God does not punish the mathematician who fails to obtain the right answer to his problem. The thought of the unsolved problem *does* punish him until he applies the right principle and thus secures the desired result. Thus sin and punishment, righteousness and salvation, are logical reactions of the Universe to the life of the individual.

When we are dealing with real Life—with thoughts, impulses, emotions, etc.—we are dealing with Causation, with original Cause, and we should be most careful how we deal with such powers and forces. In dealing with this subtle power of Mind and Spirit, we are dealing with a fluent force. It is forever taking form and forever deserting the form which it has taken. Thus a practitioner of this Science should not be confused over any given form, but should know that any form which is not of the original harmony is subject to change. The Original Spirit is Harmony. It is Beauty and Truth and everything that goes with Ultimate Reality. The Universe is not divided against Itself.

We should learn to control our thought processes and bring them into line with Reality. Thought should tend more and more toward an affirmative attitude of mind that is positive, stable and—above all else—toward a real unity with Spirit that is already complete and perfect.

We should be able to look a discordant fact in the face and deny its reality, since we know its seeming reality is borrowed from illusion, from "chaos and old night." Our standard is one of perfection. "Be ye therefore perfect, even as your Father which is in heaven is perfect" (Matt. 5:48). We should be able to look at a wrong condition with the knowledge that we can change it. *The realization that we have this ability must be gained by the application of our knowledge.*

The practice of the Science of Mind calls for a positive understanding of the Spirit of Truth; a willingness to let this inner Spirit guide us, with the conscious knowledge that "The law of the Lord is perfect" (Psalms 19:7).

And we must believe this to be a fact. *In so far as our thought is in accord with this perfect Law, it will accomplish and nothing can hinder it.* "Heaven and earth shall pass away, but my words shall not pass away" (Matt. 24:35), said the beautiful Jesus, as he strove to teach his disciples the immutability of the Law of Righteousness.

A practitioner uses thought definitely and for specific purposes, and the more definitely he uses the Law, the more directly will It respond to him. A false fact is neither person, place nor thing to the one who uncovers it, and once uncovered it has no place in which to hide. The *illusion,* seen and understood, is made negative in the experience of the one who suffered by it. While it is true that wrong conditions exist, they could not remain unless there were someone to experience them. Consequently, the experience must be in consciousness. Change the consciousness and the false condition will disappear. Conditions are not entities, we are entities. Cannot that which is conscious cast out that which has no consciousness? If we properly understood, we would be able to remove false conditions as easily as Jesus did. He *knew,* but our faith is weak. We must strengthen it and we can.

Let us analyze this: One finds himself impoverished. He wishes to change this condition. He knows that it is not in accord with Ultimate Reality; that the Spirit imposes no limitations. Therefore, he knows that his apparent limited condition has no real law to support it; it is simply an experience of consciousness. He wishes a definite result in the opposite direction. First, he realizes that the Law of Life is a Law of Liberty, of Freedom. He now states that this Law of Liberty is flowing through him and into all his affairs. But the image of his limitation persists. Here is a definite contradiction of his statements of freedom.

Right here, he must stop and declare that these images of limitation are neither person, place nor thing, that they have no power, personality nor presence and no real law to support them. He does not believe in them and they cannot operate through him. He is free from their influence, forever. He then begins to fill his thought with the idea of faith, the expectancy of good and the realization of plenty. He senses, and mentally sees, right action in his life. He puts his whole trust in the Law of Good, and It becomes very real to him as he definitely speaks It into being—into his being and into the being of his affairs. He denies anything and everything that contradicts his realization of this truth.

At this point of realization, he meets a friend who immediately begins a tale of woe about hard times, bad business conditions, etc. and, should he listen to this "tale of the serpent," he might reverse his previous affirmations and make negative his former mental and spiritual concept! This does not mean that he should refuse to hold conversation with people, for fear they will neutralize the position which he has taken in his mind, but that he should refuse mentally to accept the false position. Then he can talk with anyone and not be disturbed.

The time will come when we will let our "conversation be in Heaven," and refuse to talk about, read or think about, those things that ought not to be. But, someone will say, "Should we refuse to look at sickness, poverty and unhappiness?" This is not what we are discussing. We will not refuse to help the helpless or lift up the fallen, but we will refuse to wallow in the mud because of our sympathies. "And if the blind lead the blind, both shall fall into the ditch" (Matt. 15:14).

Of all the people in the world, the ones who have come nearest to touching the seamless garment of Truth have been the most sympathetic and the greatest lovers of the race. Jesus said, "And I, if I be lifted up . . . (not dragged down) will draw all men unto me" (John 12:32).

We are in the world and of it and it is good that it is so. The world is all right when we view it correctly. Who knows what would transpire if all men would speak the truth? It has never yet been tried, but let not the mouth of the profane hinder those who would enter, thereby keeping them from entering. The world has never yet followed the simple ethics of Jesus, yet it is loud in its proclamation that it is Christian. This statement is not written in a spirit of controversy, it is one of conviction, and will make its appeal only to those who are convinced. "A man convinced against his will is of the same opinion still."

Let us return to the man who really wishes to demonstrate the supremacy of spiritual thought force over apparent material resistance. Let us put his treatment in the first person—impersonating him for the purpose of clarity.

"I am a center in the Divine Mind, a point of God-conscious life, truth and action. My affairs are divinely guided and guarded into right action, into correct results. Everything I do, say or think, is stimulated by the Truth. There is power in this word that I speak, because it is of the Truth and it is the Truth. There is perfect and continuous right action in my life and my affairs. All belief in wrong action is dispelled and made negative. Right action alone has power and right action *is power,* and Power is God . . . the Living Spirit Almighty. This Spirit animates everything that I do, say or think. Ideas come to me daily and these ideas are divine ideas. They direct me and sustain me without effort. I am continuously directed. I am compelled to do the right thing at the right time, to say the right word at the right time, to follow the right course at all times.

"All suggestion of age, poverty, limitation or unhappiness is uprooted from my mind and cannot gain entrance to my thought. I am happy, well and filled with perfect Life. I live in the Spirit of Truth and am conscious that the Spirit of Truth lives in me. My word is the law unto its own manifestation, and will bring to me or cause me to be brought to its fulfillment. There is no unbelief, no doubt, no uncertainty. I know and I know that I know. Let every thought of doubt vanish from my mind that I may know the Truth and the Truth may make me free."

The Truth is instantaneous in its demonstration, taking only such time in Its unfoldment as is inherent in the law of a logical and sequential evolution. In this invisible law of unfoldment, we must come to trust, and although we do not see the way, we must believe that the way *is* and *is operative.* We must trust the Invisible, for It is the sole cause of that which is visible . . . ". . . and things which are seen were not made of things which do appear" (Heb. 11:3).

Healing and demonstration take place as our minds become attuned to the truth of Being. There is no *process of healing,* but there is generally a *process in healing.* This process is the time and effort which we undergo in our realizations of Truth.

The one who wishes scientifically to work out his problems must daily take the time to meditate and mentally treat the condition, no matter what the apparent contradictions may be. He is working silently in the Law and the Law will find an outlet through his faith in It. This Law is the Law which puts the act into all action. It is the invisible actor, working through us to will and to do. As a result of right treatment, the mold formed in the subjective mind by the treatment makes possible a concrete manifestation. The treatment is an intelligent Energy in the invisible world. It is a spiritual entity, working through the Law of Mind, and it is an actual force now consciously directed. Therefore, it must produce specific results.

This will not seem strange to those who have given thought to the subject. As the primordial Word of the Creator is the only thing which explains creation, so every man's word—partaking of this original nature as it does—must reproduce the creative function in his life, at the level of his consciousness of One Life back of, in and through all.

A treatment is a spiritual entity in the mental world and is equipped with power and volition—as much power and volition as there is faith in it, given to it by the mind of the one using it—and, operating through the Law, It knows exactly how to work and what methods to use and just how to use them. *We do not put the power into this word,* but we do let the power of the Law flow through it, and the one who most completely believes in this power will produce the best results. This is the Law of cause and effect, again.

When one gives a treatment for right action, and does not believe that right action will be the result, he makes his own treatment negative. Therefore, we should spend much time in convincing ourselves of the truth of our treatments. Now this is not a power of will, but a power of choice. We do not put the power into this treatment, and we will take out of the treatment *only as much as we believe is in it!*

If one doubts his ability to give an effective treatment, he should specifically treat himself to remove this doubt. He should say something like this, but not necessarily these words: "I am convinced that this word has power, and I firmly believe in it. I trust it to produce the right results in my life (or in the life of the one for whom I am using this word)."

We should work, not with anxiety, but with expectancy; not by coercion but with conviction; not through compulsion but in a state of conscious recognition and receptivity. We do not have to drive or push but we must accept and believe. We should, then, leave everything to the Law, expecting a full and complete proof of our faith. We shall not be disappointed or chagrined, for the Law is our faithful servant.

One should treat any given proposition until he proves his Principle, no matter how long it takes. We should treat until we get results—until there comes into our objective experience the actual outpouring of our subjective words. When working for someone else, speak the name of this person—into Mind—then proceed with the treatment. Should someone come to you with the question "Am I too old to find my rightful place?" what are you as a practitioner to reply? You explain that there is no recognition of age in the Truth; that everyone has his place in Truth; that God does not withdraw Himself from us at a certain age, for God is Omnipresence. In this Presence, every being is fully provided for at every age.

A practitioner consciously removes the apparent obstruction and leaves the field open to a new influx of Spirit. He resolves things into thought, dissolves the negative appearance in the condition, by recognizing only perfection. *The practitioner must know, and must state, that there are no obstacles in the pathway of Truth.* He must know that his word, being the activity of the Truth, removes all obstructions from the pathway of his patient, or the one for whom he is working.

If the obstruction is the result of a "hangover" of belief from past years, the practitioner must know that no past mistake can hinder or obstruct the flow of Divine Intelligence through God's idea—which is perfect man, manifesting the attributes of God in freedom, happiness, activity and power, and that this Truth is now made manifest in his life.

The patient should try to be receptive, not to the will of the practitioner, but to the purpose of the Universe. That is, the patient should expect results and should be willing to give up anything and everything that would hinder the demonstration. Perfect belief is the beginning and the end of all good mental work.

The mental attitude of the practitioner is one of denial toward every false condition that opposes the principle of Life as one of absolute perfection. God's world is perfect, and this is the Principle we have to demonstrate. Spiritual things must be spiritually discerned and when we are ready and willing spiritually to discern, we shall find a ready response from the Invisible into the visible. Let us do our work conscientiously and thoroughly and leave the results to that Law which is perfect.

A new light is coming into the world. We are on the borderland of a new experience. The veil between Spirit and matter is very thin. The invisible passes into visibility through our faith in it. A new science, a new religion and a new philosophy are rapidly being developed. This is in line with the evolution of the great Presence and nothing can hinder its progress. It is useless, as well as foolish, to make any attempts to cover this Principle, or to hold It as a vested right of any religion, sect or order. The Truth will out; the Spirit will make Itself known. Happy are we if we see these things which, from the foundation of the human race, have been longed for by all aspiring souls.

True thought deals directly with First Cause; and this Science is the study of First Cause, Spirit, or the Truth, that Invisible Essence, that Ultimate Stuff and Intelligence from which everything comes—the Power back of creation—The Thing Itself.[2]

The subconscious, subjective aspect of mind is here likened to fertile soil. We use it personally, and also collectively, in the respect that Ernest labels the "race consciousness" (or "race suggestion")—the sum of all human belief that exerts an influence on each of us. Yet our individual choice is supreme, able to transcend any collective limitations and when it does so, the whole collective reality is lifted up to a field of new possibilities.

The soul, being the seat of memory, already contains a record of everything that has ever happened to us. These memories, as a whole, constitute the subjective tendency of the individual life; this tendency can be changed through constant effort and a determined persistency of purpose. The soul life of all people merges, more or less, and this creates the soul life of the race—the collective subjectivity of all humanity—called by some the "collective unconscious." This "collective unconscious" contains a record of all human events that have ever transpired. We are all, more or less, subject to this collective thought, since it acts as a powerful race suggestion. The sum total of all erroneous human belief binds until the individual mentally lifts himself above the law of averages into the higher law of Spiritual Individualism.[3]

What you are deeply *feeling* is usually what you are establishing in Mind as cause; it is the pattern for what you will receive.

To make this more clear, even though you may have thought of it before, think about the soil in the garden. When you wish to produce a crop of any kind you first prepare the soil, using your best knowledge to get it into the right condition so it will bring forth what you want to grow there. When the earth is well prepared, free from obstructions, properly fertilized and in every way made ready to receive the seed; when the rain and the sun have done their part and you have carefully selected your seeds and made your plans, then you begin the planting. You plant *only* those seeds that will grow into what you want in your garden. You may want a row of radishes in between one of beets and one of carrots. Close by, in the same soil, you plant cabbages, and then next, perhaps, watermelons.

From the good, reliable, dependable soil the radish seed draws whatever is needed to produce white radishes with red skins. But, from exactly the same soil, in the very next row, you get carrots, bright orange-yellow all the way through and tasting not one bit like the radishes, and on the other side are deep red beets of still another texture and taste. All the other kinds of seeds bring forth according to their own natures and—*this is the point*—you knew they would! That is why you planted them. No one is wise enough to pick out of the soil the chemicals to produce the different results, but then no one has to. Your part is fourfold: Get the soil ready; choose the right seeds; plant them; and give the garden the right care and attention. The marvelously wise soil of Mother Nature takes charge of the processes of production.

No one can explain why or how this happens. But then, just because of lack of such understanding, do we fail to take advantage of it? No. Year after year, millions of men and women plant their gardens and know in advance what harvest they are going to have.

In the spiritual realm, Universal Subjective Mind as Law is the soil. It is just as dependable, just as reliable and functions just as naturally as the soil in the garden. It takes whatever you choose to plant in It, and It produces accordingly. You, personally, are the one who determines what kind of results you are going to have. That is one of the principles you need to keep constantly in mind. That which you decide with the conscious mind and then commit to the action of the Law, in quiet trust, in perfect confidence, is that which will come to pass for you. No one knows just how thoughts become concrete and tangible. Neither does anyone know how one part of the soil produces a carrot when the very same soil, only a few inches away, brings forth a luscious watermelon. But just because the action is not completely understood, has this kept one from planting seeds? You need to be equally wise and trustful about your spiritual planting.

Care was used in preparing the garden soil in order to get it into the proper condition. Here again the analogy is true: We must remove from the creative medium of mind all negatives. It must be at peace. It has to have removed from it everything that would obstruct the right development of the good results sought. When you are poised, calm, at peace, filled with happy expectancy, serenely trusting in the fulfillment of the highest good, you are ready to do your spiritual planting.

All summer long the warmth of the sun and refreshment of gentle rains bring your garden through the various stages of growth to rich maturity, the reason you planted it. Your spiritual garden, first planted in the soil of emotional serenity, you keep nourished with love and watered with expectancy. Do not let any weeds of doubt or anxiety hinder its progress. Give it daily attention, entirely free from worry or fear as to the outcome. Remember, you can trust the soil to do its part if you but do your part!

If there had been no soil you could have had no garden. Further, the soil had to be in the right condition. So it is with your spiritual garden. You are always planting something—desires, longings and hopes, or fears and worries. There is no special season set aside for this kind of planting. Therefore, the subjective-mind soil must be in the right condition all the time. You are always planting and you cannot afford to have the good seeds dropped into soil which contains a mass of weeds. You cannot afford to be planting bad seeds—thoughts of negation, worries, fears, angers, hates, resentments. Such seeds will grow just as rapidly as the good seeds and will bring forth a crop just as sure and abundant. The soil of the garden has no power or inclination to reject bad seeds while accepting good ones. Your subjective-mind level, the creative medium of Law, also is entirely impersonal and will just as readily take your negations and produce a crop of illness, poverty, hardship, difficulty or inharmony. Be careful about your planting!

When you first start to get your garden ready you are likely to find that it contains a good many stones, weeds, hard chunks of earth or rubbish. These need to be cleaned away if the soil is to produce as you desire. Similarly, old complexes, attitudes and habits certainly will ruin your harvest in the spiritual realm unless you get them out.[4]

Consciousness appears contagious until we make a definite stand in our own:

John Smith was humming a gay tune and seemed to exude great confidence in himself and the world as he boarded the streetcar. He sat down next to a man who was filled with fear and apprehension. By the time John Smith got off the car he was in the grip of a terrible anxiety which he could not explain.

It is possible for us to catch fear from others as much as we would catch a cold, for we are all unconscious mental, emotional and spiritual broadcasting stations. This takes us back to a thought in the Bible which says that a man's enemies shall be those of his own household, for our real enemies are our fears and phobias, our doubts and uncertainties, our anxieties and our inner conflicts.[5]

Just as each person, place or thing has a subjective atmosphere or remembrance, so each town, city or nation has its individual atmosphere. Some towns are bustling with life and action while others seem dead. Some are filled with a spirit of culture, while others are filled with a spirit of commerce. This is the result of the mentalities of those who live in such places. Just as a city has its atmosphere, so does an entire nation. The combined thought of those who inhabit a nation creates a national consciousness which we speak of as the *psychology* of that people.[6]

When Intelligence makes a demand upon Itself, It answers Its own demand out of Its own nature and cannot help doing so! In philosophy, this idea is called Emergent Evolution. Whenever the Universe makes a demand upon Itself, out of that very demand is created its fulfillment. *But that can only be when the demand is in the nature of the Universe.*

Therefore, the person who believes that God is specializing for him is right. God is specializing for him through the Law. Such a person will realize when he says, "There is a Divine Intelligence that knows the right answer," and accepts this statement as being true, *the answer to that problem is right then and there created in Mind,* and will be projected through his intellect whenever and wherever he is ready to receive it. *It is a new creation.*

God is forever doing new things, and when we conceive new ideas, it is an act of the Divine projecting Itself into Creation. There were no flying machines until man made them. The Spirit did not have a lot of little flying machine models put away in a cosmic cupboard somewhere. But the mind that conceived the possibility of the flying machine *is* God. The mind we use is the Mind of the Universe.[7]

The first thing to realize is that since any thought manifests it necessarily follows that all thought does the same, else how should we know that the particular thought we were thinking would be the one that would create? Mind must cast back all or none.[8]

Know that nothing can hinder you but yourself. If you believe that you can, you can. If you believe that the Law of Good will work, It will work. You are not changing the nature of Its power; you are merely altering your position in It.[9]

There is a tendency, on the part of all of us, to reproduce the accumulated subjective experiences of the human race . . . Realizing that the subjective draws to itself everything that it is in sympathy with, we see that anyone who is sympathetically inclined toward the race, or vibrates to the race-thought, might pick up the entire race-emotion and experience and— if he were able to bring it to the surface—could consciously depict it. Many of the world's orators, actors and writers have been able to do this, which explains why some of them have been so erratic, for they have been more or less controlled by the emotions which they have contacted.[10]

The winning or losing of what we call a demonstration lies entirely in one's state of thought or consciousness, in whether or not he is able to perceive more good than evil.[11]

Our word has the exact amount of power we put into it. This does not mean power through effort or strain but power through absolute conviction, or faith . . . Now if any word has power it must follow that all words have power.[12]

We can, if we are not careful, get caught in what I call a "cosmic trap," which I do not think is of our own making but comes from the race consciousness. It is the belief that in order to be good you must suffer, and to be in religion you must take the blows of adversity. There is nothing in our philosophy to cause us to want to be a doormat or a bookmark! We do not wish to be arrogant, either. We must have the capacity to love greatly, but justice and mercy must balance. The universe is just without judgment. It is also giving. Never let someone else decide what is right for you, because they do not know. Ask yourself if the desire or idea you have complies with the Law of Truth, of righteousness. Does it partake of the nature of Reality? If it does, then you can go the limit with it.

Every practitioner and leader in our field should be successful. Everyone in our field should be successful. The old morbid concept of suffering for righteousness' sake comes up too often in our work. You will hear someone say, "This is being given to me to see how much I can take!" That is all nonsense and we should not say such things nor believe them. Such a statement is said in ignorance of the Law, which excuses no one from its effects. It is going right back to the concept of the old man in the sky with long whiskers, and he isn't there![13]

We say there is a Universal Mind; but no one ever saw It. We say God is Spirit; but no one ever saw God. The Bible says, "No man hath seen God at any time; only the Son, he hath revealed Him." To express this idea in our language: No one has seen Cause; because we see an effect, we know there must be a Cause. Nothing is more evident than the fact that we live; and since we live, we must have life, and since *we* have life there must be Life. The only proof we have of Mind is that we think. The Eternal Principle is forever hidden.[14]

So it seems that . . .

Without realizing it we too often negate what we affirm. Take the situation of a man who owned a store and sincerely prayed, morning and night, that his business would prosper. At these times he believed and accepted without a question of doubt. But then what did he do at the store all day? All he could see were the countless people who walked past without coming in. Even those who did come in he more or less overlooked. All he could think about were the people who were not coming in! So they didn't come in, regardless of his prayers. His every thought was some form of creative prayer. He never took the trouble to see how his thoughts added up at the end of the day. But they were on the negative side and so was the business at the store. Consistency is all important. Consistent negative thought gets us into most of our trouble; consistent positive thought is the only thing that can get us out.[15]

A positive thought for us to use:

I cleanse the windows of my mind, that it may become a mirror reflecting inspiration from the most High. I do this, not with strenous effort, but through quiet contemplation, through gently reaching and affirming an inward recognition. Today I walk in the pathway of inspiration. I know exactly what to do in every situation. There is an inspiration within me which governs every act, every thought, with certainty, with conviction and in peace.[16]

Part II

The Central Flame

I had prepared a sermon based on something Ernest had said over lunch one day. When the mood was on him, Ernest was capable of platform rhetoric across a cottage cheese salad. After lunch I wrote down what I could remember in my notebook.

It went like this: In this amazing century, bursting away from so much that was slow-paced and orderly in the past, the breakthrough in the physical sciences robbed many people of cherished religious concepts and left them forlorn. But man is a religious being and there are thousands who are seeking a philosophy which can be reconciled to their own expanding awareness of the universe—a faith that will square with the century.

"Can you imagine a Nobel Prize winner holding still for an hour's talk on original sin?" he demanded. "No, people want the religion that Jesus brought to the world—if we can get back to it, through all the ecclesiastical forms. People who have left their churches to follow the mechanists have lost more than they can afford to lose. They're going to keep looking until they find a religion they can test, and prove out, and depend on."

—WILLIAM H. D. HORNADAY, *THE INNER LIGHT*

V.

The Meeting Place
of Science and Religion

THE FARER:
Before me stretched this vast and crystal sea
Between the shores of time and of eternity.
Down to the bridge that spanned the gulf I saw
The saints and sages, keepers of the law,
Lead bands of pilgrims out of every clime,
Freed from the burdened slavery of time.
Across the sands the master highways ran
Thronged by the souls who formed the caravan;
And everywhere, from south and north, from west
And east the pilgrims crossed the crest
Of mountains sloping to the sea; and on
They came, the multitudes who from the dawn
Of human day had through the troubled ages
In serried ranks been led by ancient sages
Who marched beneath the banner, LORD OF KINGS,
And all of whom bore gifts and offerings
To place upon an altar which was set
Beside the sea where earth and heaven met.

It was permitted me to view the past
And prove as *fact* what I believed, at last.
Space turned to minute form in astral lights
And from afar beyond the towering heights,
(Borne on the winds, that whirl in space
From the Eternal Dwelling Place,
As thunder rolls when lightning speaks aloud)
I heard a great voice crying through a cloud,
"The tabernacle of God is with men
And God Himself shall dwell with them
And he shall wipe away all tears from eyes
That weep, and pain shall be no more; not one
Shall sorrow for death no more shall be.
I am Beginning and the End, and he
Who turns his heart and thought to Me
Shall never thirst but ever is my son."

Then I could clearly see the ALTAR OF
THE AGES, object of devoted love
Of untold millions of the human race
Who rendered worship in this sacred place.
Behind the altar in rainbowed arcs of light,
I saw a priest, arrayed in silver-white,
Melchizedek, eternal priest and king
Of righteousness and peace, outrivaling
All priests of all the altars of the earth,
Who could not die nor had he second birth
But wore the miter placed upon his brow
By LIFE and not by LAW and took the vow
Of fealty to God from all the saints and sages
As he had done throughout the endless ages;
Not Jesus only but every seer to wait
Before the shrine had been initiate
Of the Order of Melchizedek. This

Master sage and priest whose genesis
Is hid among the stars whence he acquired
The teleois measurements which inspired
The temples and the pyramids that show
In human frames and in a flake of snow.
The first appeared Great Rama to my view
With poets and singers in his retinue
Who joined in Vedic hymns of the creation,
The first of all the faiths of correlation
Of men with God; and I beheld the morn
On blazing light where Eastern faiths were born.[1]

The Science of Mind is a science, Ernest maintained, in that the efficacy of prayer can be proven. The intuitive sense in nature recognizes only oneness. Humans, having finely honed self-awareness, appear to be both the only earthly species capable of using this sense to its fullest degree, and the only ones capable of denying that it even exists. Ernest here suggests we take a lesson from the natural world, in an often-requested reprint of a 1947 article from Science of Mind *magazine.*

Did you ever set a hen? If so, you know that you put eggs under her or put her on top of eggs. She sets there for twenty-one days, then the eggs hatch out.

What caused the first hen to set on the first egg? It evidently was not an accumulation of previous experiences which she had had or something she had consciously thought out. She had never figured that it takes exactly twenty-one days to do the job. Hens do not live by calendars or know the difference between Monday and Friday. Some intuitional sense caused her to lay the eggs and sit on them and to know what to do with the chickens when they were hatched.

What is this unconscious direction moving intuitively? It is Universal Intelligence which operates everywhere. Calmly, placidly she sets, never leaving her nest long enough for the eggs to get cold, turning them over every day so the chickens will develop normally. Instinctive omniscience is the only answer. The hen never doubts, never questions, never argues, apparently does not do any complaining. There she sets—and the eggs will hatch because the hen has followed the law of her instinct.

It is interesting to note that the hen does not try to concentrate or will anything into being. We hear so much about the development of will and the power of concentration. The hen can neither read nor write and she has never studied philosophy, knows nothing about modern psychology or ancient mysticism. No one ever heard of a hen cackling about its sins or squawking to high heaven to save its soul. It appears that she never had a guilt complex. The hen has not even studied how to become spiritual. She does not argue whether she has been reincarnated forty times and might have been forty more, if someone had not wanted fried eggs for breakfast.

The hen sets on her eggs for twenty-one days and a brood of chickens is hatched. She is not a philosopher; she is not a spiritual genius; she is not even a scientist or mathematician; she never heard of Heaven or hell . . . but she knows how to set. She keeps one idea warm for twenty-one days without ever doubting that the warmth of her body penetrating the eggs will cause them to hatch. Who is there among us who can contemplate one idea for twenty-one days, keeping it warm, alive, awake and aware, through an inward feeling which broods over its own expectation? The hen doesn't know whether she is a sinner or a savior, whether she is wise or unwise. You see the hen has not yet developed an intellect through which she can deny the divine offering or refuse to accept the creative power of her own instinctive urge.

Well, we don't wish to be hens. We act more like geese. The process of evolution has given us an intellect which makes it possible for us to deny what God has given. It did not do this, however, at the expense of the creative faculties within us. They are still there ready to operate just as they do in the hen. We have arrived at the place in our evolution where we can deny our good, even though it is always there to be accepted. We are arguing as to whether or not we are good enough. We are wondering if we know how to concentrate. Have we the spiritual enlightenment? We have covered up our instinctive omniscience through confusion, denials and negations. "They could not enter in because of their unbelief."

We think we have to follow what Plato said, or Socrates or Emerson, or some other great, good and wise man whose genius lay in the fact that he followed his instinctive omniscience. We wonder what system of thought is right and which is wrong, and argue and argue, until confusion becomes chaos, and even hope is dragged in the dust of uncertainty.

We'd better get up and shake off the dust and get back on these eggs. After all, the hen is wise.[2]

For . . .

God's will and God's nature must be identical.[3]

Law is law, and works like it, he tells us.

The Law we are discussing is simply a law of Nature, a force of Nature. It happens to be a mental force, and an intelligent and creative one, like electricity, which either lights our house and cooks our food or will electrocute us if we use it incorrectly.[4]

Science and religion meet in the territory of the mind. Psychoanalysis (then in its infancy) lays bare the interior world, while spirituality can transform what's found there. The groundbreaking article that follows, published in 1938, the same year as the revised textbook, foreshadows modern therapeutic techniques and holistic psychology.

Psychoanalysis means an analysis of the psyche, and the psyche means the subjective part of us, that repository where is gathered the sum total of all the experiences we have had plus the experiences the world has had, transmitted from one generation to another of human experience. Therefore, it goes without saying that this subconscious retention, this subjective repository of thought impulses and desire toward manifestation, is very much more elaborate and very much more vital and powerful than the intellect. That is why it is that the emotions are stronger than the intellect . . .

There is a tremendous drive and urge to express, and before man had a consciousness, that is, before his intellect said certain things are right and certain things are wrong, he did not care what he did. He was half animal and half man, and he went out and killed whatever was in sight, but he did not feel badly about it. He developed, in the logical processes of evolution, a consciousness, an idea of right and wrong. The emotional urge toward self-expression was still there, but he developed something that sat on top of it, as it were, and the intellect and the will came into conflict with the emotional reactions of the ages. He still desired to do certain things, but something in him said it would not be best. We might desire to do something today that is destructive as an emotional impulse, but when we stop and think about it we know it is not best. That intellect is given to us in our evolution that we may discriminate and no longer be led by blind emotion, because so long as the world was led by blind emotion there was no civilization, and if the world ever returns to be led by blind emotion, as we now understand it, it will disappear.

But there is a conflict between the creative emotional part of us and the intellect, the will, the reflective part of us, and all neurosis or psychosis is a result of this conflict. It is a result of a mental state where the emotion is trying to go one way and the intellect another. The feeling drive is in one direction and the reflective drive is in another. It seems a strange thing that this should happen when man evolved to a place where he began to be civilized. But it is a logical thing because he had not yet learned of this tremendous creative force within him. When the emotions come into conflict with the will, the emotions always win, but the will not permitting the emotions a proper outlet, they come up in a different channel and are not easy to recognize. Natural forces will find an outlet; consequently in the dictionary the Libido is defined as "an emotional craving for self-expression back of all things, the repression of which leads to psychoneurosis," that is, to psychic disturbances or morbid fears resulting in nervous breakdown, we will say. The nerves, of themselves, do not break down; they are merely the cohesive medium between the mental or emotional action, and the physical or objective reaction. For instance, modern medical men now are classifying many heart inactions as hypertensions, extreme nervous tension. But extreme nerve tension is the result of extreme mental and emotional tension.

Psychoanalysis is the most subtle and elusive thing on earth and only years of very careful experience would equip a person with the mental ability, the intellectual patience and human understanding to properly analyze. Most persons practicing in this field do not understand the field well enough to practice successfully, but of itself it is scientific. It has evolved the most elaborate methods of uncovering the inhibited, repressed emotional reactions, the result of an intense reality in the universe. Its problem is to lay bare, to cause the consciousness to see the reason for the neurosis, and by being self-seen, be healed. Unfortunately, in the evolution of this idea, a large number of its exponents, among whom were Freud and Adler, believed in a materialistic philosophy. They knew the mechanics of the thing, they understood the way the engine ran and how to repair it, but they did not understand how to really heal the soul of the one who was suffering. Jung says that the sum total of all human belief affects each one of us very definitely. We call it the race suggestion. It means the sum total of human thought. These men worked out the mechanics of this thing, but they did not see the necessity of spiritualizing the operation.

Now what do we mean by "spiritualizing"? Exactly what the word implies. Man, psychologically, is the result of all the mental actions and reactions that have gone before, but he is more than that, and that these gentlemen did not see. Jung has seen it, I think; gradually others are seeing it. But most of the early workers in the field of analytical psychology did not see it because their philosophy was one of materialism. They did not believe in the immortality of the soul, the reality of the spirit, but they understood the mechanistic reactions of mind. From them we get the Watsonian Theory of Behaviorism (which has already been discredited), and the idea of predetermination in psychology, which means we are all automatically reacting to thought impulses; we cannot help it. As evidence of the fact that man is not really a bunch of reactions, that determinism is a false philosophy, we have this testimony from Jung . . . that after thirty-five years of experience in analysis he has never yet known of one single permanent healing of a neurosis without a restoration of faith.

After years of work in analytical psychology and psychiatry, Dr. Link has written a book which he calls *Back to Religion*. Why? Because a man's life is incomplete unless he adds the engineer to the engine, unless he adds the perceiver to the thing perceived, the artist to the art, a Creator to creation. This is the office of religion. A nation may attempt to stamp out religion, it may attempt to create a religion founded on the ideology of a false psychology of nationalism, but it is just as destined to fail as two and two are destined never to make anything but four. Back of all psychological urges, which are real, vital and powerful, there is a culminating urge. It is an echo of the understanding that we are immortal beings, that we are eternal beings, that we are everlasting, that are we are copartners with an Infinite Intelligence and Will and Purposiveness and Personalness in the Universe. So unqualifiedly Jung says there is no healing of neurosis unless there is a restoration of faith.

In our work we start with the restoration of faith. We start where the analyst leaves off, after he has done all he can do. We know that there is such a thing as a spiritualization of consciousness and that in such degree as this spiritualization of consciousness takes place, automatically the neurosis dissolves into its native nothingness. Does not the greater contain the lesser? Of course it does. The larger a man's concept is the more it looks around the smaller concepts he may entertain, and if a man is conscious of the immortality and the eternality of his own soul, unless he includes this lesser evolution and revolution and convolution in that larger experience, it is inevitable that one of two things will happen—he will become a materialist and an agnostic, and as such a disgruntled individual, or if he still retains to the finer sensibilities and urges which instinctively seek to elevate his thought to cosmic comprehension, he will so destroy temporarily these upper convolutions of thought that he will become a neurotic. That is what is happening in the world today. There were not so many neuroses when people were religious. Spiritual emotion is just as real as any other emotion and it is just as necessary that it shall find an outlet, and that is what the religious life does. All neurosis is a thing of fear and lack of cooperative understanding, and back of that is a lack of spiritual perception, a lack of religious conviction.

Modern civilization is seeking the outlet of its new emotional trends, be they economic or political or whatever one chooses to call them—they are all psychological at their base, and all psychology at its base is a result of something that is higher, that is spiritual. Psychology is the mental action and reaction of the human mind, always colored by the religious or spiritual perception . . . Let each man have a spiritual outlook and uplift and perhaps finally the day will come when our stupidity will dim as the effulgent rays of that penetrating and mystic Divine fire enter our consciousness. Then we shall find that we are like wayfarers ascending a mountain—we know the vista is there, we know that there the eye may view the world as one vast plane and one boundless reach of sky, but not being able to look around the side of the mountain, it is only when we get to the top that we see things as they really are. Then we shall sense the representation in us of that Divine Urge which compels all evolution, all expansion, and links our own soul with the Over-Soul of the Universe.[5]

Science wonders how everything came into being in the first place, while religion simply answers, "God made it." Ernest takes the matter further, resolving the creation versus evolution debate by positing a never-ending creation consisting of involved *thought and* evolved *form.*

Evolution is the passing of thought into manifestation. To put it another way: All is Infinite Being and all is eternally becoming. Infinite Being is Infinite Knowingness; as the result of this Infinite Knowingness, there is an Infinite Becomingness or Creation. The Infinite Knowingness produces what is called involution through the self-contemplation of Spirit. As a result of this contemplation—this *Word* of the Bible—Creation is made manifest. This is evolution. Evolution is the process, the way, the time and the experience that transpires as Thought—or Intelligence, or Idea or Contemplation—passes from abstract Being into concrete expression. Consequently, *evolution is an effect of intelligence and not the cause of it. Evolution is not creating intelligence; intelligence is projecting evolution.*[6]

The original cause of the universe according to the Bible was a thought in the Mind of God. Everything that exists was first an idea, and it is the nature of ideas to take form. Some people say that they believe this because it is in the Bible. To others it appears as a logical necessity to account for things as they are. Many cosmogonists and astronomers who seek to determine the nature of the universe as a whole feel that at one time about four billion years ago there was a somewhat quiescent mass of tightly compressed particles, those particles out of which atoms are built. Then something happened. And within a very short time, a very explosive time, physical creation began and is still continuing according to inherent patterns which would have had to exist prior to that original explosive moment. "God said." Mind thought. Is there a difference? There was a cause and there was an effect. And that original causative factor did not cease to be, but is active causation still creating effects. It is without beginning and without end. Pure Mind knows no limitations.

Astronomer Gustaf Stromberg has written much on this subject and has said that when the physical world of space, time and energy was yet unborn something far more important existed. This was Mind, Cosmic Mind, or World Soul, which *was* and *is* the source of all things physical as well as the ultimate origin of our minds.[7]

Despite the colossal advances in scientific learning since their publication, these next two magazine articles remain as relevant today as when published. The first is a 1931 "baccalaureate" lecture to graduates of the Major Course, as it was then called, at the Institute of Religious Science, and stresses cooperation with all the healing arts and sciences. The second, sixteen years later, discusses the body/mind relationship.

Viewing Religious Science from its broadest meaning, we shall think of it as one of the many attempts now being made throughout the world to arrive at a more satisfactory understanding of life. It is an attempt to solve some of the enigmas of human existence. It is a seeking to solve some of the great mysteries of being, to find a solution which will give a greater hope and certainty to those who search after the Truth. The practice of Religious Science is quite different from the popular concept of it. Those who are unfamiliar with this practice often misunderstand and misinterpret its meaning. It is a popular belief that those who practice this science are a class of people who declare that everything is perfect when, as a matter of fact, everything in the objective experience of the race is not perfect and, indeed, is far from being perfect. This popular idea of the practice of spiritual science is entirely a misconception. A Religious Scientist is not one who assures himself that wrong is right, that evil is good, that limitation is freedom, that bondage is liberty or that sickness is health. He does not claim that our objective experience is an illusion, but he does make *this* claim that behind the phenomena of human and material existence, behind the slow and persistent processes of evolution there is, as Emerson stated, "One Mind common to all people." He claims that this Mind is perfect and that he has access to this Mind.

Man is an inlet to this Mind, not through choice but by reason of his nature, not through desire but by necessity. Man is an immortal being, not because he earns immortality, paying for a heavenly place through a lifetime of self-denial. He is immortal because he is made of immortal stuff. All men are immortal, not because they choose to be or because they believe in some particular doctrine, not because they are Christians, Jews or pagans, but because they are divine. Humanity is divinity wearing a mask. That which has gained self-consciousness must progressively be more and more conscious of itself. We are on the pathway of an endless expansion. We are unfolding into the Infinite . . .

The science which you are to practice is based on the theory that there is a Universal Mind and an Eternal Spirit from which all things spring. The Spirit is the Creator and the Sustainer of all that is. You have immediate access to this Divine Mind, this Universal Principle, this Creative Power. Man has access to the Great Whole and draws as much power from this source as he is capable of intelligently using. Man is not the power, *he is avenue through which the power flows.*

Your religious outlook is to be a universal one, otherwise dogmatism, creedal ceremony and superstition creep in. When this happens, men look for prayers which other men have prayed to make them whole. They look in vain. The thought of man's relationship to God should be direct, dynamic. Every man's mind is an inlet to the Divine. There is tolerance in this concept, and inclusion. The Infinite is all-inclusive, all embracing, all comprehending.

You will work in harmony with all religious beliefs, since all seek, in their different ways, the final and ultimate cause, God, to whom we have given the name of Love or Heavenly Father. The one who understands this will be tolerant, kind, sympathetic. He feels that back of every man's approach to the Spirit there is a sincere desire to reunite with the Principle from which all men spring. Your attitude toward all religious forms of worship shall be one of unity. Argue with no man, then, over his religious convictions, but let each worship in his own way. Each shall draw the picture of divinity on his own canvas with his own brush, blending his colors from the inner working of his own spiritual state. All faith is good. Never rob one of his faith unless you can give him a better one.

Your relationship to the medical fraternity should be of the same character. You will find those who are willing and ready to cooperate with you in your endeavor to relieve suffering. You will find others who will scoff at your attempts. But no man can hurt you unless your mind admits the hurt. You are doctors to the mind, wise spiritual counselors. Your work in this field is as legitimate as that of any physician or surgeon. Let the dignity of your profession be an outstanding attribute of your work. You have much to offer the medical world; offer it in the spirit of cooperation. The time will come when the healing power of thought will be better understood and more universally sought after. Already the signs of this day are approaching; already many physicians are awaiting your cooperation. If there are those who deny you the privilege of such cooperation, be not disturbed; there is still some misunderstanding which will disappear with time.

The time will come when the healing agency of spiritual thought force will be taught in all our schools. But we need not wait for that time. Meanwhile, give those who come to you such help as you have to give; the healing power of spiritual thought is based upon a principle which is transcendent of any psychological or physiological principle now being taught in our schools and universities.

Your ability to relieve suffering depends upon your ability to see, sense and feel the presence of pure Spirit in man. As the spirit heals the mind, the mind automatically reacts in the body. The healing power of this spiritual thought is greater than mental suggestion, more than willpower and transcends a mere mental determination. It is a mental penetration into that

Principle which is higher than the mind, the principle of Spirit, which principle must be discerned through the mind.

You will succeed in many cases and you will fail in many. Where you succeed you will rejoice, where you fail you should not grieve, because you will have done your best and that is all any man can do. Your work is in the realm of the mind. Leave all objective forms of healing to those who practice objectively and cooperate with all who will cooperate with you. The principle which you teach is accessible to all. It is God, the living spirit, Almighty. The spiritual evolution of people's minds has not yet reached that stage where the average man senses this Divine Presence in Its fulness. You will do the best you can "and with God be the rest."

There should be a flexibility and a willingness on your part to cooperate but there should also be a determination to prove your Principle. This determination is ever growing. It is rooted deep in spiritual soil. Its branches are forever spreading and the fruit of this knowledge is forever falling into the lap of him who knows.

You will unite with the philosophic mind, in so far as it unites with you. True philosophy is a gift of all ages to our age. You may know this, that in the pursuance of your philosophic thought you keep company with the best the world has to offer. You will find in popular philosophy much that is confusing, the reason being that much of our popular philosophy does not start with the premise that there is and must be a Unitary Wholeness running through everything. The phenomena of human existence can be explained on no other basis.

You will read every man's philosophy, reserving for yourself the prerogative of choice, knowing that any philosophy based on a Unitary Wholeness has the elements of truth. No philosophy is perfect, your own is not. Everything is evolving, growing, expanding.

In the field of practical psychology you will perhaps find a greater unity, but you will find no unity whatever with a materialistic psychology. The world of psychology will someday, I believe, realize what the late William James meant when he said that "the psychology of tomorrow will be metaphysics." But for your own enlightenment, I can assure you of this, that including all of the psychologists of the world, not one of them can intelligently explain his own science without first accepting the premise upon which your philosophy is built. So feel no sense of chagrin if the psychologist passes you by. Love him just the same and cooperate with him whenever he allows you to do so . . .

We shall never arrive at the truth through the denial of any fact. There is no reason then why you should not cooperate with all classes of people, never being arrogant. Arrogance is always ignorance. All men are of the same Spirit. Heaven has no favorites. You should find a deep and a growing sympathy with humanity, a knowledge that the *divinity* of the man must be made manifest through the *humanity* of man.

Do not fall under the illusion that there are external practices which can hasten spiritual perceptions. Do not fall into the error of thinking that there are those who can deliver to you a key of knowledge. Do not chase spiritual, mental or psychological rainbows. The pot of gold is in the imagination of the man who seeks the end of the rainbow. Salvation will never be found to be external to the mind seeking it. Do not fall under the belief that if one is to excel in spiritual things he must renounce everything that is called physical. There are those who would separate life from living. Do not make this mistake.

Take the time to weed out unbelief. Find the world to be good. See every man as an evolving soul. Let your mind be tempered with that human wisdom which rejects the lie, which separates the wheat from the chaff— but in all kindness, sympathy and compassion. Your system of thought does not deny the merit of human endeavor or intellectual attainment. It does affirm the supremacy of Spirit. It is the Spirit which creates and sustains all. The Spirit is projecting Itself through man, coming to greater fruition through him, operating directly in his mind. There comes with this belief a power, a peace and a poise, as one senses his relationship to this all-sustaining Good and Beauty which unites everything into one stupendous wholeness.

Search out your own mind. Be true to your own thought. Penetrate more deeply into your own consciousness. In the silence of your own soul you meet the Eternal and Creative Center of all. Carrying this torch of truth and reason brought down through the ages and now handed to you, advance on the chaos of unbelief and prove your faith by your works. "So shall the heart of man,/ Seeing thy flight,/ Find out the way again,/ There in the night."[8]

We are hearing a great deal about psychosomatics, which means the relationship between the body and the mind.

It is thought probably that a large percentage of physical ailments have their basis in our subconscious thought. We may take it for granted that there is an inner causative mind deeper than the intellect. There is a reservoir of thoughts and feeling which is called the subconscious, unconscious or subjective. It seems to be the creative medium through which thought and feeling work, both in our bodies and, we believe, on our environment. The sum total of everything that is in there constitutes the psychosomatic relationship, that is, the body-mind relationship, thus determining to a very great degree what our physical health shall be.

Patterns of thought are laid down in the subconscious which automatically repeat themselves, and, unless they are changed, they will go on and on with sort of a dreary monotony. This shows that this field of mind is a neutral medium. While it is creative, it is not self-directive. There is nothing in the subconscious which has not been put there. It is a creative medium with no particular purpose of its own. We learn consciously whether it be arithmetic, philosophy, or how to drive an automobile. Gradually what we learn becomes an unconscious reaction because the thought pattern has fallen into a field which repeats itself without effort.

In dealing with the unconscious, subconscious or subjective, we are not dealing with a mind in itself; rather with a mirror reflecting the images cast into it and reflecting them mathematically and mechanically. If this were not so, the whole field of psychosomatics, that branch of psychology which deals with the effect of the mind on the body, would be without meaning.

The very word "psychosomatic" means the relationship between this inner psyche or subconscious field of mind and the physical body. There is a mind principle within us which knows how to do, but does not know that it is doing; which works intelligently but not consciously; automatically but never spontaneously; receiving thought patterns but never with any selectivity; always reflecting them but never knowing that it is doing so.

We could not call this a mind in the way that we think of personal consciousness. We can only think of it as a law of mind in action. We certainly could not think of it as the person himself, as we would think of an engineer; we could think of it as an engine. We can not think of it as a gardener but we could think of it as the garden of the soul, and so it has been called throughout the ages.

Many of the ancient philosophies taught that the creative Spirit operates upon, or through, a universal Law whose business it is to receive the ideas and bring them into physical or objective manifestation. It is a self-evident proposition that the universe is a combination of directive intelligence and cosmic force, or law, and manifestation.

The very fact that there is a psychosomatic or body-mind relationship is evidence that the subconscious mind principle within us is not a person but a law. It receives the impression of that which is not a law but person. For person is not law, and law is not person. Principle and person are two different things. It is evident that there is such a principle in our individual lives. We are conscious beings with subconscious reactions. The subconscious is a law operating upon that which was once conscious. There is nothing in the subconscious but what has been put there; therefore, theoretically there is nothing there that cannot be removed.

The Greeks spoke of these two principles as Eros or the creative Principle, and Logos or the rational Principle, the knowing Principle or the word. Eros is feminine, Logos the masculine. It is the word, the projective Principle, the masculine, that impregnates the creative Principle which, in its turn, gives birth to creation. We find this same idea in the Bible where it speaks of the Spirit moving upon the face of the deep. The writers of the fifteenth, sixteenth and seventeenth centuries spoke of Anima Mundi, or the soul of the world as distinguished from Animus Dei, or the divine Spirit. Anima Mundi, the soul principle, was referred to by medieval writers as the universal medium of all creation. Esoterically it was called water. Thus, the spirit operates upon the waters and land appears. Here is the idea of a Universal Spirit, Animus Dei, operating upon a universal medium and thus producing creation. The medium, Anima Mundi, is impregnated by the divine ideas and gives birth to the patterns of thought which the creative Spirit lets fall into it.

There could be no better description of body-mind relationship than this, provided we remember that the body-mind relationship is between a conscious and a subconscious—but intelligent—Principle whose business it is to reflect, as a mirror, the images that are cast into it. It is the relationship between the conscious and subconscious, or unconscious, that we learn about in the science of psychology.

We affirm another principle under the heading of intuition, illumination, spiritual awareness or God-mind operating upon us from a higher level. It is this Spirit-mind relationship which we call Pneumatology or the Science of Spirit. This is no new discovery. It is the fundamental principle of the great spiritual philosophies—modern, medieval and ancient. There must be, and is, a unifying Spirit in the universe. This is the kingdom of heaven that Jesus talked about. This was the central theme of his instructions to his disciples, and through them to the world. This is what is meant by being transformed by the renewing of the mind, but putting off the old man and putting on the new man, which is Christ. This is what is meant by Moses going up into the mountain to receive the mandate of eternal law, or Jesus going up into a mount to deliver the ages' most famous sermon. This is the mount of transfiguration. Its practical meaning is that the psychosomatic relationship should be influenced by the spirit of charity, love, unity, reason and goodwill.

In the Science of Mind, we teach not only that there is a body-mind relationship but also that there is a direct relationship between thought and environment. Consciously or unconsciously, we are not only governing our physical bodies; we are also weaving the destiny of our fate, at least temporarily, on the loom of consciousness. It is merely a question of where we get the pattern. Shall it come from fear, strife, disunity, or shall it be drawn into our consciousness from a higher source? Pneumatology, or Spirit-mind relationship, is of more importance than just body-mind relationship, for if there is a right relationship between Spirit and mind, then the mind Principle, acting as law, will automatically reflect a right bodily reaction and an equally right environmental reaction.

We all have a mount of transfiguration but we do not always ascend into it. Moses said that the creative word is in our own mouth. God grant that this word shall first be received from Heaven. Planted in the garden of the soul, watered by quiet contemplation, fertilized by hope and cultivated through faith, it will bring forth a harvest whose planting is deeper than this earth's too thin soil. It will reach up into that purer soil of the Spirit where the flower withereth not and the plant dieth not because it is rooted in the living waters of everlasting life.[9]

He offers us this affirmation:

I see through all physical and mental obstructions to the one perfect Presence within me. I see through all apparent contradictions to the one perfect Being in every person. I see through all confusion to the one Divine Presence at the center of everything.[10]

VI.

Conviction, Warmth, Color and Imagination

THE PRESENCE:
Whose heart is fixed upon the good because
It is the good shall fill his soul with good,
And he who revels in the beautiful
Because he sees in it the beautiful
Shall grow a soul as beautiful as well.
So he who loves all things that live and breathe
Shall know the Love of Loves within the Me.
Where love is felt, there unity is known,
And all the woes that damn mankind have flown,
While he who serves but *one* has served the Whole,
God loves them all and knows them soul by soul.
Man's love is instrument of something higher,
A cosmic love to which he is the lyre.
And vain those men who in the name of faith
Exalt him most who seeks to put to death
All human love for mate or family.
For he who cleaves in purity to love, loves Me,
Unlike the sadist soul who cannot scent perfume,

Till, crushed the flower, he robs it of its bloom,

Love, like a goddess moves in mystic splendor

And with a queenly voice bids all attend her.

Obedient to love's compelling inspiration,

Man dreams, designs and builds some new creation.

From love come sculpture and the painter's art,

The poet weaves a phrase that moves the heart.

For love the soldier bares his breast in strife;

To love, in blood, he dedicates his life.

Through love of God the martyr braves the pyre

And proves his *will* imperishable by fire.

Reject the claim that earthly love is sin,

And that ascetics only can enter in

Celestial gates; each birth is virgin birth,

And each has come immaculate to earth.

Be not deceived by those who seek to prove

That virtue lies alone in flight from love.

Retreat from life to cave or hermitage

Does not convert a man to saint or sage;

The solitude in which thy God is shown

Is in the mind and in the mind alone.[1]

The Law of Mind each of us uses—neutral, automatic, receptive to whatever is given it—was only half of life's equation to Ernest. "Love points the way, and law follows" he believed. In this chapter his selected thoughts touch on love both human and divine, the role of emotion in effective prayer and what happens when the creative urge of life through us is expressed . . . or repressed. We open with one of his most often-quoted passages from **The Science of Mind.**

Love is the central flame of the universe, nay, the very fire itself. It is written that God is love, and that we are His expressed likeness, the image of the Eternal Being. Love is self-givingness through creation, the impartation of the Divine through the human. Love is an essence, an atmosphere, which defies analysis, as does Life Itself. It is that which *is* and cannot be explained: it is common to all people, to all animal life and evident in the response of plants to those who love them. Love reigns supreme over all. The essence of love, while elusive, pervades everything, fires the heart, stimulates the emotions, renews the soul and proclaims the Spirit. Only love knows love, and love knows only love. Words cannot express its depths or meaning. A universal sense alone bears witness to the divine fact: God is Love and Love is God.[2]

And from Ideas of Power:

It is a simple proposition: everyone must love and be loved or he won't be fulfilled or happy. Therefore it is believed that love looses the greatest energy in the Universe—the greatest spiritual energy—and without love there is a certain part of life that does not come to fulfillment. This is real; it is dynamic; it isn't just a sweet sentimentality.

Who do we remember in history? Alexander the Great, who at the age of around thirty was so dissatisfied that there were no new things to conquer—? Do you remember Caesar, Hannibal, Napoleon—except that they are dark spots on the pages of history?

No. We remember Jesus and Buddha and Socrates. We remember the great lovers of the human race. Isn't that interesting! Instinctively, then, love seeks its own, and there is no fulfillment without it. Consequently, emotionally, psychologically—and actually in reality—love is the only final security in the Universe; love is the greatest healing power in the Universe, and the only thing that binds people together in a community of Spirit . . .

Love—just plain love; liking everybody. We are so constituted that real love is real only in such degree as it is universal. I am not talking just about a love that says, "God bless me and my wife, my son John and his wife, we four and no more." That isn't love—it is selfishness . . .

I have watched this world twirl around quite a while, and I have observed it pretty carefully, and in nearly half a century I have counseled with so many thousands; and I'll say this: I have never yet seen a person who is unsentimental, who hasn't that compassion and that kind of fulfillment . . . that seemed very far removed from a stone image. I could hug any person here and love it, but I could not embrace a stone image—it is too unrelenting and doesn't respond. There is something in animals that knows whether you like them or not. I have never had a dog even snap or growl at me, because I love them. I have never had trouble getting along with children. Someone said yesterday that where they were going to rent a place they were asked if there were children. I said, "If it were me, I would love if there were a dozen kids on each side of the apartment; I would love to hear them yell. There is something about it that makes me feel good inside."[3]

In sensing the Presence and understanding the Law, there can be a complete abandonment of the intellect and the will. However, I think that even in such abandonment there must be the formation of some kind of a pattern, for while I believe that every object in this world is related to its divine pattern, I also believe that divine patterns are eternally being made. When you design a new dress you don't think that the dress has ever been made before, do you? Every day a new song is sung! I think that God composes all the music, and sings all the songs, but He is singing them in every singer, right now, and he doesn't have to repeat Himself, for there is no monotony in the divine Life. It is always creating a fresh and unique variation of Itself, and so I believe that as we come to sense the divine Presence, the Father, the Spirit, the something that we feel and which certainly can't be put into words, there is a great and abiding emotional feeling of Reality.

There is nothing in this feeling that will ever make us peculiar. Nothing! During the greatest spiritual experiences that I have ever had, and they are experiences that we do not talk about, I was *more* myself and not less. There was no loss of my identity but an accentuation of it. The feeling is never one of absorption; it is always a sense of immersion. You have a greater realization than you ever had as to who you are.[4]

Mind must know all things, being Omniscient; hence whatever is, Mind Knows, and Mind is the Principle back of all treatment. Treatment is enforcement of Principle. The words, thoughts, phrases and statements are the way in which one makes known his feeling of the Divine Allness at any particular time.

"Mind comprehends everything. Mind is at the center of man's body and at the center of his affairs, and comprehends both body and affairs. We are to demonstrate that this comprehension is Perfect, Harmonious, Whole, Prosperous, Happy, Complete and Eternal.

When we use such words we must feel their meaning. The feeling without the words may have a meaning but no direction, and meaning without direction will produce no creation. Feeling, organized and directed, is intelligent creation.[5]

In the method and the technique, something is said. This is a moving thing, but when we reach that other place—illumination—nothing is said . . . something is *felt*.[6]

Healing takes place to the degree that we send down the right kind of thoughts into subjectivity. We mean, by thinking consciously and with deep feeling (knowing) we implant the right idea in Mind, and Mind reproduces this idea, as effect, in the body.[7]

Our thought and emotion is the use we make, consciously or unconsciously, of this original creative Thing that is the cause of everything.[8]

Still, he wants to make it clear that ferocious emoting (like one might see on television) isn't necessary for our prayers to be responded to.

There is no peculiar sensation which accompanies a treatment, neither is it necessary that the practitioner should feel anything, other than the truth of the words that he speaks.[9]

This is because . . .

Mental treatment is a direct statement of belief into Mind, coupled with a realization that the work is already an accomplished fact.[10]

A good psychological balance is struck when the will and the emotions are rightly poised. That is, when the intellect first decides what the emotions are to respond to. After the intellect has made this decision, then the imagination is called into play and the game of living commences. It is the office of the will to determine that to which the imagination is to respond.[11]

Mind must know all things, being Omniscient; hence whatever is, Mind Knows, and Mind is the Principle back of all treatment. Treatment is enforcement of Principle. The words, thoughts, phrases and statements are the way in which one makes known his feeling of the Divine Allness at any particular time.

Mind comprehends everything. Mind is at the center of man's body and at the center of his affairs, and comprehends both body and affairs. We are to demonstrate that this comprehension is Perfect, Harmonious, Whole, Prosperous, Happy, Complete and Eternal.

When we use such words we must feel their meaning. The feeling without the words may have a meaning but no direction, and meaning without direction will produce no creation. Feeling, organized and directed, is intelligent creation.[12]

Our mental acceptances should be filled with conviction, warmth, color and imagination. The creative power responds to feeling more quickly than to any other mental attitude. Therefore we should try to feel the reality of what we are doing when we give a treatment. This reality is felt as we become more and more convinced that Spirit responds to us.[13]

That which is felt cannot be taught, while that which is taught may be felt. This is one of the most vital things in mental and spiritual science. A treatment has no Power unless it has a meaning to the one who gives it, just as we know that a public speaker cannot convey a message which he himself does not understand.

If we wish to convey a message we must feel it, just as the musician feels the atmosphere of harmony back of his technique. Yet technique is equally necessary in order that he may give definite form to his feeling.

The practitioner recognizes the whole condition as a thing of thought and in his own mind straightens out this thought about his patient. In so doing he reveals the Eternal Harmony back of the negative appearance. This straightening out of thought is *technique.* It may be taught, analyzed, taken apart and put together again. It consists of words, phrases, thoughts, ideas, all of which are understandable, teachable and learnable.

The *essence* of the treatment, the feeling which the practitioner has, his interior sense of the Divine Allness, of that Spirit which is closer to him than his own breath—this cannot be put into words, this cannot be taught. It can only be felt.[14]

Now our conviction about the mechanics of things probably exists at the intellectual level and may exist at a feeling level; but if it exists only at [an] intellectual level, remember this: a man with a good intellect may make a mold—and a perfect one mechanically, mathematically, with complete precision—but he wouldn't fill it with life. So in addition to that which he may mechanically do, there has to be a meaning; and there is no creative mold without a meaning—there just can't be; it is an unfertile seed.

So that feeling, I think, is something that while it will not deny the acceptance or rejection or analysis of intellect ... the intellect may perceive, analyze, accept, reject, deny, affirm and go through terrific performances until it builds an edifice or theoretical ladder from the earth to the skies; but it is a great question whether the intellect would ever climb the ladder, as such. *What* climbs the ladder, *whoever,* need not be repudiated by the intellect—is that clear? There is something else that goes with it ... what is meant by the philosophy of mysticism, of intuition. It is a language of the feeling which, while it does not deny the intellectual conviction, sort of sweeps it up, adds warmth and color and feeling to it, which every artists will know as the difference between a technique and a temperament.[15]

Now the practitioner who will the most persistently practice the Presence of God will be able to do the most with this technique. Why? Because he is filling it with a form, he is supplying it through his words with a form, he is filling the form with a feeling, like molten lava; and we could create all the intellectual forms forever and have nothing happen. Something has to fill what is called the spirit and letter of the law, I suppose, in the Bible. "My words fly upward, my thoughts remain below; words without thoughts can not to heaven go."[16]

As far as we are concerned, then, we shall assume that there is a thinker, an ego, an entity, a person, and that behind him is an irresistible impulsion to express Life. In a certain sense he must live or die; he must create or perish; he must express Life or the Life seeking expression through him will flow back inside him. There will then be a pressure from within out, and a pressure from without in. It is in this inner or between point that unconscious conflicts occur.

If we can accept the proposition that feeling and emotion are certain ways of thinking, and actually reduce them to thought or to Mind in Action, then we can see how it is that thought can change them. As a matter of fact this is what psychiatry and spiritual and mental counseling do. This may be done through having the patient talk his troubles out of himself with the kindly guidance of a wise counselor, or it may be done as in our method by the practitioner's thinking back to the Spiritual Reality of his patient and identifying the patient with It.

The results will be the same except that in ordinary counseling the logical implications of the Spiritual Nature of the patient are not emphasized. But if we are rooted in this deep Reality, which we know that we must be, it follows that our thought should reach back even through the feeling and the emotion to Reality Itself.

We recognize that we cannot do this by the intellect alone. Our work has a feeling about it, a feeling of the Divine Presence and the emotion of Infinite Love. As metaphysicians, or those who believe in spiritual mind healing, we do not deny physical facts or psychic facts, nor do we hesitate to affirm that there are spiritual facts. We should put them all together. The emotions affect the physical body, and the mind can be destructive or constructive according to the way it is used. For this is the Law of Mind in Action. But back of it all is the Actor.

Wise counseling leads from the act to the actor, and brings the patient to what is called self-awareness, to a place where he sees why he acted as he did and why he can just as well act differently. It takes him back through all his emotions to the place where he was when he was an infant before all of his troubles started.

But just taking him back there is not enough, even though it does have a salutary effect. He must consciously recognize his Union with the Infinite, his Oneness with Life, his Partnership with God.

Here is an interesting thought to speculate on. If feeling and emotion acting through the avenue of consciousness can produce such havoc, what would happen if the same feeling and emotion were constructively employed? What would happen if we could convert the energy of fear to faith, the energy of doubt and uncertainty into a feeling of belonging to the Universe and being safe in It? Would not the Original Artist Himself go forth into a new creation through us?[17]

In practical application, when a practitioner finds someone who is dogmatically opinionated, overargumentative and resistant, instead of setting up a barrage of audible argument, he should silently treat to know that there is no resistance to the Truth. In this way he will be treating the resistance as he would any other negative state of consciousness . . .

This calls for tolerance and love, sympathy and understanding. As a surgeon sets a broken bone with no personal opinion about his patient, seeking only to help him, so the spiritual mind practitioner readjusts thought with the same flexible tolerance and desire to be helpful . . .

The cold statement "You are already perfect and the only thing wrong with you is a false belief" will never heal. It will arouse antagonism and conflict, which will reflect back and forth, subconsciously, between the mind of the practitioner and the patient. The patient comes to the practitioner because he is sick or because he is going through some discordant or unhappy experience. He should be received in sympathy and with love, with tolerance and understanding, and never with a lofty attitude which looks down from the heights of its own conceit either in pity or condemnation. This attitude cannot heal.[18]

Here Ernest describes the sex drive in a fashion akin to the Kundalini concept of creative energy harnessed or unleashed. This is from the original (1926) edition of **The Science of Mind** *textbook.*

Life is Androgynous, i.e., It contains within Itself both the masculine and the feminine factors. The male and the female of Creation come from One Principle; all come from the One and all will return to the One: all are now in the One and will forever remain in the One.

Back of all manifestation must be the desire to create, the urge to express; this is called the "Divine Urge." But this Urge, operating as Law, produces energy. Desire gathers energy for creative purposes and utilizes power to express itself. So dynamic is this Urge that it will cause a little seed to break open the most solid earth, in order that it may express itself in the form of a plant. It is the coming forth of Spirit into expression, the loosing of energy into action, and is apparent in all Creation.

The Spirit, being Absolute, is always expressed; It has no unfulfilled desires. *It is always satisfied and happy because it is always expressed.* Creation is the result of the desire of Spirit to express Itself; It is the unfoldment of the Divine Ideas . . .

Man . . . reenacts the Divine Nature and makes use of the same Laws that God uses. We find in man the same androgynous nature that we find in God. This nature we call his objective and subjective faculties. His objective mentality impregnates his subjective with ideas; and in its turn, the subjective, gathering force and energy, projects these ideas into forms . . .

It is claimed that a large percentage of diseases is caused by the suppression of some form of emotion. This does not necessarily mean the suppression of the sex emotion, but might mean any desire that remains unexpressed . . . Things will stand just so much pressure and no more; when the limit is reached an explosion will follow, unless some avenue for expression is provided.

Human love and the affections often go hand in hand with sex desire, even when not recognized as such. An affectionate nature is generally a passionate one. Love is the most wonderful thing in the world and creates the highest form of energy known to the mind of man. It will be expressed at the level of the passions or else become transmuted into Spiritual Coin of real and lasting value. But the ideas on sex are likely to become overemphasized in modern literature along these lines. Sex is normal in its proper sphere; if it were not, it would not be; for nature does nothing without some good and ample reason.

The true meaning of love is a wonderful thing; for it is the desire of the soul to express itself in terms of creation. Creation is brought about only through the self-givingness of the lover to the object of his love. That is why, when we love people, we will go to the limit to help or serve them; nothing is too great, no sacrifice is enough. The true lover gives all and is unhappy in not having still more of himself to give to the object of his adoration.

Because of our emotional nature, love is generally expressed through the sex desire. But too great an expression of this desire is destructive, for it depletes the vitality and demagnetizes the one who overindulges. This is the meaning, and the whole meaning, of the story of Samson and Delilah. "He that hath an ear, let him hear" . . .

The sex relationship is not necessary to the expression of real love. Love is the givingness of the self, and if this givingness is complete sex will take care of itself . . .

Sex desire becomes destructive only when it remains an unexpressed longing. This theory is not put forth to encourage free love nor to advocate indiscriminate relationships, for neither the one nor the other is believed in by the writer. It is stated as a fact patent to any thinking person. "Libido" may be expressed through more than one avenue; through transmutation, freeing life's energies and lifting them into an avenue of constructive expression; or through sublimation, transfusing the essence of energy into high action and producing a magnetism that is irresistible and wonderful in its scope. The atmosphere of one thus charged is complete; for the energy then takes the form of real Love and is the highest and most powerful vibration on the physical plane.

It is very disastrous to feel that we cannot live unless we possess some one individual, body and soul. This is not love but is an idea of possession, which often becomes an obsession. No soul is really complete until he feels complete within himself.

This does not exclude the great human relationships which mean so much to all of us; but it does take the sting out of life and does free the individual to love all, adore some and find happiness everywhere.

To feel that love is unrequited creates a longing so intense that it tears the very heart out of life, and throws the one so feeling into a fit of despondency from which it is, indeed, hard to recover. This feeling is met in the Truth by knowing that Love is Eternal and Real and cannot be added to nor taken from.

This may seem like a hard teaching; but the problems of humanity deal largely with the human relationships, and until they are harmonized, there can be no lasting happiness."[19]

The subconscious mind responds to the intensity of feeling around the thought with which it's presented, and sometimes we're unaware of the pent-up feelings until they manifest in undesirable ways. These next few readings show Ernest's view of habit acquisition. These came at a time when alcoholism, in particular, was widely regarded as a moral weakness or altogether untreatable.

What is a habit? A habit is desire objectified—"the continuous character of one's thoughts and feelings"—desire for something that will give satisfaction. At the root of all habit is one basic thing: *the desire to express life.* There is an urge to express in all people, and this urge, operating through the channels of Creative Mind, looses energy into action, and compels the individual to do something. Back of all this desire is the impulse of Spirit to express. In man, this impulse must express at the level of his consciousness. Some express themselves constructively and some destructively. Suppose a man who has the liquor habit comes to you to be healed. You would not treat the *habit.* You would not pray for the man to be healed. You would know that you are dealing with a man who has the desire to express life and who, for the moment, thinks he must express it in terms of intoxication. He once thought this expressed reality to him. He now knows that it does not, but he cannot with mere willpower stop it, for the habit appears to have taken complete possession of him. (We might well remember always that unless we control thought, it will control us.)

In giving treatment, first recognize who and what this man is, saying something like this: "This man is the full and complete expression of Truth, and as such he is free from any sense of limitation. He is not bound by any sense of inferiority, which he needs to cover up, for he is a unique individuality, expressing all the attributes of God. He is free from any delusion or fear of delusion. He knows that the Spirit of Truth within him is complete and always satisfied. He has no longing outside of the longing to express his own divinity, and he has the assurance that he shall be able to gratify this: 'Blessed are they who do hunger and thirst after righteousness (right living) for they shall be filled.' This thing which calls itself the liquor habit has no power over him and cannot operate through him. By the power of this word which I am now speaking, this habit is completely destroyed and forever obliterated." Then mentally see him free and harmoniously expressing life and happiness.[20]

In most cases the habit, itself, is not the real disease. It is the unconscious attempt to escape from the real disease. The disease itself is some inner emotional state, of which the patient generally is not at all aware, but from which he unconsciously shrinks. He is impelled to seek escape through the act of self-forgetting or self-destruction. If this is the case, it follows that the habit will be healed only when its cause is destroyed. In other words, it is not alcoholism, as though it were a thing in itself, that should be attacked, but the hidden cause back of the addiction that needs to be eradicated.

If the cure is to become a real and lasting healing, it will be accomplished only by first uprooting those hidden and subjective causes which lie back of the actual disease, the elimination of unconscious frustrations, whether they occurred in early youth or in later life, for addiction is an unconscious attempt either to express what is felt but not consciously known—to escape from some subjective restriction—or else, by self-destruction, to reach an imaginary oblivion.

The alcoholic is not necessarily a mental, spiritual or moral weakling. Indeed, many of the best minds have experienced the flight into delusion, an unconscious attempt to escape from the real disease which is hidden.

Uncovering the cause—in the science of psychology this is accomplished by bringing the compulsion to the surface to be self-seen, and thereby dissipated. This is the mental surgery of psychology; the analysis of the soul, the taking apart and again reassembling of the psyche. The afflicted person has lost conscious command of himself . . .

This emotional craving for self-expression starts at the mother's breast and continues throughout life. Frustrations, then, may be of an early date in the experience of the patient, and all experiences must be taken into account if the analysis is going to be complete . . .[21]

He relates this true story:

Let me tell you about a man who was so unfortunate as to have become an alcoholic addict. This incident happened in a San Francisco hotel. Mr. Armor, one of our teachers at the Institute of Religious Science in Los Angeles, and I were visiting that wonderful city. What was my surprise, one evening, to receive a telephone call from another room in the same hotel and to hear a familiar voice, but rather a groggy one, say, "Hello, can you come over to [my] room for a few moments?"

A moment later I was knocking at his door. There he lay sprawled out on the bed, and I was greeted with these words: "I'm drunk."

"You are the first person," I replied, "I have ever known who claimed to be drunk while appearing to be perfectly sober. What are you lying on the bed for? Why don't you get up?"

"I can't stand up" was his reply. "That is one of the funny things about my drinking—I can get so drunk that I can neither stand nor walk, but I never lose consciousness. Which makes it just that much worse."

"Even though your body is drunk," I remarked, "your mind is perfectly clear. Why don't you stop drinking? Sober up and go home."

"Ah, that's just the trouble," he said, "I can't. This sometimes goes on for weeks."

"And do you always go off by yourself like this?" I asked.

"Yes," he replied. "I am a lone drinker. I don't know why I do it. Something beyond my control impels me. What, in the name of God, is my trouble? Can you help me?"

Imagine sitting on the edge of a bed talking to a man whose mentality seemed as clear as anyone's could be, and yet so drunk he couldn't stand alone!

"But what do you do when you find yourself in this condition?" I asked.

"Usually," he replied, "after a week or two I send for my wife. She generally is able to bring me out of it. But, somehow, I thought you might do this for me."

"And just what do you think I can do for you?" I inquired.

"Oh," he said, "you know, I really believe in your stuff and I think I have some understanding of it. Surely there is some power that can help me."

What a tragedy! I thought. A successful professional man overcome by a habit which, while in his particular case was not able to reduce him to insensibility, still had him cornered, as it were, beaten, defeated.

"Would you really like to give up this stuff for good?" I asked.

"That is the one prayer of my life," he said. "I have as fine a wife as ever lived and two beautiful children. It is because of them that I go away when this thing takes possession of me. After a while I wire for my wife."

My next question was to the point: "Are you sure that you wish to give up this habit for good?"

"How can you ask such a question," he said, "when you see me in this condition? Even now," he continued, "my craving is irresistible."

Perhaps you will be surprised at what we did next. We sent down to the bar for a bottle of whiskey. It is well known to those familiar with this subject, whether we call them psychologists or metaphysicians, that habits are not successfully treated through willpower. Something different than mere mental determination must happen to the emotional nature of an alcoholic or drug addict, if he is to be free from the bonds which have clamped him into his mental prison. This is why we ordered the whiskey. I told him to drink all he wished. As a matter of fact, I placed the bottle, with a glass of water, at his bedside and left, telling him if this were not enough I would secure more for him during the evening or the night.

"But," he implored, "aren't you going to help me? Is anything going to happen? What are you going to do, anyway? Shall I wire to Los Angeles for my wife?"

"No," I replied. "Mr. Armor and I are occupying rooms close to you. We will get busy and lick this thing, and we are going to do it tonight."

I wanted to get away from him, away from seeing him in his defeated condition. I wished to get that mental image out of my mind that I might see him strong, self-reliant, poised in pure Spirit, unshaken, unshakable.

It was early in the evening. We had just had dinner. I returned to my room and said to Mr. Armor, "Too bad, we won't be going anywhere tonight. We have a job to do. Mr. B— is across the hall, drunk. He wants to be healed and we are going to do it right now."

Perhaps you will be interested to know just how we went about our work. We made ourselves comfortable, relaxed. First one and then the other took up this thought for him: "This man is conscious that he is pure Spirit. He is poised and at peace within himself. There is nothing in him that craves alcohol. He is not seeking to escape from anything. He meets every issue of life without fear. There is nothing to run away from. Nothing to avoid. At all times he has a sense of well-being, of happiness, of security and of self-expression. There is no memory of ever having received any pleasure or benefit from alcohol. There is no anticipation that he can ever receive pleasure or benefit from it. The Spirit within him is satisfied. It is radiant. It never seeks to escape from Itself. It exists in Its own sense of self-adequacy. It exists in joy, in freedom and in peace."

We did our work orally. First Mr. Armor would work for ten or fifteen minutes, then I would take up the thought and continue, each speaking aloud. We worked for several hours until somehow, in a way which no one completely understands, hence no one can perfectly explain, we both seemed to have a sense of release for our friend. We seemed to feel that what we had said about him was true; that there really was no intoxicated man. There was only a glorious sense of divine sonship, free from fear, perfectly contented, happy and radiant, self-assured, united with the Infinite and one with complete satisfaction.

Early the next morning the phone rang and a steady, cheerful voice said, "Can you come over to my room for a moment?"

I was there almost immediately. He was relaxed, calm and as sober as he had ever been in his life. His first remark was "You will find the rest of that stuff in the closet."

There it was, all but about two drinks that he had taken. He never took another drink—he never had the desire.

You see, we were using the Law of Life for a definite purpose. There is no mystery about this. Anyone using the same method would have had the same result.[22]

Take the heat out from under old hurts, and what's left **is light.**

We are all marked to a certain degree by the experiences of the past. And since we cannot, or should not wish to, obliterate memory, it becomes necessary for us often to reverse our thinking about the past. For instance, let us say that someone breaks a limb, suffers considerable pain, and goes through a long and trying period of recovery. It is most certain that there is no need of forgetting that he had gone through this experience; but at the same time there is no reason why he should continually relive the memory of the pain and anguish that went along with the experience. It is for this reason that psychology definitely states that it is not the experience through which we go, but rather our emotional reaction to it, which causes us harm. However, some seem to take a particular delight in inflicting such torture on themselves.

To remove the emotional content of undesirable experiences it is often of value to calmly and coolly bring them up in memory, to quietly live them over again and recognize them as events, but definitely realize that they no longer need have any content of fear, of horror, of pain. Remember the incident, but remove and dismiss any morbidity of emotion that surrounds it. It is a fact of experience, it was lived, but there is no necessity to keep on living it mentally and emotionally today. That was life at that time, but an entirely new life is being lived today, if we will but let ourselves live it.[23]

See only what you wish to experience, and look at nothing else. No matter how many times the old thought returns, destroy it by knowing that it has no power over you; look it squarely in the face and tell it to go; it does not belong to you, and you must know—and stick to it—that you are now free.[24]

Make yourself feel that you now have, and to you shall be given.[25]

This affirmation of his invites freedom:

I now accept all that I have hoped for and believed in. There is nothing in me that can doubt that good will make its appearance in my experience. There is nothing in me that can dissipate my faith or dim its clear realization. I see in everyone that which I know to be true about myself. Therefore, everyone I think of is blessed by my thought.[26]

VII.

The Body of God

THE SCRIBE:
The Farer seemed to sleep, so still he stood,
His eyes still fixed upon the multitude
That stood before the Altar of the Ages,
But unaware of saviors and of ages.
It seemed that all his faculties of sight
Had been withdrawn—no need for outer light
Nor outer sense; as though it now sufficed
To find *within* the image of the Christ;
Nor did he know who spoke, the Presence or
The Christ or self, his soul so filled with awe
Because the Living Spirit seemed to be
His all-in-all; he *was* Eternity . . .

Then fell these words prophetic and profound,
That seemed to fill all space with soundless sound
As though Infinity Itself awoke in him
Amidst the chanting of the cherubim:

Know that flesh and blood and sinew
Are as waters of a river
Flowing from a hidden source,
As a form made up of Spirit,
Are as shadows cast forth from It
From a source no man has seen.

This Alchemy of Spirit
That the food we take in body
Should itself become a body;
This the miracle of life.

Is not this the secret meaning?
Is not this the holy meaning
Of the flesh and blood of Christ?
When of bread we take in body,
When of air we breathe in body,
When of wine we drink in body,
Is not this the eucharist?

He the one who knew its meaning
Is the one who spread the table
Is the one who broke the bread.
This He did to teach the lesson,

This He did to show that substance
Is of Spirit formed and held,
Is by Spirit freely given,
Is by Spirit gladly given,
Is by Spirit always given,
By the universal law.

This the secret of the ages,
This the wisdom of the wise men—

Body has a perfect pattern,
Body has an unseen substance,
Body has a complete likeness
In the life and mind of God.[1]

Ernest connected deeply with the Hermetic idea that everything in form has a spiritual pattern behind it, no less so the "organs, actions and functions" of the human body. He was especially enthusiastic about the use of spiritual mind treatment in redirecting the causes of physical distress. He opens with his teaching on the subject and follows with three case histories.

"We believe in the healing of the sick through the power of this Mind." Spiritual mind healing has long since passed the experimental stage, and we now know why it is that faith has performed miracles. We live in a universe of pure, unadulterated Spirit, of perfect Being. We are, as Emerson said, in the lap of an infinite Intelligence. There is a spiritual prototype of perfection at the center of everything. There is a cosmic or divine pattern at the center of every organ of the physical body. Our body is some part of the Body of God; it is a manifestation of the Supreme Spirit.

In the practice of spiritual mind healing, we start with this simple proposition: God is perfect. God is all there is. God includes man. Spiritual man is a divine being, as complete and perfect in essence as is God. When in thought, in contemplation, in imagination, in inward feeling, we consciously return to the Source of our being, the divine pattern, which already exists, springs forth into newness of manifestation. When we clear the consciousness, that is, the whole mental life, both conscious and subjective, of discord, we are automatically healed.[2]

To say that the body is unreal is a mistake. It is real but is an effect, not an entity. It may yet be proven that the mind *completely* controls the body, and that the body is but a reflection of the mind. In no way would this contradict the reality of the body nor the experience of pain and sickness, but it might help in an understanding of these experiences.[3]

You do not need to look for *a law of health as opposed to a law of disease*, for there is only One Law. This gives a great sense of relief since it means *that there is no power to oppose a treatment.* We are bound by our very freedom, our free will binds us, but as free will creates the conditions which externally limit us, so it can uncreate or dissolve them. Instead of saying, "Here is a sick man to heal, and I shall have to work very hard on this case," we should realize that there is nothing but Spirit in the Universe and, therefore, say, "I am going to conceive of this man as being Spirit, and the same power which made him sick will heal him . . ."

All thoughts of doubt concerning one's ability to heal come from the belief that it is the personality and not the Law which does the healing. Never say: "I am not *good* enough to heal," or "I do not *know enough* to heal." Know that you are dealing with Law, *It* is the Actor . . .

We must transcend the appearance, even though we admit it as a fact. We are not so cold-blooded as to say to a person with pain that there is no such thing as pain. That is not our idea or purpose. We admit the fact. *It is a quite different thing to admit its necessity.* We admit that there is unhappiness, but it would be unthinkable to admit that *one has to be unhappy* . . . Disease, accordingly, is a fact but not a truth. It is not an eternal verity. It was a fact in human experience for ages that people did not broadcast over a radio, but it was not a *truth* that they could not. It was not a divine Reality, because had they known how to manufacture a radio and talk over it, they *could* have broadcast in any age. So we must try to see and sense that always, back of the appearance, *perfection is* . . .

What should we try to heal through spiritual treatment? If we were dealing *only* with the power of a thought, we should not expect to heal anything; but if we are dealing with a Universal Principle, why should we set any limit to Its power?

Since the Law of God is Infinite, from the spiritual viewpoint there is no *incurable* disease, as opposed to a *curable* one. The Law knows nothing about disease; it only acts.

The word "incurable" means not susceptible of being cured. The root definition of *cured* is "cared for." If we say that a disease is *incurable*, we are saying that it is not sensitive to care. As long as any cell is alive it is sensitive to care, which means that as long as a person is alive, the cells of the body respond to care. Naturally, they are not being cured if they are not being properly cared for. We have already learned that disease is largely a state of mind, and we could hardly say that a state of mind is *incurable*, could we? We know that thought is constantly changing, forever taking on new ways of expression. It cannot possibly remain permanent. It has to change. Can we not, accordingly, change it to a better state instead of to a worse?[4]

Conditions are the reflections of our meditations and nothing else. There is but One Mind, that Mind is our mind now. It never thinks confusion, knows what It wishes and how to accomplish what It desires. *It is what It desires!*[5]

Since we cannot walk on the water, we take a boat. Or an aspirin.

Since our spiritual understanding is not sufficient to enable us to mentally set bones, we call in a surgeon; since we cannot walk on the water, we take a boat. We can go only as far as our spiritual knowledge takes us. Principle is Infinite, but we shall demonstrate Its power only at the level of our concept of It. Every day we have the announcement from scientists that they have made new discoveries—laws which have always existed but which have not as yet been utilized.

Do not let anyone discourage or belittle your efforts by asking, "Why don't you walk on the water? Jesus did." . . . If we had the understanding which Jesus had, we *would* be able to walk on the water. I am not at all confused by the fact we do not do this today. Someday one will come along who knows how to walk on or over water.

People say: "I can't take off my glasses." Then wear them, but begin to make the declaration that there is One Perfect Vision seeing through you. This is the Truth. *If this statement becomes a subjective realization, you will be healed, will no longer need glasses.*

If a plaster will relieve, use it. If a pill does any good, take it, but gradually try to lead the thought from where it is into the higher realms of consciousness where the soul recognizes its own I-Am-ness.

Suppose one is unable to convince himself of the Truth of the statement which he makes. How is he going to bring himself to a place of belief? By repeating his affirmation, dwelling on its meaning, meditating upon the spiritual significance of it, until the subjective state of his thinking becomes clarified. This is the only reason for repeating treatments, for *one* treatment would heal if there were no subjective doubts. Repeated treatments induce, within consciousness, a definite concept of an already established truth, even though the fact may not as yet have become objectified. This is why mental healing is scientific. There is no room for doubt in a treatment.[6]

Suppose Mary Jones has some kind of physical difficulty and we are going to treat her for physical perfection. We start: "God is Perfect. Mary is a creation of God and is living in a spiritual universe now. Her body is not separate from the Essence and Perfection of Reality. It is perfect, there is only right action; there is no inaction or wrong action, no overaction or underaction. This word is a law of elimination to everything that does not belong to her. Mary's body now manifests its natural rhythm and harmony because it is tuned in to That which is the very essence of rhythm and harmony and love. Perfect love casts out all fear; therefore, there is no longer any fear in her and she has an inward consciousness, an awareness, of life and action and wholeness. There is no condemnation in God. Mary Jones knows that she is one with God, with the universe, and with people. She has no feeling of rejection, she has no sense of guilt, she loves, is loving, and is loved. There is a radiant happiness, there is a dynamic vitality, there is an enthusiastic zest for life. Everything responds to this. Her body is a body of perfect ideas. There is perfect assimilation, perfect circulation and perfect elimination. I accept the manifestation of these ideas in her experience, right now. And so it is."

All this we must *feel*. We are not sending out anything, holding anything, or concentrating anything; we are not supplicating anything, willing anything or wishing. *We are stating and knowing the nature of spiritual Reality.* This is a spiritual mind treatment.[7]

Worry, fear, anger, jealousy and other emotional conditions are mental in their nature, and as such are being recognized as the hidden cause of a large part of all the physical suffering to which the flesh is heir. A normal healthy mind reflects itself in a healthy body, and conversely, an abnormal mental state expresses its *corresponding condition in some physical condition. Thoughts are things!* [8]

The Spirit of the Universe *cannot* change; being ALL, there is nothing for It to change into. The Soul of the Universe must obey the Will of the Spirit. The *body* of the Universe cannot help changing! This is what constitutes the eternal activity of Spirit within Itself; the Spirit passing into form—creation eternally going on. [9]

Body is a concrete manifestation, existing in time and space, for the purpose of furnishing a vehicle through which Life may express Itself. The physical Universe is the body of God; it is a manifestation in form of the Mind of God. It is that Creation which—while it may have beginnings and ends—of Itself neither begins nor ends. The manifestation of Spirit is necessary, if Spirit is to come into Self-Realization—hence, Body. [10]

It is necessary that Soul and Body should exist because Spirit, without manifestation, would construct only a dream world, never coming to Self-Realization. In order to express, there must be a medium through which Spirit manifests and there must be a manifestation, hence, Soul and Body. The teaching of the great thinkers of all time is that we live in a threefold Universe of Spirit, Soul and Body—of Intelligence, Substance and Form. [11]

In order that Nature may be coherent and come into self-expression, there must be an objective, a manifest world; but *that which is physically outside of us still exists in the same medium in which we have our being, and the intelligence by which we perceive it is the same intelligence that created it.* [12]

Nature made a chemical laboratory within us to take care of our health. In a sense we might say that there are little intelligences within us acting as though they were little people, whose business it is to digest our food and assimilate it, to circulate our blood and get rid of its impurities. There are millions of these little people inside our bodies whose purpose it is to keep us physically fit. But there also are other little people who are not so kindly minded and they try to tear things down and disrupt the work of the good little people.

Every doctor knows that when he can get the good people inside working with him, things are going to come out all right. We break a bone and when it is set nature gets busy and all the good little people begin to knit the bone together again, and all the time they are causing the blood to circulate so there will be no infection.

One of the most popular psychologists in America told me that he once suffered from indigestion and the thought came to him that he could talk to these little people inside him and tell them that it really was their business to take care of his digestion. So he talked to them for a few moments every day and told them how wonderful they were and how much he appreciated what they were doing and that he wasn't going to interfere with them anymore. He was going to be happy and he knew they would take care of everything for him. He praised them and blessed them, and in a few weeks his physical condition cleared up.

Well, this is a body-mind relationship. It is reducing psychosomatics to its simplest common denominator. There is an Intelligence hid at the center of everything and we are intelligent and the lower form of intelligence responds to the higher form. The intelligence in the physical body is a subconscious intelligence. It works creatively, but within certain fixed limitations. It is like a man sent on an errand and told what to do and knowing only to do what he is told.

But we are learning that we can interfere with the good little people inside us because they are subject to a greater intelligence than theirs, which is the person himself. They are supposed to be working for us and with us, but we can so disturb them that they work destructively instead of constructively.

This can be carried to such an extent that the wrong direction given to these little people produces a large part of our physical diseases. But right direction can reverse this process and produce physical well-being instead of disease. And we now know that while hate, animosity and confusion can produce discord, love can heal it.

It is helpful to imagine and feel that all the little people inside that are working for us and with us are connected with the Divine Intelligence which directs them—the very Power that created them. This brings us back to the need that we all have for a faith, a calm assurance and an inward sense of well-being.

Not only is there an Intelligence directing the activities of our physical bodies; this same Intelligence is also directing everything we do. Not only does man operate against himself, physically; he does so in every activity of his life. How many of us really expect to be happy tomorrow? How many of us, when we lie down at night, relax and let the bed hold us up? How many of us have confidence enough in God to sleep in peace, wake in joy, and look forward to the coming day with gladness?

What we need is a conscious cooperation, and a glad one, between ourselves and the Power which, if we let It, would rightly govern everything. But man is so used to operating against himself, so used to thinking of himself as detached and separate, he has so completely taken the whole burden of life on his own shoulders that he has almost lost the ability to cooperate with that Divine Presence which seeks to be a partner to all of us. In our ignorance we have not only operated against ourselves; we have contradicted the supremacy of God. We have denied ourselves the privilege of working with rather than against the Power that put us here.

We know that we did not set the stars in their courses; we did not cause the sun to shine or the rain to come; however, we can cooperate with this Power back of us. But we cannot unify and cooperate with something we do not believe in. So the starting point, the very beginning of the reeducation of our minds, must be a deep conviction, a firm faith. And since, in a sense, life is a stage on which each plays a part, there is no reason why we should not dramatize our relationship with the Infinite.

Just think of all these little people working inside us! God put them there. Why not hook them up in our imagination with the living Spirit and recognize their presence, praise and bless them and even tell them what we want them to do. And each day think how wonderful it is to be cooperating with God! Surely this is the greatest drama of all.

But we must not forget the Director of the play, the One who knows how to make each separate line and act become part of the whole piece until something complete is produced. God is the Great Producer, the Great Director and the One who knows all the parts and where each one belongs. And we must learn to believe in this Producer and Director, even though He is invisible. We cannot see the little people inside us but they are there, and in our imagination we can sense them.

Therefore, say to yourself, quietly and with deep conviction:

My body is the temple of the living Spirit. It is spiritual substance now. Every part of my body is in harmony with the living Spirit within me. The Life of this Spirit flows through every atom of my being, vitalizing, invigorating and renewing every part of my physical body.

There is a pattern of perfection at the center of my being which is now operating through every organ, function, action and reaction. My body is forever renewed by the Spirit and I am now made vigorous and whole.

The Life of the Spirit is my life, and Its strength is my strength. I am born of the Spirit. I am in the Spirit. I am the Spirit made manifest. And so it is.[13]

Here, Ernest again distinguishes fact from truth. The facts are the diagnosis, or present situation; the truth is the prognosis, or anticipated reality, drawn from the limitless field of Eternal Reality.

Physical pain is not necessarily an enemy, since it calls attention to serious conditions which need to be changed, thus enabling one to take the proper steps in rearranging his life. Therefore we should not be bitter over it nor become melancholy through having experienced it. On the other hand, we must be equally certain that we do not fall under the mistaken idea that illness is imposed upon us by some deific power, as though God were tantalizing us or clubbing us into acquiescence to the Divine will. All experiences should tend to enlarge our awareness of the real purpose of life and help us to arrive at a greater realization of the Spirit that is within us.

A negative condition or limitation is a definite experience, more than imaginary. We cannot consider physical pain or want as being illusions.[14]

Some schools of metaphysical thought believe it is wrong to seek medical assistance under any circumstances. And while we hold no controversy over this subject, it is entirely fitting that we make our position clear. The Science of Mind has no superstitions, holds to no dogmas, but believes in the good in everything. We sincerely believe that any undesirable physical condition can be bettered through the proper use of prayer, faith or spiritual affirmation. We are equally certain that not all people who have asked for such help have finally been healed. If one is able to say to a paralyzed man, "Take up your bed and walk," and have the man actually take up his bed and walk, then there is certainly no point left to argue over. But what right have we to deny anyone whatever help he can find?

Possibly someone will ask, "But are you not resorting to material means in order to assist the Spirit?" The answer is "Not at all." There are no material means so far as Spirit is concerned. Divine Intelligence has conceived and created everything. And everything which God has made must be good if we could only understand its true nature. The mental attitude that one cannot receive spiritual benefit if he is being attended by a physician seems to us to be built upon superstition. Rather, we believe in the most complete cooperation among all of the healing arts; the complete cooperation between the physician, the psychologist, the metaphysician and the spiritual counselor.

We know that the ultimate in healing is spiritual healing. This spiritual healing may be a result of earnest prayer, of exalted faith or of spiritual affirmations. It is useless to quibble over terms. We know that faith and conviction must be arrived at, and it does not seem fruitful to argue over what methods one should use, or to say that one method is right while another is wrong. Any method which is constructive is right, if it finally arrives at the desired goal. Why not combine them all and thereby, happily, enjoy the greatest possible good.[15]

Practitioner training materials at one time contained fairly elaborate practitioner/ client scenarios in a supplement called the "Clinical Course," written in the 1940s.

Most of these were fictitious, created by Maude Allison Lathem (who could have done well as a novelist), or loose composites of several real situations. This one, though, was inserted by Ernest himself, and is factual. Then it becomes **true.**

She seemed to be losing her eyesight, and yet there was no apparent physical reason. But there was a definite psychological cause for her trouble.

She was compelled to live in an environment which was distasteful to her even in its minutest detail. One of the particular points brought out, in our first conversation, was that her husband had insisted on choosing all the furniture for their home. She didn't like this furniture. The patterns in the rugs were too large and nothing harmonized.

She had merely made up her mind to grin and bear it. Unconsciously she was saying to herself, "I detest everything about this home in which I live, but if it must be, then it must be. I resign myself to it." All of which was very grand, so far as the intellect was concerned, but the emotions are not so easily coerced. She still silently and unconsciously detested what she was physically compelled to look at; therefore, unconsciously her emotions said to her, "All right, look at it, but don't see it." After a while she noticed that she really couldn't see the pattern in the rug at all. It was all a blank.

She had reached a stage where it was impossible for her to travel around the city alone. Surely this was a case of putting on blinders in a very definite way. Of course, the whole process was unconscious; that is, it was subjective.

Her thought was healed by knowing that wherever she looked she would see beauty. It is impossible to look away from the Spirit. As has truly been said, "Wherever you will go you will find me, wherever you look you will see me." I never did know whether or not they changed their furnishings, but I do know that her vision was completely restored. Where was this vision during the interim? It must always have been there. An emotional veil had been drawn before it.

I have known similar cases where people have gradually lost their hearing through refusing to listen to that which they did not wish to hear. I remember also the case of a young lady, emotionally desiring to be with her parents and yet being compelled to go away to a boarding school, who developed such a serious physical condition that it was impossible for her to go. This went on for several years until it was corrected. There are many cases of hysterical blindness, deafness and dumbness which can be attributed to just such an emotional block. We may attribute many physical maladies to the same cause: an escape mechanism, an unconscious compromise, the battle between the intellect and the emotions, a flight from reality into fantasy.

It is necessary for us actually to understand, believe and more completely accept the world in which we live, and to enter more abundantly into a life of self-expression. There is nothing chaotic about this, for proper self-expression never infringes upon the rights of others. It gives to each the same privilege which it asks for itself. It is liberty without license.[16]

These stories of treatment for mental and psychosomatic turbulence come from **This Thing Called Life.**

The larger part of our consciousness is functioning independently of our conscious mind, as is shown in the following case history:

She was about sixty, cultured, traveled and educated. She was amply provided for financially and appeared to have good business judgment in handling her affairs. But . . . voices talked to her. It seemed as though invisible entities were tormenting her. Had I believed in spirit obsession, I should have felt that she was really obsessed. Some months before I met her, she had learned to use a ouija board and she was delighted with the messages she received. They were helpful and contained considerable philosophic discussion of no little merit.

Gradually she found that she could dispense with the ouija board and communicate directly with these alleged invisible presences. But the day came when these influences, which had been so benign, became quite vicious. They began to persecute her; to tell her that because of sins she had committed, she must be punished until the sins were atoned for. It would be impossible to know just how she felt inwardly, but her experiences were real enough, so far as she was concerned. She suffered actual physical pain as a result of her inward conflict; she was not allowed to sleep at night.

Her torment had reached an excruciating stage when I first met her. I tried to tell her that these voices she heard emanated from her own subconscious self; that perhaps she had some deep-seated but unconscious sense of guilt, and that this was the way her mind was talking to condemn her. I do not think she had ever done anything very bad in her entire life, but so often we find well-meaning, honest and constructive people who entertain this deep sense of guilt. I have often felt that it might arise from the race consciousness itself; the theological condemnation of the ages; a misuse of conscience; a misconception of the beautiful relationship which the soul should have to the universe.

I found it impossible to get anywhere with this method. She insisted that she was dealing with vicious entities; that they would have to be destroyed or she would lose her reason. She feared insanity. Finding it impossible objectively to explain to her what I believed to be the seat of her trouble, I began a process of silent treatment which I felt sure would deliver her from her torment. I was thoroughly convinced then, and still am, that she was talking to herself.

I followed the line of thought that since there is but One Spirit, One Mind, which is complete and happy, and since each of us is an individual center of this God-Consciousness, there was nothing in reality that could torment her. I reasoned that there was no power, person or presence, in the flesh or out of it, which could obsess, possess or suggest anything to her, good, bad or indifferent. I took the thought that the One Mind controlled her and that the whole theory of spirit obsession or of the obsession of mental suggestion, was entirely foreign to the Truth, could not operate through her, had no power over her, no reality and no appearance of reality.

The thing did not happen in a minute. Her trouble was very deep-seated and it took some time for her to find complete emancipation, but gradually the influences waned, the voices grew less distinct. Finally, one day she met me at the door with a joyous expression on her face, exclaiming, "You know, I have had the most wonderful experience. I know that I am going to be healed. Last night the voices told me that they were not people at all; that I had been laboring under an hallucination and that you were entirely right—it has been my own subjective self that has been talking to me."[17]

Power that is unused remains dormant; it is merely a possibility. But we are using the Power of Life at all times whether or not we are aware of the fact. Here is the case of a woman who was using It wrongly.

I have never seen a funnier spectacle than she presented, stretched out on the bed with a hot water bottle poised on her stomach. I couldn't help it, I sat down and burst out laughing. If she hadn't had a sense of humor she never would have liked me. But that was many years ago and she has been one of my best friends ever since.

We were living in a small cottage at the beach and one day when I was in Pasadena (twenty miles from where we lived) lecturing, my mother phoned me and said that a Mrs._____ had arrived bag and baggage, with the declaration that she had come to be healed. Naturally, my mother told her that we were not running a private sanitarium and it was impossible for us to receive guests since we only had a small cottage. But all to no avail. I have always admired her persistence. She just wouldn't take "no" for an answer; therefore, she didn't have to. She came and she stayed.

When I returned, just before dinner, my mother said, "She is upstairs."

It all seemed quite ridiculous and absurd, but up I went and there she was, spread out on the bed. She was fully dressed. Great tears were streaming down her face. She was a large woman and that hot water bottle perched on her stomach was one of the funniest things I have ever seen. I should have had to laugh if she had died that very moment. Perhaps this is one of nature's ways of relieving a tense situation. Tears and laughter—what relief they often bring. Naturally, she was surprised at my laughter.

"What in the world are you laughing at?" she asked.

"You," I replied. "I am laughing at you. I can't help it."

She really had a great sense of humor—a God-given gift. She burst out laughing, too, even in the midst of her pain and tears.

The history of her case: Several years before this incident, it had been necessary for her to have an abdominal operation. It was believed at that time that she could not possibly survive. She came out of the anesthetic into a moment's consciousness just long enough to hear one of the nurses remark that in all probability she would pass on between four and five o'clock in the afternoon. She again lapsed into an unconscious state. However, she lived and apparently got well. She had been operated upon by one of the finest surgeons in America and he was in no way responsible for what followed. It was just one of those things that happen, but it does have great significance in showing us how the laws of mind work.

She recovered from her operation but about three months after that, every afternoon between four and five she would be seized with severe abdominal pains, excruciating agony, tremendous gas pressure and a physical discomfort which racked her whole being. Possibly it was all in her imagination, but it certainly appeared to be in her body. What difference does it make where the pain is, if it hurts? You will never heal anyone by merely telling him that his trouble is just in his mind or imagination, for whatever the seat of the trouble is, it must be dealt with intelligently.

Fortunately, in this case, within an hour we had a complete analysis and apparently a correct one, since she was healed that very night. Within two weeks she was perfectly normal and the physical symptoms from which she had suffered have never returned.

I explained to her that when she regained consciousness in the hospital long enough to hear one of the nurses say she would probably pass on between four and five that afternoon, that remark registered in her subconscious—that part of her which acted as though everything she heard were true and which tried to make everything which she believed come true in her experience. We might say that her pain was psychic, and so it was in its origin, but it produced its physical correspondent with mathematical precision and exacted an awful toll from her physical and mental endurance.

In this instance, very little silent treatment was necessary. The explanation seemed to be sufficient to meet the case, to uncover the cause and to enable her to regain her psychic equilibrium. I often wonder how many of our internal disorders are of similar nature.[18]

There is an infinite Intelligence which gives birth to our minds, and if our minds are in league with It, then we arrive at the reason for the power of thought. Does it not follow that the creative power of thought does not repose in the human will, but in the Divine Presence? And should we not have an entirely different conception of spiritual healing if we knew that it had nothing to do with mental suggestion, but with the silent recognition of the

Spirit already resident and inherent in the individual for whom we are working? You and I, by taking thought, do not do anything other than line ourselves up with that which is the Father of thought. But could it be other than that "the highest God and the innermost God is One God?" When we seek to heal spiritually we are seeking to release the spiritual Principle inherent within the individual needing healing.[19]

Here's a powerful practice, whatever we're faced with:

If bodily illness confronts you, do this at least twice a day: Get as comfortable as you can, releasing all tension. Resolve that at least for a few minutes you will forget the bodily discomfort, the pain, the fever or any other symptom which distresses you. Try to let go—to relax—all over, so that all tenseness disappears from your body. Close your eyes and know that your body is the house in which God dwells, that God is in you as you, that God is what you are. Then quietly, very slowly, with ample time for a deep realization of every word, say:

"There is One Life, that Life is God, that Life is perfect, that Life is my life now. My body is a manifestation of the living Spirit. It is created and sustained by the One Presence and the One Power. That Power is flowing in and through me now, animating every organ, every action and every function of my physical being. There is perfect circulation, perfect assimilation and perfect elimination. There is no congestion, no confusion and no inaction. I am One with the infinite rhythm of Life which flows through me in love, in harmony and in peace. There is no fear, no doubt and no uncertainty in my mind. I am letting that Life which is perfect flow through me. It is my life now. There is One Life, that Life is God, that Life is perfect, that Life is my life now."

You will notice that here no particular discomfort was named. You have not asked for anything. You have been trying to *realize* what you already *are.* This or a similar meditation should be used often during any period of illness. The big job you have to do is to *convince yourself* of your natural perfection. When all negation is wiped out of your consciousness and you feel that you are a specific part of the Infinite, a child of the One Father,

141

with His qualities, you have then planted the idea of health in your mind and it will come forth in your body. This is what effective meditation or prayer does.

To bring healing to pass is, indeed, exercising your rightful dominion over your state of health.[20]

How about a treatment for just a good night's sleep?

The Spirit within me is in perfect rest. The center of my being is quiet and poised. I let my inner spirit fill my whole being with peace and stillness. With this word, I now relax in body and mind. I let the Divine Tranquillity fill me.

My mind now releases all sense of burden or strain. Nothing can hurt or disturb my spiritual self. I am free and safe. All plans and ideas can wait until later. The Divine Wisdom works through me and I am protected from mistakes. My mind is quiet, calm and deeply still. All tension is released and the great inner peace flows out through every nerve. My body rests in the still silence of the Spirit. I bless my body and my mind, for they are good and worthy of my love.[21]

VIII.

What Is Known at One Point
Is Known Everywhere

THE FARER:

Arjuna sat as one entranced, and love
Enveloped him as in a cloud. And he
Who wills can read in the Celestial Song
Of him on whom the light of Krishna fell,
Of how he understood the mysteries
And dared to pit his sun-god strength against
The lunar gods and devil-worshippers—
A history set down in script in after-years
In that same century when Moses heard
Jehovah's voice proclaim the Unitary God
Whom Krishna had made known.
How great
Thou wert and are, O thou whose beam of light
Celestial falls across the pages of
All faiths; who reaffirmed the Trinity;
The Manifested Word, assurance of
A life beyond the grave and spoke these words:

"Know then, that soul which has found God is freed
From death, rebirth, old age and grief."

Of Krishna I can say no more save that
I saw the primal substance, weaving, form
The pattern of his death, which he forecast,
And so designed, a sacrificial act
To set his seal upon the doctrine of
The soul. Beneath the cedar tree he knelt
To pray. The archers of the king and of
The lunar priests fell back abashed and filled
With fear when they beheld his raptured face,
But when at length they bound him to the tree
Insulting him and casting stones, he made
No effort to escape, and when at last
An arrow pierced his flesh from which the blood
Gushed forth, he cried out words of victory.
Transfixed again, he called to Devaki,
"My radiant Mother, grant that those who love
Me enter with me in thy light." And at
The third, he cried out with a single word—
"Mahadeva," and with the name of God
Upon his lips, fell into bliss.[1]

Ernest's use of the term "practitioner" refers to two different sets of people. One is the men and women he or others have trained and licensed to serve in the churches, primarily by performing spiritual mind treatment, accepting as already accomplished the desires of clients who request it. Since treatment is affirmative prayer rather than intercessory, these licensed practitioners are not doing something the client can't also do. It's just easier sometimes, when faced with a problem in life, one's mind swimming in confusion and doubt, to enlist the aid of another person in affirming the highest good. By "practitioner," though, Ernest also means everybody, and his instructions and suggestions to the first group are excellent tools for living for all of us.

We should be careful to distinguish daydreaming and wistful wishing from really dynamic and creative treatment. When we treat we do not wish, we *know*. We do not dream, we *state*. We do not pray, we *announce*. We do not expect something is going to happen; we *believe that it has already happened*.[2]

What is it that must be felt in spiritual practice, the feeling which is beyond words, statements and phrases? It is the essence of Life, the Spirit of the thing from which the mind automatically draws an intellectual conclusion. This feeling results in words which are an activity of the feeling, the enforcement of the Principle back of it. In this way the word becomes Spirit and life.

The practitioner assumes that the Truth is all there is; hence all appearances of evil are but wrong interpretations of the Truth. They are not the Truth in reverse, neither need we consider them as opposites to the Truth, because the Truth has no opposites. Negation is a false statement of the Truth, a false belief about the Truth.

Treatment corrects the wrong use through its right knowing. Right knowing is an intelligent activity of mind which plunges beneath the surface and reveals pure Spirit as the Invisible Cause of creation. The words that a practitioner uses should imply a feeling which lifts him above the appearance he wishes to change.

The practitioner makes a series of statements about the Truth. The feeling that he has must be that the Truth is all there is, and he must sense that the words that he speaks are the enforcement of this allness. Hence he must feel something which cannot be merely stated in words; he must feel the allness of his treatment, not as mental suggestion but as spiritual realization.

In such degree as he does sense this allness his word will have Power.[3]

There is a vast difference between "holding thoughts" and holding things in thought. One is the attempt at an impossible coercion; the other is a mental acceptance. To hold thoughts, as though we were forcing issues, does no good and utilizes but a fraction of the creative power at our disposal. To hold in thought, as though we were *letting* something happen, is to use the greater power . . . the greatest power of all.[4]

In mental treatment we should feel as though the whole power of the universe were running through the words we speak. The words must become "Spirit and Life" if they are to overshadow the thoughts and actions that have brought about a discordant condition. As much conviction as we have, *that* we may use.[5]

Healing is not *creating* a perfect idea or a perfect body; it is revealing an idea which is already perfect. Healing is not a process; it is a revelation, through the thought of the practitioner to the thought of the patient.[6]

For instance, suppose we have received a request for help for a physical condition. Immediately we take the name of the person in consciousness— as every man maintains his identity in Universal Mind, just as he maintains it in the physical world—and we declare the truth about that man, the truth about the *spiritual man,* and we know that the truth about Spiritual Man is the truth about that man's condition right now. First, recognition; second, unification. We continue to do this until something comes into our consciousness which says, "Yes." We know the work has been accomplished. This is the third step: realization. This is what a treatment is.[7]

It is the practitioner's business to uncover God is every man. God is not sick. God is not poor. God is not unhappy. God is never afraid. God is never confused. God is never out of His place. The premise upon which all mental work is based is perfect God, perfect man, perfect being.[8]

Never say: "I am not sure that I have enough power to treat." You can never heal with this mental attitude, *for that implies that you think you are doing the healing.*[9]

These next passages reinforce the point that treatment is done within the mind of the practitioner, expressed silently or verbally. It's not something done to the person requesting it.

Treatment is the act, the art and the science of inducing thought within the mentality of the one treating, which thought shall perceive that the body of the patient is a Divine, Spiritual and Perfect Idea . . . As a result of this treatment, Subjective Mind—which is Universal and Omnipresent—accepts the images of the practitioner's thinking, and reflects them in the direction he specifies . . . to his patient.[10]

A practitioner should think of his patient as a perfect entity, living in a perfect Universe, surrounded by perfect situations and governed by perfect Law.[11]

In the silence of your own consciousness, alone with the great Reality, you balance the account. Not in the other person's mind to see whether he should be an alcoholic or a consumptive, but in your own mind to see whether or not you have true love and givingness, and more conviction to bring to bear, not to influence the Law, but *to be operated upon by the Law* with a mathematical and mechanical certainty at the level of your conviction. If you cannot depend upon the Law with mathematical and mechanical certainty, then you have to wait for the moment of inspiration.[12]

The practitioner loves his patient back into his own center. With technical knowledge of practice he removes the blocks which obstruct the passage of Spirit in the patient's experience. He does not establish the patient in Truth, in God or in Life. He merely takes him by the mental hand and leads him back into himself. His entire effort, whether it be audible explanation or silent practice, is to establish the patient in his own spiritual center.

Spiritual mind practice is a combination of mental technique and spiritual consciousness which establishes a faith and a conviction in the reality of good. The practitioner should never condemn his patient, or say, "You are suffering because you have done this or that or something else." Unless the practitioner can rise above both the mistake and its consequence, he will heal neither. He cannot rise above the mistake while he attaches it to his patient any more than he could rise above a mistake in his own personal life if he attaches it to his own spirit.

There can be no permanent healing without a spiritualization of consciousness. A permanent healing takes place in such degree as consciousness turns inward to the Source of being and finds itself united with life, with love, with God. This is what we call spiritual awareness and it is fundamental to all permanent healing.

The patient must be shown that he has personal and immediate access to all the presence and all the power there is in the universe. A practitioner's work is good only when he has grounded his patient firmly in a consciousness of his own personal contact with Reality. Always the practitioner is seeking to free the patient from the necessity of having a practitioner, from the belief that he must depend upon anything but the Truth.[13]

The practitioner does not send out thoughts or suggestions; he realizes, in his own mind, the truth . . . *The practitioner treats the practitioner, for the patient, always!*[14]

The practitioner thinks within himself, about someone; after definitely stating for whom this word is spoken, he seeks to realize the spiritual, mental and physical perfection of this person. He does this in his own mind; and since his mind is functioning in the Universal Mind, in which each individual mind functions, the realization will rise to fulfillment in the one desiring help according to his receptivity.[15]

How do we know when we have treated a patient long enough? How would one know when to stop seeing him if he were a doctor? When he is well he will need no more treatments; until this time comes, treat every day for a realization of perfection. Begin each treatment as if you had never treated the patient before, trying to realize each time that this particular treatment is going to do the work . . . perfectly.

Does it make any difference whether or not the patient is taking medicine? Not at all. If it gives him any relief, he should have it. We need all the relief we can get. The patient is healed when he no longer needs medicine. Some think they dishonor God when they take a pill. This is superstition. Discard these thoughts and give your entire attention to realizing perfection for your patient.[16]

Abundance in every area of life was something Ernest believed to be available to any-one—through a newfound acceptance made in consciousness.

Suppose I do not say I am poor, but that I came into the world with an unconscious thought of poverty. So long as this thought remains, I am likely to remain poor. I may not understand the Law, but it will be working all the time. We come into this world with a subjective tendency toward conditions, but we must not forget that *we are also dealing with a subjective tendency toward ultimate good*, because in spite of all conditions, the race believes more in good than in evil; otherwise it would not continue to exist. This is the eternal hope and sense of our life.[17]

He regarded licensed practitioners as professionals in every sense.

Although I know there are people who think that you shouldn't be paid for spiritual mind treatment, I do not believe that there is anything wrong in being paid for the work that we do. I would suggest that these people examine their thinking, examine the underlying motive of this belief. They might be surprised as to what they will find![18]

These next two articles, from The Philosophy of Ernest Holmes, *were two halves of one lecture given to Institute students in April 1958, in which Ernest gives an account of the histories of both the New Thought movement and Religious Science. He traces New Thought into ancient times and portrays it an eclectic philosophy comprised of the mystical elements in and around the world's religions.*

I wish to start with the history of the New Thought movement because there would be no Religious Science had there not at first been a New Thought movement. We are one of the New Thought groups of America, which have come up in the last sixty years and influenced the thought of the world and this country more than any other one single element in it—that is, spiritually, religiously, theologically, psychologically too. But the New Thought movement itself, which originated in America, had its roots in a very deep antiquity. We would have to go back, because it has drawn its knowledge from all sources; it is not just a Christian philosophy, although it is a Christian denomination.

It draws many of its sources from India. Now India did not have any one outstanding prophet or revealer as most of the religions have had, such as Buddhism or Christianity or Judaism. India never had a great prophet or a great savior—never claimed any. Rather, their teaching is an accumulation of generations—thousands of years, probably—of wise people. (They didn't even call them saints, but *sages.*)

In looking over these generations of the teachings of India, we find a very great concept of the unity of all life. They believed in one God and only One. They didn't call it God; they called it the Absolute, or Brahma; but it doesn't matter what you call it. They believed in one Presence and one Power, and only One in the Universe. They believed (which later came out as a theosophical teaching) in the mind that sleeps in the mineral, waves in the grass, wakes to simple consciousness in the animal, to self-consciousness in the human and to cosmic consciousness in what they call the upper hierarchies, or an ascending scale of evolution, ad infinitum.

They believed in the theory of involution and evolution, "the spark that ignites the mundane clod," or the divine idea which exists in everything—*everything*—a Something that all things are impregnated with. It is called involution, or the passing of Spirit into substance prior to the passing of substance into definite form to begin an endless round of evolution or unfoldment, cycle after cycle (if they believe in reincarnation, as they do), over and over here, until they have learned what there is here, and then on and on and on.

I personally happen to believe in the upper hierarchies. For all we know, planets are individuals; we don't know that they are not. As intelligent a man as Dean Inge, who was the greatest living exponent of Platonism, and who probably understood Platonism better than anyone else in his day . . . said it didn't seem strange; it was rather rational to accept that all planetary bodies are individuals. Now, whether they are or not doesn't make any difference; I don't know; that is a part of their teaching. If you would like to take the time to read the best single volume on what Hinduism is, the ancient teachings of the *Bhagavad Gita*, the Upanishads, and the Vedas, you will find it one volume of about nine hundred pages . . . called *The Life Divine*, by Aurobindo . . .

[Walter T.] Stace, in a book called *The Destiny of Western Man*— professor at Princeton, I believe—said the philosophy of Christianity is a combination of what he called Palestinian impositionalism (which means "Thus saith the God from *up here*," as the Hebraic prophets said) and what he called Grecian immanentism ("Thus saith the God from in here"), while Dean Inge said that the philosophy of Christianity is twenty-five percent from Judaism and seventy-five percent from the Greeks. You see, the Hebrews were the greatest line of emotional prophets the world has ever known. They were terrific people. They believed that God is One: "Hear, O Israel, the Eternal, the Lord thy God is One God"—*but One.* Absolute monotheists.

The ancient Hebrews (and still today; they haven't changed in their doctrine) and the ancient Hindus (they haven't changed) were, together with certain phases of ancient Egypt which I wish to mention, the first people to perceive a unitary Cause. Whatever it is, it is one and not two ultimates. If they were alike, they would destroy each other. If they were unlike, they would coalesce, amalgamate and come together and be one; there can't be two finalities. The Truth is one, undivided, and indivisible.

But fifteen hundred years prior to the time of Moses we find the Hermetic doctrine—Hermes Trismegistus (Thrice-Great Hermes). In this teaching we find a great deal that Moses taught (because Moses was educated in the Egyptian court, in the Egyptian temples. He was brought up by the Egyptian priests, the hierarchy of nobility), and he was a "top guy," as history has shown.

We find in the Greeks a rehearsal of the Hermetic teaching, particularly in their concept of what Emerson called the Law of Parallels and Swedenborg called the Law of Correspondences, because the Hermetic teaching had said, "As above, so beneath; as beneath, so above." What is true on one plane is true on all—which really means (and this is where we got the idea) that for every visible thing there is an invisible pattern to which the visible is attached.

One of the latest words in modern physics I read within the last two or three years is a book on an explanation of Einstein and Eddington by a very prominent man (accepted by both of these people), in which he said, "Modern physics has become metaphysics"; and the view of the physical universe (which we used to call the material universe) in modern physics is that what we see is not a thing in itself. Whether it is a mountain or a planet or a wart on our finger, it is more like a shadow cast by an invisible substance . . .

This Law of Parallels which Emerson said he believed in—for he said, "Nature has but two laws, but she plays the familiar tune over and over again"—is Hermetic. That would be in line with concepts of Swedenborg where he said, "There is the celestial correspondent to every terrestrial thing." And the Bible says, "How is it that the dead are raised up and with what body do they come? . . . There are bodies celestial and bodies terrestrial . . . so also is the resurrection of the dead . . . The body is sown in weakness, it is raised in power; it is sown a natural body, it is raised a spiritual body. For there is both a natural body and a spiritual body."

And Plotinus, whom Inge called "the king of the intellectual mystics of the ages," said that every organ in the physical body is attached to a cosmic pattern. Now, you see: the pattern is generic, the organ is individualized. A generic pattern means a universal pattern. There is a pattern of man—not the individual but the generic or the universal. This is what is meant by "Christ" and by "Buddha" and by the "illumined," the "one Son," whom Eckhart said, "God is forever begetting, and He is begetting him in me now."

Every organ, Plotinus said, is attached to its pattern, and when by reason of any fact it seems to become detached, it gets in pain and longs to get back. Augustine, speaking of it in a different way and with a different motivation, said, "Thou hast made us, Thine we are, and our hearts are restless till they find repose in Thee."

Probably fifty percent of the best philosophy in the Catholic Church came from Augustine, and he was consciously referring, as Eckhart did, to those whom they called "the pagan philosophers," by whom they meant the Greeks . . . Observe Greek art and see how perfect it is. You will not find a piece of Greek sculpture, unless it is something running, where it doesn't have to overcome the gravitational balance and attraction; but if you could draw a line right straight through the center, you would find it is in absolute balance, as is all their architecture—but it is an intellectual concept, it is kind of cold; yet it is beautiful.

Then look at Roman art: it is all warmth and color but grotesque in form, isn't it? You know, all these guys who painted the pictures of the little Madonna and Jesus—Jesus looks like a strange creature, to say the least. Four times as big as a baby ought to be, and legs as big as an elephant's.

We have to put all these things together—art, science, philosophy and religion—to find out what makes it tick. No one system, no one teacher, no one person has given the world what it knows. It is very significant, because this is what Religious Science stands for.

So we have Buddhism, which plays an important role in the New Thought movement. Just as Christianity is a combination of the Hebrews and Greeks—drawing much through Egypt, because Hermes was an Egyptian—so Buddhism stems from Hinduism . . . [The Buddha] was a Hindu. He was born a prince, and his father would never let him go out in the world to see the horrors, poverty and death. But one day he got out and saw them, and then he went out to try and find out what it was all about—and that is how he got started . . .

He, sitting there at the Banyan tree . . . had tried both paths. He found asceticism didn't work, because he became emaciated and fell over almost dead, and someone had to take care of him. He followed what he called the Middle Path; as he sat in contemplation, there was supposed to have been revealed to him the Law of Cause and Effect. The Law, Annie Besant says, binds the ignorant but frees the wise. There was supposed to have been revealed to him the endless chain of cause and effect, karma, the karmic law . . .

So we get this sequence of cause and effect from both the Buddhist and Mosaic teaching. Moses said, "The sins of the fathers are visited on the children to the third and fourth generations of them that hate God." There was much also in Zoroastrianism.

The great contributions toward the New Thought came from Hinduism, Buddhism, the Old Testament, Judaism, the New Testament (of course) and the Greeks. The philosophy of Emerson is a combination, a compilation, a unification, a putting together of all these things, because he had studied them all his life. You find continual references, if you know where to find them and know what they mean. He had studied all these things and that is why he was so great. And then he had added to that which he had learned and synthesized it . . .

So we find these ancient sources coming down, stemming from things before them, and in their turn contributing to what followed after them, gradually formulating certain concepts which do not necessarily agree with each other in detail but which, in the main, agree. We shall find out of them, a synthesis—the best the world knows spiritually, I would say.[19]

Now we come to our own movement. Our movement is also in a certain sense a Christian denomination. It would be classed as that, but it is very much more than a Christian denomination, remembering again that the philosophy of Christianity is a combination of the Jews and the Greeks. "The God without and the God within," the mystics said, "the highest God and the innermost God, is One God." I changed that a little and said, "God as man in man *is* man." It is more simple, more direct and means the same.

I have to make certain personal references. I don't like talking about myself. Anyone who thinks about himself hasn't very much to think about. It is like someone who thinks he owns something. If he does, and cares very much for it, it will own him. Emerson said, "Cast your good on the four winds of heaven. Only that can increase and multiply which is scattered." I don't think I own anything. These are our playthings here. We exist for the delight of God and we will play with other things somewhere else. And no thing and no era in history is of any value other than as it expresses some ceaseless, incessant Urge which presses against everything, that It shall express Itself for the joy of Its own being, the delight of Its own being, to sing a song: *creativity.* That is what everything exists for.

I have to refer to myself because I happen to have been there when it happened—but I consider Religious Science a thing of destiny or I wouldn't be here. I have given my life to it. I never even made a living out of it, because it doesn't interest me in that way. I think it is a thing of destiny. I believe that the evolutionary process, periodically in history, pushes something forward as a new emergent to meet a new demand . . .

But I did get born in Maine and didn't go to school, because I didn't like it—hated it—and quit when I was about fifteen. I didn't go back except to study public speaking . . . At any rate, I rebelled against authority and didn't want to be taken care of, so I went to work when I was a kid. What I have gathered has been from reading, studying and thinking, working—it is a long, laborious, tough method, but it pays off. I don't believe there is a real *other* method. What you are going to learn after you take these classes—which is the best we have to offer—or in any good reading you can get: what you will really learn will be what you tell yourself, in a language you understand, that you accept—giving yourself a reason that is rational enough to accept, reasonable enough to agree to, inspirational enough to listen to with feeling, profound enough to sink deep, and light enough in it to break away the clouds. Because there is a place where the sun has never stopped shining in everyone's mind, and there is ever a song somewhere and we all have to learn to sing it.

Well, I didn't see things or have hallucinations; I wasn't strange in any particular way. When I was a kid, I began to study Emerson. I was from the beginning a nonconformist, asking so many questions my relatives hated me—every time I visited them I drove them crazy. I was, fortunately, brought up in a family by a mother who refused to have fear taught in her family. She was an old New Englander—born a hundred years ago—and New England, theologically, was pretty strict. However, she was a smart woman and she determined we should never be taught there was anything to be afraid of. I had to grow up and be almost a man before I knew that people actually believed in Hell. I don't know now what they believe or how they think; I only know this: that anyone who does, if he will ever get to the place where there is complete forgiveness for himself and heal his own unconscious sense of rejection, will never believe in Hell and never condemn anybody else. You can only project *yourself*.

So I studied Emerson, and this was like drinking water to me. I have studied Emerson all my life. Then I went to Boston to school to study speech for a couple of years, while working to pay my way through this very wonderful school. The people were Christian Scientists and very good ones; the head of it was a reader in the Mother Church. Here, naturally, I heard wonderful things. Some of my own classmates were Christian Scientists, and I asked if what they believed was true and they said yes, and then I said, "I can do it." Anything anyone has ever done, anybody can do—there can be no secrets in nature. This I have always held to. There is no special providence; there is no God who says—to Mary or Ernie or Josie, or anybody else—"I am going to tell *you* what I didn't tell the other guy." There is no such being.

So coming out here to L.A. forty-five years ago or whenever it was [1912], I came in contact with New Thought students. Here is where everything was taught—everything; more here in the earlier days than now. They used to say everyone here was a screwball, but they weren't; they were very remarkable people. When you get someone who gets up and moves to another place, tears up all their background, you at least have a progressive person . . .

Well, here was occultism and theosophy; they had their schools—much more than they have now. The New Thought movements were flourishing. Julia Seton was here, and I became acquainted with her. She was one of the early New Thought teachers. Many of them came here to lecture, and I often lectured with them after a few years, and I began to read and study everything I could get hold of—no one thing. I started from the very beginning with the thought that I didn't want to take one bondage away from myself and create another. I have always been very careful about that . . .

We happen to have the most liberal spiritual movement the world has ever seen, and yet it is synthesized and tied together by the authority of the ages and the highlights of the spiritual evolution of the human race, all of which I have been familiar with, since I have spent fifty years studying it and thinking about it.

I was always studying; and since I had to make a living, I took a job as purchasing agent for [the city of Venice]. A street superintendent asked me what all the books were I had around my office, and I said they were books on philosophy and metaphysics, the occult, New Thought—everything you can think of. He said, "They look interesting to me." I said, "You are an engineer and wouldn't be interested"; but he thought he might. He borrowed some of them and after a while said, "How would you like to come over to my house and I will invite a few people one evening and you can just talk to us—?" I said that would be fine—and we did.

These were the first talks I ever gave, in two homes. During one of these evenings a lady came to me and said she was at the Metaphysical Library (we used to have a big metaphysical library at Third and Broadway, and I used to get books out of it) and she said, "I told the librarian you would come up next Thursday and talk." I said, "Talk on what?" And she said, "Like you talk to us! You are really better than the people we hear up there."

I went, and the librarian said, "You have a class this afternoon at 3 P.M." I said, "I wouldn't know how to teach a class." She informed me I could pay a dollar for the room and charge twenty-five cents a person to come. I decided to teach [Thomas] Troward. I had read *The Edinburgh Lectures.* I believe I had thirteen in the class and got home with a five-dollar gold piece above my rent. Within two years I was speaking to thousands of people a week and never put a notice in the paper. They just came.

This went on for a number of years, and I thought I would like to see how it worked in other places; and for several years I went to Eastern cities and around and discovered that wherever there were people, they wanted it and were ready for it. I had already started on what I consider our great synthesis, putting the thing together.

It has always been my idea that the greatest life is the one that includes the most—that we have to study what everybody has to say, we have to be the judge principally of what we think is right or wrong, good or bad, or true or false. There is nothing else, and we must not live by authority. We must have no more prophets or saviors. Now I say this guardedly, and not out of disrespect to the saviors of the world. The Gita says, "The self must raise the self by the self." Shakespeare said, "To thine own self be true and it shall follow as the night the day, thou canst not then be false to any man."

This is true. You learn from yourself in doing. So I decided that to kite around the country wasn't good for me; I didn't care for it. I had a beautiful home here and had made many friends, so I came back to L.A. after several years' of being out of this local field. In 1925 we took the little theater which used to be in the Ambassador. It seated 625 people. We put an ad in the paper and started on a Sunday morning. Within a year the people couldn't get in. Then we took the Ebell Theater and within a year were turning people away from there. It seated 1,295 people.

Then Bob Bitzer came from Boston where I had met him. I started him in Hollywood; he was very young. I said we would take the Women's Club on a Sunday afternoon; we invited everybody to come. We had about eight hundred people. I told them we were going to start their own church over there and Dr. Bitzer was to be the head of it. That is the way that church started.

Then, because we needed space, I took the Wiltern Theater, where Dr. [William H.D.] Hornaday now speaks—and we turned away many, many hundreds every Sunday. This was during the time of the Depression, and probably many people were looking for help even more than ordinarily. I had a big radio program too, which was a big help.

I want to go back before this happened. I came back here in 1925, and in 1926 some friends of mine said, "You should organize this." But I said, "No, I don't want to do that; I don't want to start a new religion or be responsible for it; I don't want to tell anyone what to do. I don't know what to do myself, so how can I tell anyone else?" But they argued that this was something they thought valuable and the greatest thing in the world, and they finally convinced me—and we became incorporated thirty-one years ago last February as a nonprofit religious and educational organization. The Institute of Religious Science and School of Philosophy, it was called.

Finally I said, "This can't be done this way. If we are going to have a church and there are more people, let's have more churches." So I asked everyone in Pasadena to come to the Arroyo Seco Hotel on Sunday nights and everyone who went to Glendale to come Tuesday nights there. I carried this on for about six months and started churches. I did the same thing in Long Beach and in Huntington Park and Santa Monica and Redondo Beach and other places. That is how our churches got started; they were surpluses from Wiltern services. We started classes, trained them and so on. This is merely the way the movement originated. It grew up; it wasn't a planned thing.

It wasn't until it had many, many, many branches that I really thought to myself, Something is going on here, this really is a thing of destiny; it is really going to become the next spiritual impulsion of the world—and I believe it. I finally came to see that it had to be organized so it wouldn't fall apart . . .

Now what do we teach? It is very simple: God is all there is. There isn't anything else; there never was and never will be. That is what I am. There is nothing else I can be; I am compelled to be That. I have nothing to do with it. I have no virtue great enough to make It and no vice bad enough to destroy It . . .

I am ready to introduce new thoughts and new ideas into our movement, starting the first of the year, which I think will be transcendent. But I believe we are just starting. I believe we can do something to ourselves psychologically that will yield the same faith and conviction in our science and our truth that the electrician has when he wires a building: when we press a button, we will get a light. Did you ever stop to think of that?

Faith is an attitude of mind accepted and no longer rejected. No one can accept it but himself. No one can accept it for him; no one can reject it for him. We have to have the same faith in what we teach and preach and practice that science has or the gardener has. And when that terrific and great simplicity shall have plumbed and penetrated this density of ours, this human stolidness and stupidity, this blindness which we seem to be born with, this drunkenness, this debauchery of the intellect and the soul—then something new and wonderful will happen. It is the only thing that will keep the world from destroying itself.

I think we should feel as though we are on a mission. Not a mission of sadness to save souls—they are not lost; if they were, you wouldn't know where to look for them—but a mission that glorifies the soul. Not to find we are here for salvation, but for glorification—the beauty, the wonder, the delight of that Something that sings and sings in the soul of man. "Build thee more stately mansions O my soul,/ As the swift seasons roll!/ Leave thy low-vaulted past!/ Let each new temple, nobler than the last,/ Shut thee from heaven with a dome more vast,/ Till thou at length art free" (Oliver Wendell Holmes).[20]

Finally, this statement of Ernest's, as quoted by George P. Bendall in his introduction to **Ideas of Power:**

If you ever get to that place of stillness—out of it everything comes: the uncreated creativity; the creative possibility of the individual out of the uncreated; the voice that was not spoken, yet is ready to articulate—something new and fresh, a creation that never existed and need never again be. But in the passing movements of our present fancy, the word shall become flesh and dwell among us as long as it ought to and dissolve when it is no longer necessary . . .

You and I as practitioners can throw all of our theories and all of our books and all of our previous prayers out of the window now, because they are evermore *about* it and *about* it and *about* it. They are necessary and they are fine . . . but now that divine moment is come. Emerson said, when it happens, throw out all of your theories, leave them all as Joseph left his coat in the hands of the harlot, and flee—for this is a transcendent moment; this is the moment of a new creation . . .[21]

. . . Which we can internalize through affirmative statements like this one:

Today I enter the limitless variations of self-expression which the Divine Spirit projects into my experience. Knowing that all experience is a play of Life upon Itself, the blossoming of love into self-expression, the coming forth of good into the joy of its own being, I enter into the game of living with joyful anticipation, with enthusiasm.[22]

Part III

The Veil Is Thin Between

To the end of his expression on this place of experience, he constantly searched for new plateaus of understanding and wisdom, always keeping in mine his lifelong premise, "There is only one Life and one Law, from which all things come."

In his later years, in those many hours each day of meditation, some of his experiences bordered on the purely mystical, and I am sure he was aware of flashes of so-called cosmic consciousness. These experiences further confirmed his faith, his certainty in regard to the convictions at which he arrived through his intellectual search.

He did not talk about these glimpses of Reality and would not admit to being classified as a mystic, but his inspirational writings are evidence that, in truth, he was . . .

I believe it was this inner awareness which was felt, consciously or subconsciously, by all who contacted him, listened to his lectures, or studied his works. I often thought that his listeners were getting the mental atmosphere of the man, that inner awareness, rather than whatever words he was speaking.

—REGINALD ARMOR

IX.

The World Has
Suffered Enough

THE FARER:

Why should Celestial Powers
So hide the real that none can view the truth
That what they seem to see should be illusion?

THE PRESENCE:

This is not part of a creative *plan;*
The growth of knowledge must depend upon
Man's own awakening to what he is;
He learns to read the mind of God and to
Translate what he has read in terms of law
Or principles. The Unseen Cause itself
Must then await for man's awakening.
The mask or mist that seems to cloud
The truth is not on Nature's face but on
Our own. Some day the eye will penetrate
The mystery and will reveal there is,
In fact, no mystery and no illusion.

Then shall we find that what "things" are is but
Symbolic of reality which waits
For our perception.

THE FARER:
O glorious day,
When I shall rouse from my long sleep and see
The light of truth! My soul is anguished. I die
To learn the meaning of it all.

THE PRESENCE:
Perhaps
It is more simple than you think. Restore
Your childhood's attitudes of mind, before
The clouds of doubt closed in and hid from view
The *living* things whose voices spoke to you,
The roadside roses, the birds that seemed to say,
"Be of good cheer, this is a happy day";
Go back, I say, to those half-pagan days
Before reality was hid in haze.
Learn once again to view the airy wings
Of conscious life, the very soul of things.
As artists see the aura which they paint
Around the head of master or of saint,
So he who penetrates the outward screen
Shall view the unseen hid behind the seen.
God speaks in thunder; His tender voice is heard
By tiny nestlings of the hummingbird.
He laughs with children playing on the beach;
The sea is His, the spuming waves His speech.
Behold Him as the Cosmic Mother-Love
In ev'ry mother's face that leans above
The infant nursing at her ample breast;
And it is He who gives the child its rest.

The whole wide world is whispering his name
He is the altar, offering and flame.

The Lord is present, the single and the Whole;
When least aware He floods the seeking soul.1

The Science of Mind is a personal use of universal, spiritual law. Its use can change conditions for the individual, and when individuals recognize themselves to have a choice in their lives, the world seems a better place. Emma Curtis Hopkins, who was called the "Teacher of Teachers" because the founders of the Divine Science and Unity movements, as well as Ernest, had at some time sought her counsel, wrote that "all evil is done in the name of good." By this she meant that people do hurtful things not because they choose to from a perceived field of limitless choice, but because they feel they have to, given apparently very little choice within which to maneuver. In this chapter, Ernest discusses the theological problems of evil, suffering, war and other world events in the context of his time and his country.

The world is beginning to realize that it has learned all it should through suffering and pain. Surely there can be no Intelligence in the Universe that wishes man to be sick, suffer pain, be unhappy and end in oblivion. Surely if God or Universal Intelligence is imbued with goodness, then It *could not* ordain that man should ultimately be other than a perfect expression of Life.

We must know definitely and consistently that the Universe is for us and not against us . . . We shall have to learn that evil is neither person, place or thing of itself, but is an experience which we are allowed to have— because of our divine individuality . . . If man takes his images of thought only from his previous experiences, then he continues in the bondage which those previous experiences create. If we talk about discord, we shall become more discordant. The more the world arms for war, the more certain it is that that there will be war . . . Eventually we shall understand that all human bondage is an invention of ignorance.[2]

Someone may say, "I cannot imagine *God not caring.*" I cannot either, but we are dealing with Law. Does the law of electricity care whether it cooks the dinner or burns the house? Whether it electrocutes a criminal or warms a saint? Of course, it does not. Does the Urge which impels people to express care whether a man kneels in ecstasy or lies drunk in the gutter? We are dealing with Law, and it follows that since we are dealing with Law, It will ultimately bring back to us the result of the forces which we set in motion through It.[3]

This whole idea of morbidity that goes with religion is based on a sense of insecurity, on a sense of not being at home in the Universe, not being wanted, needed and loved, not belonging.[4]

All evil is either a misuse of this Power or a misunderstanding of It. Everything that is wrong in our experience, whether we call it pain, sickness, poverty or unhappiness, is a denial of the allness of God.[5]

There is no way under heaven whereby we can think two kinds of thought and get only one result; it is impossible and the sooner we realize it the sooner we shall arrive.[6]

We have no responsibility for anyone except ourselves. Get over all ideas that you must save the world; we have all tried and have all failed . . . In this you are not selfish but are simply proving that law governs your life. All can do the same when they come to believe, and none until they believe.[7]

There is no one who believes more in faith, more in prayer or more in the necessity of the Divine Will being done than he who practices daily the Science of Mind. He has relieved his mind of the morbid sense that the Will of God *can* be the will of suffering; for if there were a suffering God, and if we are eternal beings, then we should suffer through all eternity. But a suffering God is an impossibility. We suffer because we are not in both conscious and subjective communication with the affirmative side of the Universe. All human misery is a result of ignorance; and nothing but knowledge can free us from this ignorance and its effect.[8]

How do we know what the Will of God is? We do not, other than this: The Will of God cannot be death. Why? Because if we assume God to be the Principle of Life, the Principle of Life cannot produce death without destroying Itself. The Will of Life has only to *be* Life . . . Therefore, we should interpret the Will of God to be everything that expresses life without hurt.[9]

In our ignorance of the truth, we have misused the highest power we possess. And so great is this power—so complete is our freedom in it, so absolute the domain of law through it—that the misuse of this power has brought upon us the very conditions from which we suffer. We are bound because we are first free; the power which appears to bind us is the only power in the universe which can free us.[10]

We must be careful, in the transition from the old to the new, not to knock props from under us which perhaps we still need; not to rob people of their God unless we can give them a better one, for that is the most destructive thing in the world. I would rather see someone with a poor idea of Deity than to see him have no concept of Deity at all, because we must all interpret God through our perception of the Divine Being. In the transition, then, let us be careful that in place of every false supposition which we once had, we shall find a divine reality which is an eternal verity.[11]

If we seek to combat evil we should be careful that we do not make the evil real. There is a place in the mind which intuitively knows that good overcomes evil and there is a place which knows no evil to overcome. Our argument, then, is between the experience of evil and a solid conviction that good is the only reality. The law of life cannot produce death. Wholeness cannot will to create apartness. Omniscience cannot will ignorance and God did not make the devil.[12]

If we mix the concept of good with the concept of evil, the result will fluctuate between the two. If we mix a concept of peace with a concept of confusion, the result will be both peace and confusion. If our thought fluctuates, our external world will fluctuate also . . . We cannot expect to convert our whole consciousness in a moment, nor is it necessary. But if we take the mental stand that evil and negative conditions are not things in themselves, and constantly and consistently affirm that good alone has constructive and lasting power, is a spiritual entity and has a real Law to support it, and that good *is* active in our experience, then we will demonstrate our theory, no matter what the existing conditions to the contrary may be.[13]

All do not learn the laws of life and the rules of the game of living in the same hour. Is it wrong that we should have the benefits of electricity because Solomon and Moses knew nothing about them? Are the comforts of modern invention evil because antiquity did not enjoy them? The great lesson is that life delivers itself into our capacity to receive it. The outpouring from the cosmic horn of plenty can only fill the cup that is lifted up toward it. A pail turned on its side cannot be filled with rain from heaven.

The lord of the vineyard stands for the love of God and the givingness of the Spirit. The vineyard represents the fruits of life. We are the laborers, and the reward, the compensation, is the law of cause and effect which measures to each according to his acts. The ones who came in at an earlier hour represent those who have gained some slight knowledge of spiritual things before others. They are indeed fortunate. But the ones who came in at the third, the sixth and the eleventh hours also entered into the Kingdom and their reward must be equal to those who came first.

If yesterday we did know that God is love, then yesterday we could not enter into communion with that love. If we do not discover this until late in the afternoon of tomorrow, then we may know that all the yesterdays of hurt and fear will vanish. In the hour of recognition love comes full-orbed into our present experience. This parable is a lesson of hope. We are all searching, we are on the pathway of self-discovery. This self-discovery cannot be separated from the discovery of God, for God is the supreme Self, the everpresent Reality. We have always been living in the divine sea of life but we have not realized it. The awakening is not to God but to man.[14]

I was fortunate in being reared in a home where no religious fears were taught, and where every attempt was made to keep away from superstition and ignorance. It was, however, a religious home, where family prayers were said, the Bible was read daily and grace was said at mealtime. But it was never suggested we fear God or the future.

I was a natural candidate for the New Thought philosophies that have sprung up in this country. Having read Emerson, it was easy to realize that Unity is at the base of everything.

Over a period of several years it was my privilege to study the ancient systems of thought, the mystical writings of the Middle Ages and the modern movements such as Theosophy, Spiritualism and the various branches of New Thought. I found great interest in trying to synthesize these various systems, with the purpose in mind of finding the thread of unity running through them. It became my persistent desire to put them all together in one system, realizing that we inherit the great thought of the ages and may enjoy the privilege of entering into its meaning.

Probably no one could have had less desire than I to organize or launch a new religion. I am a great believer in all religions, and am firmly convinced that every man's faith is good for him and that the form it takes is best for him at the particular time he follows such form.

I am certain that the great spiritual leaders of the ages, having given their lives to meditation, prayer and communion with the Spirit, have left a great spiritual legacy to the world. Taken as a whole, they have come nearer to discovering God than any other group of people. Claiming very little originality of thought and not particularly desiring any, I have always been in a position to learn from all sources. Truth cannot belong to any individual, and there can be no religion higher than the Truth.[15]

The three great enemies of mankind are war, disease and poverty, and we believe that these three great enemies must finally be overcome, as Divine Wisdom and Infinite Intelligence find a more complete outlet through the mind of man. We are conscious that peace is the power at the heart of God, that at the very center of the universe there are equilibrium, poise, peace, love, truth and beauty, and on this Armistice Day we feel that we would draw closer into this beauty, into this Divine Presence, into the realization of this eternal Peace which must finally triumph over all war, which must finally heal all disease and which must finally destroy every sense of lack, of limitation and of want.

We know that it is not a natural order of things for people to be at war with one another. We know that the human heart is instinctively kind, that it desires peace, it desires self-expression, it desires liberty and it desires happiness. If we would promote the idea of peace in the world we must begin with our own individual consciousness. The whole nation and the whole community of nations, making up as it does a community of humanity, all are aggregates of individuals like we are. All nations are made up of groups of individual centers of thought, of will, which we call personality, for personality is really will, intelligence and volition fused into one, making possible an individual mind and a personal expression.

We must think peace if we wish to express peace. The mind that is always confused and distraught is not at peace; the mind that is continuously upset and agitated by the little, petty things of life is not at peace; it is at war with itself. It is only when the individual mind ceases combating itself that it will stop combating others. We do not know when that far-off Divine Event will transpire which shall heal the world of the wounds of war, the memories of ancient strife and the anticipation of future struggle. All we know, as individuals, is that it is within our power to control our own thinking, to so order our own mind and thought that we, as individuals, shall be surrounded by peace.

Peace comes from the absence of fear, from a consciousness of trust, from a deep, underlying faith in the absolute goodness and mercy, the final integrity of the universe in which we live, and of every cause to which we give our thought, our time and our attention. If we would have peace outwardly, we must first realize peace inwardly. Peace is greatly to be desired; nations at war with each other destroy themselves finally. We, in America, hope and pray and wish and think and work that there shall be no more war, that peace shall come to the nations. It is not in our power to control the thought of other nations. We only have the power to control, first, own our thought and, finally, through that, the thought of our nation. In a world tortured by fear and superstition, doubt and suspicion, we feel comparatively safe in the community of nations, but there is no final safety until all nations are in peace. We cannot compel peace in foreign lands. We can think, act and become peace at home and in this way provide a lesson for all other races.

Those of us who believe in peace should work toward this end. Let us never forget that the very impulse of that movement is in the silent contemplation, the prayerful meditation, the sincere expectancy in our own minds. Are we ready for peace? When the world is ready for peace, it will have peace. When the individual is ready for peace his thought will be so composed that he will find himself living in peace, even though to the world he appears to be in the midst of chaos and confusion. Let us contemplate this thought: "I live in peace with God as a partner. I live in peace with the great Creator, the Maker and the Sustainer of all. He is the Parent Mind; He is the Divine Source in which my life, and in which all life, is rooted. I seek to persist in a belief of this perfect unity with the Divine. Divinity, my Divinity is at peace within God.

As we contemplate these words and meditate upon their meaning, with prayerful thoughtfulness, there wells up from within us, as though from some subterranean source, some unplumbed depths in our own mind, a new vision, a vision which has power to offset hate, to destroy discord, to still anguish, to obliterate fear. There wells up from within us a trust, a consciousness that we are surrounded by an Infinite Goodness; and that thought of peace spreads itself beyond the confines of our own consciousness and helps that much in healing a sick world of the belief that it must fight. First, at home, in the silence of our own thought, let us heal ourselves of fear, of doubt, of uncertainty. Let our lives be peaceful; let our lives be whole. So shall the thought of man, "seeing Thy light, find out the way again, there in the night, and let that Peace which is God abide with us forever."[16]

I presume that everyone would rather have peace than anything else on earth. If everyone really is desiring peace, and if desire were an effective prayer for peace, then we would have had peace a long time ago. There are not many people in the world who are opposed to having peace; there couldn't be, particularly in an age when anything other than universal peace would lead to universal destruction.

We are at that place in scientific discovery where it is possible for the world to destroy itself. I am not worried about that, because if it does, it does, and if it doesn't, it won't. We will all be somewhere. However, I do think it would be rather an inglorious final exit from this mundane universe, and undoubtedly an unnecessary thing.

We shouldn't view the state of the world with fear, because we shouldn't have any fear. We shouldn't view it with timidity, because we shouldn't be timid. But we should view it with intelligence, because the only sin is the lack of intelligence. "There is no sin but a mistake, and no punishment but a consequence." The money that is now being spent in preparing for war would completely abolish poverty from the earth. It is a terrific thing that, right now, the world is in a position to do away with impoverishment!

I am not a pacifist, but, when only six percent of the national budget is for the alleviation of impoverishment and seventy-two or seventy-three percent is for destruction, one knows there is something wrong in the worldly state of affairs and in the state of the human mind. When we stop to think of these things, we know that there is something lacking, there is something missing, there is something that we have overlooked.

When we view the universe scientifically we find that it is one system. Modern science has never discovered any law in nature that could destroy itself. This is what Jesus meant when asked if he cast out devils by the prince of devils and he said, "How can Satan cast out Satan? . . . if an house be divided against itself, that house cannot stand." God is all there is, he said in effect, and if I use another kind of power, if I use another kind of an intelligence, if I use a higher power and a higher intelligence then that is the kingdom of God, and it is come among you. You believe that there are two kinds of power in the universe. One is good and the other is bad. You believe there is a God and a devil. I don't believe that! . . .

The structure of our whole philosophy is based on two things: the universe as Law and Order, and the universe as a Divine Presence. The one with which or whom we may commune; the other that we may use. I believe God is the only Presence there is, infinite, intimate and personal to each one of us; present with each one of us, and in each one of us as what we are. Our word goes out as law. This is a glorious concept, for it teaches us that at any moment we may transcend the past no matter what happened . . .

All we have said applies to war and peace, for we are discussing the possibility of a spiritual power which, consciously used and directed, can change the destiny of the world. I believe in it as I believe in life, and if I didn't believe in it I should have no confidence in life . . .

So the principle, I believe, is as definite as one, two, three. It is as definite as mixing paints and knowing what color you will get. It is law and it is as definite as any other law in nature. The use of it is by prayer—as petition believed in, no matter who does it; or as affirmation affirmed and accepted consciously and definitely. I believe that affirmation has more power, but I wouldn't argue about that because I think the prayer of faith absolutely accepted is an affirmation believed in, and the affirmation believed in does the same thing as the prayer of faith and they will both work because there is something which corresponds.

We want peace? Then it has got to begin right where I am, for me. I, myself, must believe in my own prayer—"When ye pray, believe that ye receive." You and I as a group must believe in our prayer . . . What possibilities if people in America only knew that it is possible to teach one hundred and fifty million people how to do this! . . .

We so want peace on earth? Then let us pray for peace in our hearts, let us affirm peace in our own minds. Let us live as though peace were the mandate of God, because it is. Together let us affirm it and let us encourage others to, no matter what the opposition appears to be, for it is a fundamental reality of God . . . Let us face the future without fear, but let us also face it intelligently as men and women who are not afraid of anything. There is nothing in the universe to be afraid of. Some things could be avoided. Let us realize if the world is healed of war and brought into peace it won't have been because guns were bigger and better, or more of them. We need them until it does heal itself, but that will come to pass only because somewhere along the line the balance of the scales of eternal truth shall fall on the side of peace.

Let us, you and me, pray for peace and let us make our hearts fit to accept it when it comes. Let us make our intellect, and our soul, and our will and our feeling ready to receive it and embrace it even before it comes. Let us in the stillness of our own soul go back to that ineffable Presence which is Peace and proclaim It even in the midst of confusion—that peace which is the Power at the heart of God.[17]

"Spiritual Armament," which follows, was a sermon Ernest first delivered on his radio program, This Thing Called Life, on August 6, 1950, in the early days of the Korean Conflict. It won him an award from the Freedom Foundation.

"Long may our land be bright, with freedom's holy light. Protect us by the might, great God, our King."

Democratic leaders, in this and in other countries, have asked that we pray for peace, for everyone realizes that we and the world are in a period of great crisis—a crisis which many feel can mark the beginning of a new and united effort toward world peace.

The overpessimistic are afraid that this crisis might lead to complete world devastation, but those with hope and faith should not feel this way. Rather, we should feel that this crisis can lead to something permanent and good, something which will make the world a better place in which to live, with individual and collective safety, personal liberty and freedom and justice for all.

The greatest responsibility that ever came to a nation—and with it the greatest opportunity—has come to our great country, which, with other democracies is making a united effort to preserve those values which are dear to all freedom-loving people throughout the world. And as we arm for this conflict, we may have the inward assurance that right is on our side. And we should clear our minds of all confusion about this, for there is not, and never has been, any political or economic system that can equal democracy.

And it is democracy we are fighting for—democracy which alone can give freedom to the world and make possible of realization the great hope of humanity. In this effort we all should unite. There is no sacrifice too great to make for it, and indeed, such sacrifices as we on the home front are called on to make should not be considered sacrifice at all, but rather, as an opportunity that is placed before us to join in this great aspiration for human freedom.

But freedom is something that is won with difficulty and kept only through eternal vigilance. And what does freedom really mean, as it works out through the only instrument that can maintain its purpose—the instrument of government, other than the idea that all people are equal before God; that every man is an individual in his own right, and that each should have the privilege of self-expression provided his desires do not infringe on the rights of others. Democracy is a great cooperative enterprise through which this is made possible.

Since time began, and throughout all the ages, this has been the hope and the dream of mankind, first finding expression in the Magna Carta—where the right to govern was seized from despotic rulers—and finally coming full bloom in our Declaration of Independence and the Constitution of the United States of America, the two greatest human documents ever written.

These instruments were conceived in faith—the faith of great and wise and good men, men who were not only great enough to give birth to our country, but also were students of history—men like Jefferson and Adams, Franklin and Washington. These were men of great intellects, great souls and great faith. That which they conceived has borne the fruit of human liberty as no other system ever did.

It would be advisable for us to reread the Declaration of Independence and the Constitution of the United States and try to think out their meaning all over again, line by line and word by word. For here we find not only the supreme ideal in government, but the specific and definite directions for working it out. And it is simple enough—a federal union so organized that it may protect the interests of the common good without infringing on the rights of the individual citizen.

Our forefathers were wise indeed when they worked out a system which bound all together in one common purpose without overlooking the fact that each is an individual, that every state and each political subdivision down to the precinct in which you and I live, should be able to preserve its identity and integrity from the largest to the smallest.

In doing this, those who wrote these two great documents surely did so under Divine guidance. For all you have to do is to look about in nature and you find that while everything comes from one source, everything bears the stamp of a unique individuality. The great lesson that Life is trying to teach us is that we are all rooted in God, but each is an individualized center in the Divine Being. We have what Emerson called unity at the center and variety at the circumference.

But unity does not mean uniformity. Unity means a oneness of purpose. Unity means what is best and safe for the majority without losing sight of each individual member of that majority and each location in it. And so we have a federal government, a *United* States, within which union we have states and counties and townships and municipalities, right down to the smallest unit, each free from the tyranny of the other. And we have checks and balances so that no one group at the top can dictate the policies of the lesser groups down the scale of our political system.

This is the system upon which our country has grown and prospered. No doubt there are many defects in it because, after all, we are all human beings. But it is infinitely stronger than it is weak and upon its preservation rests the hope of the whole world.

Amidst the present-day confusion we should not lose sight of another great and wonderful thing that is happening. For the first time in the history of the world, democracies everywhere are uniting against aggression. Fifty-two out of fifty-nine nations have made a solemn pledge to uphold the hands of freedom, to protect the idea of liberty and to do their utmost not only to preserve the freedom that they now have, but to safeguard it for all time.

We must not lose faith in the purpose of the United Nations, for it is going through the first pangs of a new birth, the travail of bringing about that which is really a continuation and expansion of the very idea conceived in the minds of our ancestors. For there will always be great nations and small nations, just as in our country we have some states larger than others.

We are now seeing the necessity of a world law, to the maintenance of which all nations, great or small, shall contribute the best they have that the strong shall protect the weak without overpowering them; that the great shall live with the small without subduing them; that cooperation shall take the place of aggression; that government shall rule without tyranny through the common consent of the governed and that individual freedom shall unfurl its flag of liberty on the ramparts of a world union whose motto shall read: "Of the people, by the people, and for the people," and whose strength shall guarantee that such a united people will not perish from the face of the earth . . .

That which was born in faith must be kept through faith. As never before, our thoughts, our meditations, our hopes and our prayers must rise in one common accord. And you and I should form the habit of taking definite time each day to pray for peace with justice—for there is no peace possible without justice. We should take time each day to pray, to know and to meditate on the thought—and to meditate affirmatively, with complete acceptance—that our leaders everywhere are being guided by the all-sustaining Wisdom and upheld by the all-sustaining Power of Good. And we should pray for the peace of our own minds, that we shall not become confused.

But faith without works is dead. We should not only pray, we should act, each contributing the best he has to the common purpose, each willing to make any sacrifice necessary—not a sacrifice reluctantly made, but as one who offers all he has for two great purposes—one, in a certain sense, a selfish one, for we all desire self-preservation, but the other in the greater sense that there can be no individual self-preservation without the preservation of all . . .

For if the whole nation works together and prays together, a great moral and spiritual power, an actual soul force, will penetrate the whole world, helping to bring confidence and calm judgment and right action until the crisis shall have passed. Freedom need never be ashamed of itself, nor liberty bow to despair. God is always on the side of right and faith will always conquer fear.

We cannot doubt but that the great masses of humanity in every nation desire peace. And our country is trying to inform those behind the Iron Curtain that we have no ill will toward them, as citizens. We wish to bring them peace and justice, and in our prayers we should know that this idea is being received and accepted. I believe there is a silent communion of mind with mind and that every one of us has ample enough evidence of this in his everyday life . . .

The world is perhaps at the point of the greatest crisis in all human history, and there seem to be two attitudes we can assume. One is calmness, faith and conviction; the other would be despair. And despair is unthinkable. Let each, in his own way, dedicate his time, his service, his hope and his spiritual conviction to the common cause of liberty and justice for all. And let's work without tiring and pray without ceasing. We know that on the battlefront and in the rear guard, something alive with meaning is taking place, something vibrant with hope is happening, something latent with the possibility of the future is being conceived.[18]

My Prayer for My Country

Believing in the Divine Destiny of the United States of America and in the preservation of liberty, security and self-expression for all, I offer this, my prayer for my country:

"I know that Divine Intelligence governs the destiny of the United States of America, directing the thought and the activity of all who guide its affairs.

"I know that success, prosperity and happiness are the gifts of freedom and the Divine Heritage of everyone in this country; that they are now operating in the affairs of every individual in this country.

"I know that Divine Guidance enlightens the collective mind of the people of this country, causing it to know that economic security may come to all without the loss of either personal freedom or individual self-expression. I know that no one can believe or be led to believe that personal freedom must be surrendered in order to ensure economic security for all.

"The All-knowing Mind contains the answer to every problem which confronts this country. I know that every leader in this country is now directed by this All-knowing Mind and has the knowledge of a complete solution to every problem. Each is impelled to act upon this knowledge to the end that abundance, security and peace shall come to all.

"And I know that this Spiritual Democracy shall endure, guaranteeing to everyone in this country personal liberty, happiness and self-expression."[19]

Ernest was able to be a proud American while embracing the world community and everyone in it. Here he uses an event in the life of Jesus to illustrate his belief in our connectedness as childen of the One Spirit.

It is related that while Jesus was talking, he was told that his mother and brethren waited to speak with him. "But he answering said unto him that told him, Who is my mother? and who are my brethren?" He then told them that whoever does the will of God is his mother, sister and brother. We are not to suppose, by this, that he did not care for his earthly parents or friends. He was explaining that anyone who lives in harmony with the Truth automatically becomes the brother, the sister or the mother of all.

This is a lesson in the brotherhood of man. God is the Androgynous Principle, the Father and Mother of all. Our earthly parents symbolize this heavenly parentage. Jesus was a consciously cosmic soul, who recognized his unity with all. He knew that love must become universal before it can reach its maturity. Hence he said that all who live in harmony with the Truth are brothers in it.[20]

This is ours for the accepting:

Today I enter into my Divine inheritance, shaking my thought clear from the belief that external conditions are imposed upon me. I declare the freedom of my Divine sonship. I possess the Kingdom of God in all its fullness. I look long, sincerely and simply, upon every object, every person. I wait at the doorway of my expectation until my acceptance grants me the privilege of beholding His face forever more. I shall not wait long, for today I expect to see His shining presence, I expect to don the "seamless robe" of Divine union. Today is my day. I let it live itself through me.[21]

X.

Jesus and the Christ

THE FARER:

It seemed so simple and so real that I
Could scarce repress my eagerness to cry
How all the wisdom of philosophy
That I had gained had failed to bring to me
Such depth of faith, such sure and deep release
From earthly doubt; nor had it brought such peace
As came to me in these etheric spaces
Where I could hear these words and see these faces.
Akashic vision telescoped the years
And I was back with Jesus in those spheres
Where he brought forth such truths as rocked the ages;
So simply said for children, yet the sages
Have not explored their depth, nor breadth nor height
Save those who read the message in the light
Of that transcendent doctrine of the One
In Trinity, the Father, Mother and the Son,
And see in Jesus Christ the twofold being.

Behold the Son of Man! yet in your seeing
Behold the Son of God!

O Golden Son of God, the minted mold
Of Heaven, the coin of life struck off to show
Two sides; the seal and sign of God enscrolled
On one; the face of man to see and know
Upon the other—between them purest gold!

In Him behold the man!—god-man ideal,
The prototype of heaven and the real!
Then deeper look and turn your gaze within
Yourself, the Christ that is or might have been!
And still is there though feeble seems the flame,
Thou art the Son of God and Christ thy name.
Such simple words, Forgive and be forgiven!
Blessed are the pure in heart. In heaven,
The childlike soul shall see the Father's face . . .
Search not for Heaven in some other place,
But in your heart . . . You need not beg for bread,
Ask and receive . . . He who believes is fed.
And all his wants are met . . . who plants the seed
Shall reap the harvest he has sown . . . No need
To pray a mournful sacerdotal prayer,
Or search for God on some high altar-stair,
But in your heart and He will meet you there.[1]

Ernest loved the words and works of Jesus, yet felt he had been misunderstood and the bulk of his point missed. He drew a distinction between Jesus as a man, and Christ as a principle, a path by which to attain a state of conscious union with God. Jesus was one who had shown us the way—probably the greatest spiritual teacher of whom we have record, Ernest believed, and now it was up to all who came after to follow that path on our own, by loving, forgiving and realizing that this world and its forms are just the tip of the iceberg in the universal scheme of things. We are made of Spirit, clad in form.

This first selection is Ernest's Easter message entitled, "You Are Immortal," from the Science of Mind *magazine issue of April 1952.*

This month we celebrate the most memorable event in human history—the day when the light of eternal life penetrated the tomb and set the captive free from the thralldom of death. "For he is not dead, he is risen." All of us have had friends and loved ones, who, during the last year, have left this world. And something of us has gone with them.

Jesus said, "In my Father's house are many mansions: if it were not so, I would have told you." And St. Paul said, "There are celestial bodies and bodies terrestrial . . . So also is the resurrection of the dead . . . the body is sown in weakness; it is raised in power: It is sown a natural body; it is raised a spiritual body. There is a natural body, and there is a spiritual body."

The great hope and expectation of all of us is that we shall live forever, that that which makes us alive, awake and aware shall continue beyond the grave. When the disciples of Jesus asked him: "What is God's relationship to the dead?" He answered by saying, ". . . he is not a God of the dead, but of the living: for all live unto him." In other words, Jesus was saying: God is Life, and Life cannot produce death. God is Love, and Love cannot create hate. God is Peace and Joy, and God is right where you are. Not only in this world, but in another world, which was as real to him as this one is to us.

As wonderful as were the words and works of Jesus, the miracles of love and compassion which he performed, the climax of his whole mission was to prove that the spirit of man is indestructible, immortal and eternal. Jesus plainly taught that the Kingdom of God is at hand, here and now; that Divine Love can protect us, here and now; that Divine guidance can lead us, here and now.

He also taught that that which we really are, the spirit incarnated within us, is some part of God and will live forever. His teaching would have been incomplete unless this were true. It would merely have been a wonderful code of ethics, or morality, a high example of what every human being ought to be. But there was so much more to it than this. It was the final triumph of the spirit which he demonstrated, the complete emancipation of man from the limitations of the flesh.

Jesus was not talking of himself alone. Perhaps the real reason why he raised Lazarus from the dead, to be followed by his own triumph, was to show that all men are immortal. Not just some men, because of their particular belief, but all men. This is why he said to the thief who died with him: "Today shalt thou be with me in paradise."

. . . Immortality means that you and I shall not only continue to live after this life, but that we shall continue to be the same individuals that we now are, retaining everything that makes for the warmth and the color of what we call the human personality. And that means that we shall carry our entire consciousness with us, the ability to know and be known, to see and be seen, to commune with each other.

This is why Jesus showed himself to so many persons after he had left the tomb forever behind him. And I wonder if sometimes we haven't been just a little too morbid about the thought of death. To Jesus it was the triumphant procession of the soul, the ongoing of the spirit, the expansion of the mind. He knew that this is not the only life, or the only world . . .

Who can doubt but that Jesus, who so definitely forgave people, was trying to show us that all will finally arrive at the same goal. Perhaps we have yet to learn that there is but one race, which is the human race; one family, which is the family of God, and that there is but one God, Who is the God of all people.

I often wonder just what would happen to us if this were a firm conviction in our minds. Would we not be more tolerant of each other's mistakes? Would we not be more forgiving? And would we not all come to realize that this life, after all, is but a temporary thing in a vast and eternal expansion of the soul?

What would be your reaction and mine if we knew the only thing we could take with us when we leave this world would be that which we really are? Would not our reactions be more kind and gentle? Would not our very possessions seem of less value? And should we not come finally to realize that the only things that are really worthwhile are those things which cannot change? And, above everything else, should we not come to live as though we were immortal beings now?

That this would bring about a vast change is self-evident, and even the event toward which we all must look forward would be robbed of any sense of morbidity or fear. We should know that our friends who have left this world have gone into another one, to which we someday shall go, to become reunited with all to whom the natural law of attraction draws us—just a going on into a fuller life, into greater activity and into a more complete self-expression.

Perhaps this is why Jesus, on one rare occasion, took some of his closest followers into a secluded spot and permitted them to commune with others who had passed on. Immortality means that our entire personality persists beyond the grave. In this world we associate our personality pretty much with what we call the five physical senses, plus this subtle something which we call the mind, the consciousness or the spirit.

Now the realist might ask: "What evidence do we have that these qualities will really persist?" So, let's analyze them and see what happens. Biology is the study of the physical organisms and the life principle that makes them work. Has anyone ever seen this life principle? Does anyone know what it looks like? You cannot weigh it or measure it or analyze it, yet no one doubts it is there. It is as simple as this: I know I am alive. All the biologists in the world do not know what life is.

Psychology is a study of our mental actions and reactions. And yet, all the psychologists put together haven't the slightest idea what the mind is. Physics is a study of energy, and yet, no physicist can tell us what energy is or what it looks like. Theology is a system which tells us about the spirit of man, and yet, no theologian has ever seen this spirit. Philosophy is a study of values and realities, and yet, no philosopher has ever seen these realities.

So here we are—living in this world with almost no knowledge of what we are, and yet, to deny our existence would be utter absurdity. And this was what Jesus was trying to demonstrate to us. He was trying to get us acquainted with the fact that we are spirits right now, just as much as we ever shall become. It is this spirit, this mind, this consciousness, this invisible thing about us, that persists after we have left this world. It is entirely non-physical. And being non-physical, is not subject to the laws of this world; it is transcendent of them.

Perhaps one of the most interesting things that has happened in the last twenty years is the demonstration, in a psychological laboratory, that even while we are in this world, under certain conditions we are able to reproduce all the activities of the physical senses without using the organs of the senses. If you knew there was something about you that can see and hear and communicate and travel and exist independently of the physical body, even while you are in this world, don't you think this would be sufficient evidence that God has put something in you which is as eternal as His own spirit? Of course it would.

Here is a thought I love above most other things that Jesus said: "It is your Father's good pleasure to *give* you the kingdom." You and I have never done anything personally to earn this Kingdom. It is the gift of Life to us. And you and I cannot believe—in fact, we dare not believe—that we could do anything really to destroy it. We may be able to delay the day of our emancipation; we may be able to deny the reality of our own spirits, because we are individuals; but surely, that which God has made, you and I cannot destroy.

Jesus understood this so perfectly, and demonstrated it so completely, that we need have no fear. For Jesus knew that which you and I yet have to discover—that all men are divine. And he knew that the universe is founded in love, as well as reason. And we cannot conceive of love desiring to destroy or annihilate that which it has created.

All of our actions are drawn from an invisible source, and in reality the personality itself is not really seen—it is only felt. We feel the contact of each other, we commune with each other, and yet, all we see in this physical and objective world is merely a token of that which is invisible. No artist has ever seen beauty—he feels it. No lover has ever seen love, but he realizes it. No mathematician has ever seen the principle of mathematics, but he uses it.

At the center of every object, and at the center of every personality, there is a spiritual presence which makes itself known. And in you and in me this spiritual presence is personalized, is individualized; it comes to a point of conscious awareness, and lives and moves and thinks and acts from an invisible energy, from a Divine Intelligence which you and I never created, nor can we destroy . . .

Why, then, should we wait to become immortal? The Apostle John said, "Beloved, *now* are we the sons of God." He didn't say by and by we are going to become sons of God. He said we are that now, today, this moment. "Now are we the sons of God, and it doth not yet appear what we shall be: but we know that, when he shall appear, we shall be like him; for we shall see him as he is."

Suppose we transpose this into our own language, and if so, we should be saying, "Beloved, you are a spirit already. You are the son of God today." And while it doesn't quite appear this way, so that we are indefinite as to what we are going to become—"it doth not yet appear what we shall be"— "When he shall appear," that is, when we shall know ourselves as we really are, "we shall be like him," we shall discover that we are spirits in the Kingdom of God. We know that we shall be like him, "for we shall see him as he is"; in other words, when "he," which is the Spirit within us—the Christ incarnated within us—shall appear, and when we see him as he really is, we shall know that we are like him. We shall understand that we are one with him forevermore. And all our yearning and longing will pass into the certainty of actual experience.

It is this thing which we really are that is immortal, for, as Jesus said, flesh and blood do not enter into that Kingdom which is beyond this world. Flesh and blood belong to this earth. And when, for any reason, this physical body is no longer a fit instrument for the soul, then the Spirit severs itself from this body. For "never the Spirit was born, the Spirit shall cease to be never. Never was time it was not; end and beginning are dreams. Birthless and deathless and changeless remaineth the Spirit forever. Death hath not touched it at all, dead though the house of it seems." Life is an eternal progression, never less, but always more itself.

But we are all human, and we all miss those whom we have loved. We all long for the touch of a vanished hand or the sound of a voice that is stilled. But even in the moment of grief there should be no despair, for we know that our friends have passed on to a greater, deeper and fuller life. They have carried everything that makes for the warmth and color of human person-ality, and God can make no mistakes. This is right, or it would not be so.

There is something about us that is limitless and triumphant and eter-nal, and it will not suffer beyond a certain point, or be restricted beyond certain limitations. Its very nature causes it to break the bonds of the flesh, and to enter the momentary tomb of apparent dissolution, only to find it-self emerging in the sunrise of a new day. As Longfellow said, "He is gone, the sweet musician, he the sweetest of all singers, He has gone from us for-ever. He has gone a little nearer to the Maker of all music, to the Master of all singing."

So we can say of all of our friends who have gone from this world, leav-ing behind them the atmosphere of their presence, which, like sweet rose-mary, lingers with us for remembrance: "They have drawn closer to the eternal light and laughter of love, and today they walk in the Garden of God," and, I believe, waft back to us a kiss from the Kingdom of Heaven.[2]

Too long we have held the teaching of Jesus in a vague and abstract way, not realizing that he told us how to live, right here and now, in happiness, in wholeness and in prosperity.

He never would have healed the sick unless he had known that disease is unnatural to the Spirit. He would not have fed the multitude unless he had known that Divine Providence ordained that the food we need to sus-tain physical life should be provided.

He never would have forgiven people their sins to the last moment of their human existence, as he did with one who died with him on another cross, unless he had known that the eternal Heart forever forgives and unless he knew that all men are immortal and destined to live forever, somewhere.

Jesus, the kindest soul who ever lived, would never have misled people by telling them that there is a Power for good greater than they are that they can use when he said: ". . . as thou hast believed, so be it done unto thee" unless he had known that there is a spiritual Law that can be used for every good purpose.

He had no long-drawn-out dogma, no set of creeds. He was a person who was acquainted with God, who was able to feel and see God in every-thing and in everyone. We should return to the simple teaching of this en-lightened man who gave the world the greatest truth it has ever had.[3]

We are now as much the son of God as we can ever become, and no mo-ment in eternity is more important than the one in which we now live. If God ever had a creation, if God ever had a son, He has that son in each of us this day. He is begetting himself in us now![4]

When the Bible says, "Let this mind be in you, which was also in Christ Jesus," it is referring to that Spirit within us which is our personal share of the universal Spirit. The Christ Mind does not refer merely to a personality who lived two thousand years ago. It also refers to the innermost principle of our own being. It refers to the Divine Presence centered in us. We have been told to put off the old man and put on the new man, which is Christ. This new man is our innermost self. Pure Spirit exists at the very center of our being, at the innermost part of our mind. It is our true and eternal Self. Such life as we have flows from It. There is nothing to our real being other than Life and what It does through us.[5]

Mental science does not deny the divinity of Jesus; but it does affirm the divinity of all people. It does not deny that Jesus was the son of God; but it affirms that all men are the sons of God. It does not deny that the kingdom of God was revealed through Jesus; but it says that the kingdom of God is also revealed through you and me.[6]

Jesus used this Power directly and spoke It into being consciously, and because he had perfect faith in It, he performed miracles. He healed the sick, raised the dead, stilled the wind and waves and brought the boat immedi-ately to the shore. You and I can do the same thing if we believe that we can. Jesus said that all things are possible to those who believe. Jesus viewed the world, not as a solid fact, but as a liquid form. He viewed life not as a phys-ical fact, but as a set of spiritual laws.[7]

Here Ernest takes a familiar story and delves into its metaphorical relationship to every person's life. This comes from The Bible in Light of Religious Science, *long out of print, and appears in a slightly different configuration in* The Science of Mind *textbook.*

This story [of the Fall in the Old Testament] taken literally would be so ridiculous as to be positively absurd; hence, it is necessary to look for a deeper meaning. The writer was trying to teach a Cosmic lesson. He was attempting to teach the lesson of right and wrong.

The Garden of Eden typifies life in its pure essence. Adam means man in general—generic man. Man exists in pure life and has all of its agencies at his command. This is the meaning of his being told to till the soil and enjoy the fruits of his labor.

The Tree of Life is our real being and the tree of the knowledge of good and evil means the possibility of dual choice—that is, we can choose even that which is not for our best good. Man is warned not to eat of the fruit of the tree for it is destructive.

Eve, the woman in the case, was made from a rib of Adam. This story suggests the dual nature of man as a psychological being. The woman is made from the man. She must have been in him or else she could not have been made out of him, and the story clearly states that she was taken from his being.

Adam and Eve are potential in all of us. The serpent represents the Life Principle viewed from a material basis and beguiles us in this way; he says that evil is as real as good; that the devil has equal power with God; that negation equals positive goodness and that the universe is dual in its nature. From the acceptance of this argument we experience both good and evil. And should we come full-orbed into individuality without having learned the lesson of unity, we should live forever in a state of bondage. This is the meaning of God saying, "he shall become as one of us and live forever." The Eternal Mind does not wish us to live forever in bondage, and this is what would happen unless we first learn the lesson of right and wrong.

And so that part of us which can be fooled eats of the fruit of dual experience and in so doing reveals its own nakedness. The native state of man is one of purity, peace and perfection, and it is only when he can compare these with impurity, distress and imperfection that he is revealed as naked. Emerson tells us that virtue does not know it is virtuous. It is only when virtue tastes of impurities that it becomes naked and must hide from itself.

The voice of God, walking in the Garden in the cool of the day, means the introspective and meditative part of us, which, in its moments of pure intuition and reason, sees the illusion of a life apart from God or Good.

Error is ever a coward before Truth, and cannot hide itself from Reality, which sees through everything, encompasses all and penetrates even the prison walls of the mind with Its clear effulgence.

The conversation between God, and Adam and Eve in the Garden of Eden represents the arguments that go on in our own minds, when we try to realize the truth. These arguments are familiar to all and need not be enumerated.

The expulsion from the Garden is a necessary and logical outcome of tasting of dual experience. If we believe in both good and evil we must experience both.[8]

Christ is the embodiment of divine Sonship which has come, with varying degrees of power, to all people in all ages and to every person in some degree. Christ is a Universal Presence.

We do believe that in the unique personage of Jesus, this Christ was more fully orbed than in anyone of whom we have record. We do believe that in the person of Jesus more of God was manifest. We also believe that Christ comes alike to each and all. There is no one particular man predestined to become the Christ. We must understand the Christ is not a person but a Principle. It was impossible for Jesus not to have become the Christ, as the human gave way to the Divine, as the man gave way to God, as the flesh gave way to Spirit, as the will of division gave way to the will of unity—Jesus the man became a living embodiment of the Christ.

If we can look upon Jesus from this viewpoint, we shall be able to study his life as a living example. What is more inspiring than to contemplate the consciousness of a man who has the faith to stand in front of a paralyzed man and tell him to get up and walk, *and to know very well that he is going to get up and walk;*

or to stand in front of the tomb of a dead man and tell him to come forth! Such an example as this is worth something, but if the whole performance were enacted in the mind of a man *entirely unique and different from us,* then it would mean no more to us than studying the biography of hundreds of other men.[9]

Jesus was either the great exception or the great example. If he were the great exception, there is little we can do other than admire the spiritual altitude from which he spoke. If he were the great example, we should follow his teaching and seek to make it practical in our everyday living. He chose to think of himself as the great example, saying that what he did we too can do if we follow the same rules, if we believe in God and have faith.

We shall not understand his teaching unless we keep in mind that he was placing himself in a relationship toward God that all men should assume. He was demonstrating to those of his day, and to those of our day, that there is a spiritual power which we may use. In no way did he intimate that God gave him a power that is withheld from others. He said, what I do shall you do also, and greater things than these shall you do.

One thing is certain: The claim of Jesus has never been disproved. It would be a weak argument to deny the possibility of something which we have not tried. As a matter of fact, those who have even partially imbibed the spirit of Christ have found comfort and a sense of well-being. It is indeed a good thing for us to reevaluate and reemphasize the whole teaching of this master mind, individually and collectively. Since other methods have failed, we should follow his instruction, daring to leave the results with God.[10]

"I am the light of the world." Jesus was not referring to his human personality, but to the principle inherent in generic man. They who follow this inner principle shall have the light of life; for this principle is life.

"I Am" has a dual meaning. It is both individual and universal. God was revealed to Moses as the great "I Am," the universal Cause, the Causeless or self-existent One. Moses taught that "I Am" is the First Principle of all life, and the law of cause and effect running through everything. The whole teaching of Moses is based upon the perception of this "First Principle."

Jesus said that he came, not to destroy the law of Moses, but to fulfill it. How could he fulfill it except by teaching the relationship of the universal "I Am"—to the individual—I. In all the sayings of Jesus we find this thought brought out, that God is universal Spirit and man is his image and likeness, an individualization of His eternity.

Therefore, when we understand our own—"I"—we shall walk in that light which lights the world unto the perfect—"I Am."

We can consider this from another viewpoint. Man is the only self-knowing mind of which we are conscious; a self-knowing mind is conscious of what it knows. Man, the only self-conscious being in this world, must be the light of the world. To know this and to understand why it is so is to know *that* truth which alone can make free. Truth is eternal and eternity is timeless; hence, if one knows the Truth he will never see death.[11]

The vision of Jesus we should catch is not merely one of a glorious figure who so calmly and majestically trod the human pathway, but of the lesson he brought: "Behold, I am with you always, even unto the end of the world." This "I Am" is the presence of God at the center of every person's life. It is this Divine Presence which is with us always. The inspired personality of the Great Teacher has long since departed. The presence in which he consciously lived and with which he communed, and the Divine Law which he so compassionately used, is ours for the taking, today and every day.[12]

Here again he plumbs the depths of metaphor for useful tools for all time:

And he spoke about a Pharisee and a publican who went up to the temple to pray. The Pharisee prayed aloud, saying, "God, I thank thee that I am not as other men," while the publican smote his breast, saying, "God, be merciful to me, a sinner." The Master told his followers that the publican and not the Pharisee was justified in his attitude toward God, "for everyone that exalteth himself shall be abased, and he that humbleth himself shall be exalted." Jesus did not condemn the Pharisee. He did praise the publican. The prayer of one was spoken to be heard of men; the prayer of the other was a confession of weakness seeking divine strength.

There should be a true humility in our approach to life and to God—a humility based on the grandeur of things; the humility of a man of science approaching a principle of nature or a mathematician trying to measure the unimaginable reaches of space. It is the humility of a surrender of the lesser to the greater, of a part to the whole.

To sin means to make a mistake. We all make mistakes, therefore we all sin. To deny that we make mistakes is but a psychological attempt to cover up our unconscious sense of guilt because of the mistakes we have made. To gain relief from this sense of guilt we may scream our prayers into the infinite, we may boldly assert that we are not as other men. This self-righteousness, however, is but a psychological aggression built up as a defense mechanism against an inward sense of guilt. The publican who came down from the temple, having humbly proclaimed himself a sinner, had found a release from psychic tensions and burdens which the arrogance of the Pharisee never could have found.

True spiritual humility is not humbling oneself before a despotic power which seeks to avenge itself against our shortcomings. It is a submission of the lesser to the greater, of the finite to the infinite. This submission makes possible a more complete, conscious union with God. Throughout the ages and in many modern spiritual institutions confession is a common practice, and a salutary one. But possibly there is a deeper catharsis of the psyche than this—a searching of the soul which no one can do for us but ourselves; an inward sense of being right with the universe.[13]

This is the most perfect lesson ever taught by the Great Teacher. "When he was yet a way off, his father saw him and ran, and fell on his neck, and kissed him." This means that God turns to us as we turn to Him. A more beautiful thought could not be given than this! There is always a reciprocal action between the Universal and the individual mind. As we look at God, God looks at us. Is it not true that when we look at God, God is looking through us, at Himself?

God comes to us as we come to Him. "It is done unto us as we believe." "Act as though I am and I will be."

The great lesson here is that God never reproaches us and never condemns.

God did not say to the returning son, "You miserable sinner, you are no more worthy to be called my son." He did not say, "I will see what I can do about saving your lost soul. I will spill the blood of my most precious son in hopes that by his atonement your life may be eternal." He did not say, "You are a worm of the dust and I will grind you under my feet in order that you may know that I am God and the supreme power of the universe." No, God did not say any of these atrocious things. What the Father did say was "Bring forth quickly the best robe, and put it on him: and put a ring on his hand and shoes on his feet." Here Jesus is showing that God is Love and knows nothing about hate.[14]

There was a discussion the other day as to whether or not we are a Christian denomination, and I said of course we are a Christian denomination, and several said we are not; I said we are a Christian church, and they agreed to that, because we believe in and follow the teachings of Jesus, the greatest of all Jewish prophets. There were no Christians when Jesus was around; Jesus never heard of a Christian, and he would be amazed if he could come here today and see what we have done to what he said.

It was very interesting to me. As far as the world is concerned, we are a Christian denomination and we wish to be, but Mark [Carpenter] explained to me that we are Christian insofar as we follow the teachings of the Bible and of Jesus, but we are not Christian theologians, because we do not accept what has been attached to it by theology—much of it—and that is rational, I think. We don't believe in devils, in hell, in purgatory or limbo; we don't believe God chose some people to reveal something to, and didn't to others, because that is ridiculous. We believe in *divine patterns*, and not *divine plans*. But all of this Jesus taught together with all other great teachers.

I have been waiting for some years for something like this to come up in our movement, merely to clarify it—because I have never once imposed a personal opinion on our church movement. Whatever I believe I do not try to impose on our ministers or say, "This is what 'we' believe." In my mind we do not believe anything unless we all agree that there are certain things we do agree on. I wouldn't want to be any part of starting another closed system. But having this question come up through a ministers' meeting, now I can tell them what I believe, and they probably will say they believe it; and then we will arrive at what we believe without my imposing what I believe on what they believe, and no one will know the difference. And this is the way to get your own way, if you just have patience.[15]

I was trying to explain to a man last night that the universe as such—the manifest universe—must exist, as Aurobindo said, for the delight of God, and that the universe as such has no purpose as theology teaches purpose. The only purpose an infinite and unobstructed Being could have would be to express Itself as what It knows Itself to be. It hasn't the purpose of saving Its own creation, because It doesn't know that Its creation is lost.[16]

The Church of God is not built with hands; it is eternal in the heavens; it is not lighted with candles; its dome is heaven and it is lighted by the stars of God's illumined thought, and each member in his separate star "shall draw the thing as he sees it, for the God of things as they are." When you can look upon all creation as the perfect work of a perfect God, you will become a member of this church. I doubt very much if the church universal admits members from the church individual. When you can see in the saint and the sinner one and the same person, when you can realize that the one who kneels before the altar and the one who lies drunk in the street are the same one, when you can love the one as much as you do the other, no doubt you will be able to qualify . . . The expanded thought will never wish to join or be joined to. Nothing human can contain it. It feels the limitation of form and ceremony and longs for the freedom of the Spirit, the great out of doors, the Great God of the everywhere. Alone in the desert, the forest, or by the restless ocean, looking up at the stars, man breathes forth these words, "With only my Maker and me."[17]

Here's an affirmation as fresh for today's use as when Ernest wrote it in 1948.

There is no judgment, no condemnation, no criticism. I know that any belief in a power that damns, or a hell that waits or any devil, is false . . . There is no damnation, no judgment coming in or passing through me.

There is justice, knowledge, right government, divine guidance without judgment . . . Divine Intelligence operates through me without confusion, calmly, forward moving, progressive, upward spiraling, outward reaching. I am guided by Infinite Wisdom into that Light which is eternal. My soul is jubilant.[18]

XI.

Untapped Powers
in the Self

PYTHAGORAS:

The great enigma in which all nature slumbers
Can be resolved, reducing it to numbers.
The number "I" assumes a point in space
Which moves to form a line, the line will trace
A plane which moves to form a cube: dimension
Is but the number "one" in full extension;
The line is "two," the surface "three," while "four"
Denotes the solid—thus "number" is the core
Of knowledge; appearances of sense
Are then reduced to essences, and hence
The mind of you can be aware and know
The "real" from which "substantial forms" must flow.
So from the elemental noumenal
Is built the "solid" world phenomenal.
The "holy tetracity" have I designed
To form a pattern for the human mind
By which the number "four" is clearly shown

To hold all numbers cased within its own.
For "1" plus "2" plus "3" plus "4" are "10,"
The "perfect number" whose numerals again
Will add to "one" in which all things begin.
All science then from numbers is evolved:
Philosophy is thus to "principle" resolved:
Those who interpret numerals with skill
Reduce the universe into the terms of "Will."
The "four" is square, four-square, and so is shown
As Truth or Justice. "One" (I) is aptly known
As Monad, sentient soul who journeys through
A trackless world but when its hour is due
Returns at length to feel the warm embrace
Of Father-arms, eternal dwelling place.
It is by knowledge that man rules his fate,
The knowledge of the One; its correlate
That *man is mind* and can participate
In cosmic life. When freed from base desire
His soul is luminous with Living Fire.
He holds dominion in the world of things,
Who knows that mind moves on itself; and flings
His word out where the cosmic forces swarm
Which give it soul and bring it forth in form.
Man is a spirit who builds himself a soul
Out of the substance of the cosmic whole,
Creation's fluid, a form ethereal
Surviving death—a body spiritual.
Man has the power to make, remake, and evermore
Return to earth or reach the Farther Shore.
The *subtile chariot* will bear the soul
Into the realm of light, if pure and whole,
Or it will fall once more to the embrace
Of matter, forced again to run life's race.

As Moses formed the Tetragrammaton
To seal and yet reveal the Three in ONE
So I perceive the universe as three
Immersed in One to form a true Quaternion.
All things resolve to numbers, the first four
Include them all—nor is there less nor more
Than ONE which manifests expressing endlessly
In man and matter and cosmogony.
The universe itself is BEING; soul
On soul are stars and planets (for the whole
Wide solar system is a living thing)
Which unsupported through the ethers swing
Around the sun as they run they sing.
The spheres are tuned in space to number seven,
The lyre is but a replica of heaven,
Harmonic intervals unfold the plan
By which the *monad* moves up to the man.

Celestial Monad, who from sphere to sphere
Through endless ages reached thy natal year,
Born into time but drawn from timeless space,
Thou hast on earth a moment's dwelling place;
Entombed in matter; yet now aware of soul,
Thou shalt take wing, let heaven be thy goal![1]

Awareness and deliberate use of Science of Mind principles can free us from limited conditions—and there's a lot more to it. Ernest was passionately interested in all areas of mind science, including the psychic realm (which he thought of as no more or less than an augmenting sense to our usual five) and more so mysticism, our glimpse of the Infinite that bursts unasked and unforeseen into ordinary moments. In this and the final chapter, we hear the words of someone who has seen the Infinite and, like an advance scout, bids us follow down the trail and see for ourselves.

The Temple of Truth

The Bible tells us that certain universal principles are at the root of every-thing. The realm of nature, the world of man and the Divine world all have fundamental laws unifying and coordinating the inner relationship of the parts with the Whole. In this way each plane reproduces the one just below it on a higher level, or reproduces the one just above it on a lower level; the same laws obtaining on all planes, or, as the Hermetic philosophy states, "What is true on one plane is true on all, as above, so beneath . . ."

It was Troward's belief that the Bible, using many and varied illustrations, is ever pointing to a few central facts and that no matter how "deep the mys-teries we may encounter . . . Everything has its place in the true order of the Great Whole." Now, of course, ignorance of the true order would not ex-empt us from suffering the results of a misuse of its laws, hence ignorance binds us until we become redeemed by the Truth. This is the meaning of sin and salvation. Since sin means making a mistake or missing the mark, salva-tion must stand for the correction of the mistake or hitting the mark.

The laws of nature of themselves never change, and Troward tells us that "the only question is whether through our ignorance we shall use them in that inverted sense which sums them all up in the Law of Death or in that true and harmonious order which sums them up in the Law of Life." He also states that Solomon's Temple symbolizes "this Grand Order of the Universe." Before this temple stood two pillars, Jachin and Boaz. These pil-lars were in no way connected with the Temple but merely stood in front of it. Jachin stands for "The One," while Boaz stands for "The Voice," or "The Word." Jachin, then, stands for a mathematical principle in the universe and Boaz for the Word which utilizes this Principle. We enter the Temple of Truth only by passing between these two pillars which symbolize "the com-bined action of Law and Volition." It is the purpose of the Bible to teach us how to pass between these two pillars and into the Temple that "the inner secrets of the sanctuary . . ." may be open to us.

The Temple refers to man's mind, consciousness or being. "Know ye not

that ye are a temple of God and that the Spirit of God dwelleth in you ...
The Temple of God is holy, which temple ye are." Emerson said, "God builds
his Temple in the heart on ruins of churches and religions." And Seneca affirmed, "Temples are not to be built for God with stones piled on high; He is
to be consecrated in the breast of each." St. Augustine wrote, "A pure mind is
a holy temple of God and a clean heart without sin is His best altar."

The New Testament states that "if our earthly house of this tabernacle
were dissolved, we have a building of God, an house not made with hands,
eternal in the heavens." Does this not mean that the human body has a
divine pattern in Heaven, a spiritual prototype? Since Jesus described
Heaven as an interior state, we know that we are to be clothed upon, not by
some power external to the Self but by some creative agency already within
the Self.

The building of the Temple is something which takes place through a
recognition of one's true relationship with the Universal Wholeness. Not
that one awakes to a recognition of the Universal Wholeness to the exclusion of his individual being, but that as he as an individual is immersed in
pure Spirit. "The children of the I Am" are also individualized "I's" within
the "I Am," each recognizing his greater Self to be the Universal Wholeness.

It is this unity with Life which makes our thought creative. Thought is
creative not by will, wishing, longing, prayer nor supplication, but merely
because it is its nature to be creative. Man is a microcosm within the Macro-
cosm, a little world within the Big World. But because man is an individualized expression of God-Consciousness he must consciously enter the Temple.
That is, he must come into conscious union with the Spirit. This is "the secret place of the Most High," which brings him into "the shadow of the
Almighty." And, according to the Law of Cause and Effect, it is only when
one recognizes his union with the First Cause that he may consciously partake of the harvest of such a union.

Since Harvest symbolizes a gathering in of the fruits of wisdom, it follows that man with true wisdom must consciously unite himself with Good
before he can become a conscious "builder of the Temple." Troward tells us
that when we enter this Temple a "Divine Interpreter will meet us on the

threshold." Threshold is described as "a symbol of higher planes of Mind which are the entrance to Spirit." Thus we see that being met "on the threshold" means entering into a conscious union with Reality.

"Each individual is a Temple in himself." Within this Temple, before the altar, stands the high priest "Advarya," priest of the mind, and "Hotri," priest of the speech. Before the altar stands the mind which perceives and the law which executes. The true priest is one who knows there is no gulf between God and man. It is the business of the priest to become the conciliator, the mediator between this inward Principle and Its outward manifestation. It is written that there is no mediator save Christ, which means that there is no mediator save our own true nature.

No one can enter the Temple for us but ourselves. No one can offer the sacrifice but ourselves. No one can receive the blessing but ourselves. Thus ancient wisdom tells us that the altar, the sacrifice, the one who makes the sacrifice and the one to whom it is made are identical. It was this same perception of unity which Whitman disclosed in his great poem to himself. It is only when one recognizes that each must become his own priest that he truly stands before the altar; it is only when he has renounced all disunion that he has made the proper sacrifice, and it is only when this has been done in love that the sacrifice is acceptable. Thus, one greater than Moses said that it is useless to lay our gift upon the altar while we have anything against our fellow man. This does not mean that God becomes angry with us but, rather, is an affirmation of the Law of Cause and Effect. In other words, we can enter into the Nature of Reality only by first complying with such Nature. The giving up of everything which denies this Nature is the great sacrifice.

If we wish to enter into a less limited experience, we must sacrifice our limitations. It is impossible to do this unless we realize that Spirit is independent of all conditions. It is self-evident that if we are dealing with Causation, we are dealing with that which creates conditions and therefore could not be limited by them. But because our images of thought are too often merely reflections of our external environment, we automatically limit the gift of Spirit. Consciously we say that since we have never experienced much happiness, we probably never shall; unconsciously we affirm that joy and prosperity do not belong to us; unconsciously we create our patterns of thought after those borrowed from others, not realizing that the act of thought is independent and that conditions flow from thought. Effect reflects cause.

When we shall learn to receive our visions of Reality as a result of having entered that "temple not made with hands," then we shall truly become liberated. The tabernacle which Moses erected in the wilderness will have disappeared; the temple made of wood and stone which Solomon built will have crumbled. The real Temple, the spiritual prototype of our external forms will be revealed.

The Bible story of the building of the Temple does not in reality depict some ancient happening, nor yet "some far off divine event"; it is the story of every man's life as he lives it here and now. What is the dominant belief in our consciousness? Are we looking merely at the external? Is our prayer one of the intellect only, or have we passed between the pillars of Jachin and Boaz? Have we understood the meaning of the Law and of the Word, and have we realized that these pillars must be arched by love and unity? If so, we stand on the threshold of a greater Reality. The doorway to the Temple is open and we may advance, not with fear and trembling, but with confidence, in peace and with perfect trust. Petition has now become transmuted into communion, which is conscious unity with the Divine Creative Spirit. Hate, fear and uncertainty have been left behind. The gift which we lay upon the altar of our faith is now acceptable because it unifies with Life, merges into It; hence our request will be answered.

We would miss the whole meaning of the teaching if we failed to realize that the true Temple is in our own consciousness and that the consciousness of good which we entertain is not different from, or other than, the essence of Goodness Itself. It is not separated from the Power which both creates and projects.

Our Temple is the Self; our altar is faith; our sacrifice is a renouncing of negation; our gift, which is acceptable, is the supreme affirmation "I am that I Am beside which there is none other."[2]

To live by inspiration means to sense the divine touch in everything; to enter into the spirit of things; to enter into the joy of living.[3]

Consider the Spirit as a warm, pulsating, reciprocal thing. It presses against us, It flows through us. It is our intelligence. It is a great universal urge and surge. It is a warm colorful thing. It is a beautiful thing. It cannot be put into words. You can only feel it. But consider the Law as a cold fact, nothing else. It has no motive of its own. It is just a power, a blind force, but it is an intelligent, an executing and immutable force. The law is the servant of the Spirit. Consider creation—whether it be the vast body of the Cosmos, or the suit of clothes or dress we have on—as some effect of intelligence operating through law and you have the whole proposition as clear as can be that there is a power in the universe which knows, a law which does, a creation which corresponds. Creation does not respond; it only corresponds. Now that is what we mean when we speak of Divine Principle. Divine Principle is not God any more than electricity is God. It is a law of God, just as electricity is a law of God. It is a mental law of cause and effect. When you impress your thought upon it, it is its nature to take that thought and execute it, exactly as you think it. If there is destruction in the thought, it must destroy. If there is good in the thought, it will execute goodness or healing. This is the principle governing *spiritual science*, and, unless such a principle were, spiritual science could not be. Know that there is something more than law; an intelligence to which we may come for inspiration, for guidance, for direction; a power responding to us, a Presence pressing against us, an animation flowing through us, a light within us.[4]

Spiritual experience is a fact. Spirituality may be defined as an atmosphere of good, the realization of God. It cannot—and does not—borrow its light from another, no matter how great or noble that other may be. It springs from within, coming from that never-failing fountain of life, which quenches every thirst, whose Source is in eternity; the well-spring of self-existence. It is a revelation of the self to the self, putting one back on the track of his own self-dependence on Spirit, his own at-one-ment with Reality.[5]

Two years before the atom bomb fell in Japan, at about the time they were experimenting with it down in New Mexico, I was giving a treatment one day. In the middle of the treatment I seemed to be sitting on the side of a hill overlooking a town. All at once there was an explosion. I saw a cloud rise and mushroom high in the sky exactly as it did later when the A-bomb fell on Hiroshima, and I looked down at the town and said to myself, "This isn't destruction; this is annihilation!" Part of London had just been destroyed but I realized this that I saw wasn't like that kind of destruction, because the city was there and then in the next instant it was gone. I knew this was going to take place and end the war. I didn't know where or when but I knew it was going to annihilate a city. So I recorded this experience and explained it to five people, who witnessed the manuscript by signature, and then I put it safely away.

Now this incident is an example of a psychic experience. It was psychic because the causation of that bombing had already been set in motion, which, mathematically, had to produce the exact result that took place unless it was intercepted. There was nothing fatalistic about it . . . It could have been that those scientists, after they had seen what this energy could do, would have shuddered and said, "We will not use it." Then the causation would have been intercepted and a city would not have been destroyed. Was what happened good or bad? I do not know. We are not discussing moral issues here.

Chains of causation can be set in motion, individually or collectively, which produce their inevitable results unless they are changed. *They can be changed.*[6]

Probably in our field of thought more than in any other field, for instance, we are apt to become confused over the two entirely different ideas of psychic hallucination and spiritual illumination.

I have watched Dr. Hammond and Dr. Hill perform. They were two of the most outstanding authentic scientific investigators in the field of psychic phenomena. During seances, which they conducted, I witnessed nineteen materializations as solid as my body, which apparently had flesh and blood and circulatory systems. We could weigh them, shake hands with them, and talk with them. They wore clothes and were *apparently* real, but of course I do not believe they were real at all! They were real as phenomena, yes. There was no doubt about that, for no chicanery was performed, and these materializations were not illusions. An illusion cannot be produced, as a manifestation, that has weight, substance and a voice, whose heartbeats can be measured, unless there is some form of circulation.

I have also seen the precipitation of the most beautiful pictures imaginable—landscapes, seascapes and perfect portraits of people in color . . .

I have heard beautiful music, and once I heard a whole mass in Latin. One other time, just after Valentino and Jack Pickford had died, we asked, through this medium, for Jack to appear. All of us present had known him. We asked him, when he apparently appeared, what he was doing and he said he was writing a play with Valentino!

Any person who knows anything about such phenomena will not deny their existence. The person who denies them is ignorant of their significance. The phenomena do exist. I have seen things come through solid walls that you could take home and keep. One group which investigates these forces, as they are called, has a whole museum of such phenomena . . .

We must accept the premise that psychic phenomena exist but we must interpret them in a dispassionate and sane manner.[7]

Can you imagine a power so great that it is both an infinite presence and a limitless law? If you can, you are drawing close to a better idea of the way Life works. Most of the bibles of the world have said that all things are formed by Its word. This word has been called the Secret Word, the Lost Word. It is said that some of the ancients had a holy scroll upon which was inscribed the sacred and the secret name of life. This scroll was supposed to have been put in an ark, in a chest, and laid away in a place which was called the Holy of Holies, the innermost room of the temple.

What do you suppose was inscribed upon this sacred scroll? Just this: the words "I Am." Here is a concept of the pure, simple and direct affirmation of Life making everything out of Itself. This is why most of the scriptures have stated that all things are made by the Word of God.[8]

A mystic is not a mysterious person but is one who has a deep, inner sense of Life and of his unity with the Whole . . . A mystic is one who intuitively perceives Truth and, without mental process, arrives at Spiritual Realization. It is from the teachings of the great mystics that the best in the philosophy of the world has come.[9]

The teaching of the mystics has been that there should be a *conscious courting of the Divine Presence.* There should be a conscious receptivity to It, but a *balanced* one.[10]

The mystics, or those who were illumined, have all had an experience in common: They have seen the Cosmic Light. That is why it is said that they were illumined. They have all had much the same experience, whether it was Moses coming down from the mountain; whether it was Jesus after the resurrection; whether it was Saul on the return to Damascus; whether it was Plotinus, who, according to his pupils, had seven distinct periods of illumination.

Emerson, walking across the Common at Concord, suddenly became conscious of this light; Whitman refers to it as that which stuck its forked tongue into his being as he lay on the grass; Edward Carpenter, after leaving Whitman, walked across the bridge, and looking up, thought all of New York City was afire; and there are recorded many lesser degrees of illumination.

The mystics have all sensed this light, and we all do at times. In varying degrees we do enter into this mystical sense, this illumination. I feel that if a spiritual mind treatment could be seen, it would be seen as a pathway of light. All spiritually minded metaphysical practitioners, when they are treating, often experience a light about everything, and feel that they are immersed in light . . .

The mystics, having seen the light, have never been the same afterward, but they have been perfectly normal human beings. There was an added something, an atmosphere about them, that everyone felt. It is that atmosphere that we sense about people who are evolved spiritually—they have a sense of calm and certainty, a contact with Reality which all people arrive at to some degree. It has been the vitality of every religion, no matter what the dogmatism of its theology may have been.

So we find that people who spend a great deal of time in prayer, meditation or communion with the Spirit gradually take on a new atmosphere, a new sweetness, a light which all people sense. As Plotinus said, this is a gift which all men have but which few men use.

The Old Testament often refers to a light always shining over the altar in the temple. This light, of course, is a symbol of the Life that is never extinguished. "The spirit of man is the candle of the Lord . . ."; "Ye are the light of the world . . ."; "Let your light so shine before men, that they may see your good works and glorify your Father which is in heaven."

We find many references to light in the sacred scriptures of the world. Numerous Catholic saints make mention of it. St. Teresa said that the light was so strong that it was complete darkness, implying that the light was so bright that all else was dark in comparison. When Moses came down from the mountain, which is probably a symbol, there was a light around him so bright the people could not look at him, so he used a veil. There was also a light around Jesus. The light of Jesus has been sensed by artists so completely that they have depicted it as an aura, an atmosphere of light. It also appears around the heads of saints in paintings.

Now this light is real. There is such a light at the center of everything. During the ordinary course of affairs, without attempting to, you might see this light. Some day you may look up and there it is, the Substance Eternal falling so fine that you think it will drift across the sands of time and enclose all objects, only to discover that it falls through them. Infinite, lighter than light and brighter than bright, you can look right through it like you can look through a pane of glass. This is the Divine Stuff of which we are made. You might see it everywhere and in all things.

Symbolically, we must think a lot about light. I do not know exactly how to put it in words, but everything must become light. There is nothing outside this light; everything exists in it. Even though it may not appear to exist, it is there just the same.

There is a light at the center of everyone. This light is never obliterated, but it does seem that it is often obscured by various reasons. Jesus said to never put your light under a bushel, but to let it shine. On occasion you might be looking at someone and suddenly see him enveloped in light. At least this is the way it would appear to you. But he is always in the light, only you have not seen it before.

Some people have the ability to see a person's aura, a light enveloping their body. It is said that it varies in color and in shape according to the habitual physical and emotional state. This light that encompasses everything can to a certain extent be photographed around the human body. The picture is often murky due to the fact we are covering it up with a bushel; however, there is a deeper light that if let come through will clear up any adverse condition.

So there is a light over the altar. We should consider ourselves as the altar and that there is light within ourselves as well as everything. Just as Moses saw the bush give light, so may you. This was not an illusion of his but a reality. At the center of everything there is fire, celestial fire, caught from heaven. Every bush would blaze if we unified with that central spark which is the cause of all evolution, all advancement, everything we know, everything we shall ever attain.

It seems that in all forms of healing all that can be done is to let an inner light flow to restore us to our original pattern of perfection. All that any human ingenuity can do is to help restore us to that pattern, a pattern which we did not make. In Genesis we find the reference to the generation of the time when the plant was in the seed before the seed was in the ground.

We need to discover another language to use, a language beyond the words we now use, or else we can never enlarge our capacities. We need to break down every precedent, for beyond all our human mental states, beyond all our human experiences there is a light that we must follow. Otherwise we shall merely be going round and round in a vicious circle, caught in a beautiful cage, trapped in a beautiful trap, living still pretty much under a law of illusion or delusion, whichever it may be. Remember, this was the genius of Moses and Jesus: They did not break the law, but transcended it. This is what we have to do. We need to break out of our shell of monotony and discover within the light that lights every man's life . . .

There is a Divine imagination, a light that lighteth every man's path.

Every great creator has found it, and every great composer has found it, or it has found them. Emerson said that sometimes the muse, too strong for the bard, sits astride his neck and writes through his hand. This is the only great writing there is. All great writing, great poetry, great music, great acting and great everything is done under the inspiration of that Thing which is the only final writer, the only thinker and the only doer there is . . .

Do not be afraid to seek this Consciousness, to experiment with It. Do not feel you are silly if you believe in It. It is not hallucinatory, It is real, It is a light, I have seen It many times. This is the Mount of Transfiguration; this is the secret place of the most High. This is the light of illumination—the thing Jesus and Moses saw until a halo was visible around their heads and an aura of light around their bodies.

All at once there it is! You do not know where it came from, you cannot say it came, you hardly know what it is, but it is a light that is ineffable in its beauty and apparently flows in and through all things in a softness that dims the light of the sun. There is nothing hard about it. It does not cloud the vision and it seems as though you are a part of it. I can well understand at least something of the meaning of Jesus when he said: "I am the light of the world."

Jesus was one who walked fully in the light. There is a light that permeates the world, but we have not sensed it. We need, in the silence of our own contemplation, to take time to feel that light and to see it. We have to hitch our earthly wagon to a spiritual star because if we do not we are going to hitch it to a make-believe life, something that has no light at all. The only light there is the Light Eternal.

Very frequently I sit down all alone for two hours and listen to the silence and it speaks, and look into the darkness and it turns light—it is there and there is no question about it. God is warmth, Spirit is colorful, the Universe is filled with light. A voice speaks from everything—running brooks, stones and trees, animals and moon and stars, deserts and stillness. And you can listen to the stillness until it speaks to you.

Back of us the Infinite searches, finding manifestation through us, as us, and all that we are. It is what we are and we should never deny It. When we surrender to It we are not surrendering to a foreign agent, but we acquiescing consciously to a Divine host, a celestial visitor, a universal individualization.[11]

We are individual entities in a Universe which furnishes the background and the foreground for each of us, but each is unique, different yet fundamentally alike. Why then should it seem strange—if this whole differentiation of the physical universe is but a difference of form, distinguishing objects one from another because of arrangement—that the enlightened should see back of this arrangement the Word of God?[12]

Intuition is Spirit *knowing* Itself. Opinion is our *estimate of Reality.*[13]

Spirituality is natural goodness. God is not a person; God is a Presence personified in us. Spirituality is not a thing; It is the atmosphere of God's Presence, goodness, truth and beauty. Religion is a life, a living. If we could forget that philosophy is profound, that religion is spiritual and life serious—all of which may be true—but if we could forget all these things, and approach Reality as normally as we go about our daily affairs, we would be better off.[14]

Reality approached normally is still full of surprises. These next three quotations discuss the immanence of Spirit in all things—where our spiritual quest may lead us in the future; and close with a profound experience of "direct knowing" in Ernest's life while speaking at a church dedication in Whittier, California, in February 1959 that he never tried to publicly explain or even describe.

So close is the union of creation with the Creator that it is impossible to say where one begins and the other leaves off. Emerson tells us that nature is Spirit reduced to Its greatest thinness; and Spinoza says that Mind and matter are the same thing; while Jesus proclaimed that the very words which he spoke were Spirit and were life. Robert Browning writes of the spark which we may desecrate, but never quite lose, and he further announces that all are gods, "though in the germ." Wordsworth sings that Heaven is the native home of all mankind, and Tennyson exclaims that more things are wrought by prayer than this world dreams, while Shakespeare perceived sermons in stones and good in everything.[15]

While there is liberty in the evolving principle, it is always in accord with certain fundamental laws of necessity. It seems as though behind evolution there is an irresistible pressure, compelling more, better, higher and greater things.

If we study the evolution of locomotion from the rising of man from the clod, we see him riding upon a horse, in a cart, then in a wagon, and so on to the automobile and the airplane. What is this but the evolution of locomotion, the unfolding through man's mind of the possibility of travel? If we watch the evolution of travel by water, we find the same thing from the raft to the ship.

What is the inevitable end of locomotion? We shall ultimately do away with every visible means of transportation. That which is the principle back of evolution will not be satisfied with the process through which we now go. When we shall have unified with Omnipresence, we shall be omnipresent.

When you and I know enough and are in Los Angeles and wish to be in San Francisco, we shall be there. When we know enough to want to pass on to another plane of existence and come back again, we shall be able to do so. When we know enough to multiply the loaves and fishes, we shall do so. When we know enough to walk on the water, we shall be able to do that, and it will all be in accord with natural law in a spiritual world.[16]

. . . We are a teaching order, not a preaching order. We are a practicing order, not a proselytizing order. The world has waited long for something to happen. Now the healing power of the unseen magic of the Spirit can be made evident. This is the basis of our cornerstone.

We have not yet done what I believe we should do with our membership. We are here tonight to dedicate a church, a physical building. I think it is beautiful, I think it is wonderful, I think it is a miracle, but I know why it is here. It is here because you are here and because the consciousnesses of all of you wonderful people has moved together. And what happened? Power! Like the weaving of a rope where one strand will hold no weight but many strands united will hold terrific weight. We have yet to see what the multiple consciousness of a church body can do *if* the members are properly trained, if they permit someone to exercise authority over them—not over their theology, not over their private lives, but over one thing only: their spiritual concepts. There is a Law of Good; there is a Power in the universe greater than we are and we can use It. And It will multiply Its effects a thousand times through the united consciousness of a group.

I have had so much inward conviction about this the last year. There are so many wonderful religions in the world. We are not better than the others. We are not more spiritual, we are not more evolved, we are not anything other than this one thing—

Here his voice was said to change . . .

We have cojoined our consciousness with the eternal guarantee of the Universe that the everlasting and eternal Father of all life and the Mother of all creation, forever begetting the only begotten, is begetting him in us, right now. And that the word of our mouth is a word of Truth in such degree as it emulates and embodies the Truth which sanctifies the word to its unique service of healing, not only the sick, but the poor in heart.

We are dedicated to the concept that the pure in heart shall see God, here; that the meek will inherit the earth, now; that one with Truth is a majority; that every one of us in the secret place of the most High, in the center of his own consciousness, has the secret with the Eternal, the Everlasting, the Almighty and the Ineffable. God and I are One. And I see uniting in one great inner praise, one great union of effort, one crescendo of song and one enveloping light of consciousness—

. . . I see it!

. . . O God!

. . . The veil is thin between.

. . . We *do* mingle with the hosts of heaven.

. . . I see it!

. . . And I shall speak no more.[17]

215

We are all "fourth-dimensional" people, he tells us, in a life that's more than meets the eye.

Somehow or other you and I—I guess nobody can do it for us—have to see. I gave a treatment this morning that is to work through a whole organization, in which thousands of people are engaged. There are many departments, heads of departments, stenographers, janitors—everything that goes with a big organization; and I said to myself: This statement is in every branch of this organization; there is no difference between the person who runs some department and the one who sweeps the floor—it has to affect everything and everyone for good; it has to remove every negation, every error and everything that causes it and every belief in it, everyway; and I think I got my mental arms around the situation enough to embrace. And if I did, it will heal the whole thing just as easy as one part of it, because there are no parts in unity. Isn't that right?—and I think we don't quite realize enough the sweepingness, the all-inclusiveness of what we do.

So we are fourth-dimensional people. We are spiritual beings. We are transcendent agencies living in a dimensional world, which we will always live in somewhere, and there is nothing wrong with it or we wouldn't be here. But it will not always have to obstruct us. As long as consciousness is aware, it will produce that of which it is aware. Probably we will always have a body somewhere—we are not just going to slide off into thin air, where nobody can find us. The laws of nature will persist. But we can have one that doesn't get congested and doesn't have pain and doesn't limit us and weigh anything (it doesn't have to weigh anything); it will be just as articulate.

Now we have recognized we are fourth-dimensional beings, and let's do it without being stupid and pulling a long face and looking in the mirror to see how spiritual we look and won't read anything but the Bible—and before it was written, what did they do? . . .[18]

Then he presents us with this magnificent thought—the simplicity of it all, and how the human mind, while complex and mysterious, is nevertheless entirely sunlit.

In this respect we should regain in our consciousness that spontaneity which we had as a child. The child who was in us, before we learned to be so sophisticated, is not dead, is not asleep. We have crowded so much experience, so much negation into our lives that not he, but we, have forgotten that celestial palace whence we came.

Each of us should seek that beam of light within and follow it to the great Light—the Light that is in everything. We must acquiesce to It, and surrender all that has made us unhappy, all that has isolated us from It. Only then can God fully pronounce Himself through us and in us, and personalize Himself as us.

We must awaken ourselves and rediscover the lost paradise; find within us that child who was not afraid of the universe in which he lived, who did not deny himself or his God, and who had not listened to the dull monotonous tune of condemnation.

There is a place on the side of the mountain we are all ascending where, having gone beyond the peaks that obstructed the Light for us, our ascent reaches an apex where no longer any shadows are cast. This is the Light that is spoken of, that lighteth every man's path, and you believe that you live, believe you are that Light. As you believe in the possibility of your own soul, believe it is God. As you believe in God, believe in yourself.[19]

So may we affirm:

I realize that there is a Divine Presence at the center of my being. I let this recognition flow through my entire consciousness. I let it reach down into the very depths of my being. I rejoice in this realization. The Perfect Life of God is in and through me, in every part of my being. As the sun dissolves the mist, so my acceptance of Life dissolves all pain and discord. I am free because the Spirit of Life in me is perfect.[20]

XII.

The Banquet Hall
of Heaven

THE FARER'S QUERY:
"What is the secret key that will unlock
The mysteries of Egypt?"—This did I ask,
And softly heard—
"There is no mystery
For him who knows the Mysteries. Hid in
Himself the answer lies, for none but *self*
Can find or know the self; the goal is not
To *know* but *be*, for knowing leads thee to
Becoming. Thou art soul and now possess
Those buried qualities, that hidden sense
Which can be brought to life and consciousness."
This is the object of the mysteries,
And the initiate can enter here
On earth into the knowledge and the life
Of God.

The pageant of the mysteries
Portrays the journey and provides the keys

By which the soul can reach Amenti's shore:
The bold initiate must pass the door
Where Isis sits, "whose veil no mortal hand
Has ever raised"; escape the burning brand,
The fiery furnace and the stagnant lake;
And lured by singing harp-strings, he must take
The path that skirts the bower wherein lies
A temptress whose beauty, fit for Paradise,
Conceals a peril deeper than the pit,
The promise of fulfillments exquisite.
Though willed his step, his eyes are backward turned
To that fair form for which his senses yearned.
But fairer still the vision in his soul,
He lifts his eyes and gazes on his goal.
He wins! He comes at last to his release
And at the feet of Isis finds his promised peace.

. . . The streams conjoin in Egypt, each alike
Proclaims one law of conduct, and the soul
May not attain Nirvana nor the bliss
Of its absorption into God nor can
Return unto the Father's House until
It pass the test imposed upon itself.
If good outweighs the evil of his days,
If he has been a father and a friend
To those in want, he need not dread the end;
He cannot enter to a world of bliss
Unless he first begins it here in this.
But if his works were good, then he can claim
Identity with God and take his name—
"Known as Osiris, he has become as He"
And enters life throughout eternity.
The soul by which its works is purified
In Brahma's bosom ever will abide.

The *names* of God and gods shall pass away;
No more the need of rites or "Passion Play";
Old Night shall yield to the Eternal Day.
Not death but life—of gods, shall be but One;
Look deep into the West when day is done
And you shall see the East, *the Rising Sun.*[1]

This final chapter contains three essential elements of Ernest's belief and the work that stemmed from it. First, he details his belief in the immortality of the soul together with his opinions about the next experience, or "afterlife." Then we read the main part of his "Sermon by the Sea," given at the Asilomar conference in Pacific Grove, California, in the summer of 1959, that points a direction for and urges onward the movement he started and would soon leave in the hands of others. And we close with "A Fable" that needs no elaboration.

From the standpoint of immortality we may have a body within a body to infinity. When this physical body is rendered useless and is no longer a fit instrument through which to function, another one may be already there![2]

It is not merely pleasing and satisfactory to suppose that we pass from this life to the next, in full and complete retention of our faculties: it is logical. Jesus revealed himself to his followers after his resurrection, *to show them that death is but a passing to a higher sphere of life and action. To know that we maintain an identity independent of the physical body is proof enough of immortality.* This, together with the fact that remembrance maintains a constant stream of recollection; and the realization that mentality can operate independently of the body—performing all of its normal functions without the aid of the body—and that the new theory of matter and ether furnishes proof of the possibility of a body within a body to infinity, and that the inner man is constantly forming matter into the shape of a body; all of these evidences should prove to us that *we are not going to attain immortality,* but that *we are now immortal!* Our contention is not that dead men live again, *but that a living man never dies . . .*

There are thousands of cases on record where people have penetrated the veil of flesh and seen into the beyond . . . There is certainly more argument and evidence in favor of the theory of the possibility of spirit communication than against it, and so far as we are concerned, we are entirely convinced of the evidence . . .

To suppose that we can compel the attention of anyone out of the flesh, any more than one in it, is an absurdity, and if we could, what would we hope to gain? *People out of the flesh know no more than they did when in the body.*[3]

Some suffer, some are happy, some unhappy, according to the way they contact life. No one judges us but ourselves. No one gives to us but ourselves and no one robs us but ourselves. We need not fear either God or the devil. There is no devil, and God is Love . . . We need fear nothing in the Universe. We need not be afraid of God. We may be certain that all will arrive at the final goal, that not one will be missing. Every man is an incarnation of God. The soul can no more be lost than God could be lost. We should neither be disturbed by the wailing of prophets, nor the anathemas of theology. We cannot believe that because we have subscribed to some creed, we have thereby purchased a seat in heaven, nor can we believe in any vindictive or malicious power in the universe, which damns us because we have erred through human ignorance. We believe in God and that He is Good. What more can life demand of us than that we do the best that we can and try to improve? If we have done this, we have done well and all will be right with our souls both here and hereafter. This leaves us free to work out our own salvation—not with fear or even with trembling—but with peace and in quiet confidence.[4]

I believe in the continuation of the personal life beyond the grave, in the continuity of the individual stream of consciousness with a full recollection of itself and the ability to know and to make itself known. I wish to feel, when the experience of physical death shall occur, that that which I really am will continue to live beyond the grave. I wish to feel that I shall again meet those friends whose lives and influences have made my life happy while on earth. If I could not believe this, I would believe nothing in life; life would have no meaning and death could not be untimely, unless it were long delayed. If personality does not persist beyond the grave, then death would be an event to be devoutly longed for and sought after . . .

I do not believe in the return of the soul to another life on this plane. The spiral of life is upward. Evolution carries us forward, not backward. Eternal and progressive expansion is its law and there are no breaks in its continuity . . . I can believe in planes beyond this one without number, in eternal progress. I cannot believe that nature is limited to one sphere of action . . .

It is human to grieve over the loss of dear ones. We love them and cannot help missing them, but a true realization of the immortality and continuity of the individual soul will rob our grief of hopelessness. We shall realize that they are in God's keeping and they are safe . . . So we shall view eternity from the higher standpoint, as a continuity of time, forever and ever expanding, until time, as we now experience it, shall be no more. Realizing this, we shall see in everyone a budding genius, a becoming God, an unfolding soul, an eternal destiny.[5]

The Sermon by the Sea

Our religion is not something to be lived merely here at Asilomar, as much inspiration as we receive from it, but rather to take that consciousness which we have arrived at here back with us into whatever activities we may be engaged in. I do not believe Life is separated from Its living, anywhere.

There is nothing in the world that can take the place of love, friendship, appreciation and cooperation in our lives. I have thought so much about this all week because these are the only things that have any meaning in the eternal values in which we are so interested . . .

I do not believe there is a single fact in human history, or a single manifestation in the universe, which is or could possibly be anything other than a manifestation of the One Divine Mind, the One Universal Presence, the One Infinite Spirit.

It seems to me that it is only as we view all life, everything from what we call great to what we call small, important or unimportant—it is only as we view the whole thing as "one stupendous whole, whose body nature is with God the soul" that we shall really enter into communion, into sympathetic oneness and rapport, with the reality of all that is about us. Someone asked me: "What do you think God is?" I looked out the window and said, "I think God is that tree." And there was a squirrel running up the tree and I said, "I think God is that squirrel."

It is going to be absolutely impossible for us, with our finite comprehension, to have the intelligence to divide the indivisible and to say this is real and that is unreal. The marketplace is as real as is the temple. That is why Jesus said that it is neither in the temple at Jerusalem nor in the mountain, but in yourself that the secret of Life is discovered, that the Soul of the Universe is consciously entered into, and the Divine and benign Spirit which indwells everything is loosed in Its splendor and power through you—through your partnership with the Infinite, through your oneness with God the living Spirit.

Everything that lives proclaims the Glory of God. Every person who exists manifests the Life of God. There is One Spirit in which we live, One Mind by which we think, One Body of which we are a part and One Light that lighteth every man's pathway.

We are a part of the evolution of human destiny; we are a part of the unfoldment of the Divine Intelligence in human affairs. It has reached the point of conscious and deliberate cooperation with that principle of evolution and outpush of the creative urge of the Spirit, on this planet at least, to bring about innumerable centers which It may enjoy. Also we may enjoy It through that Divine interior awareness which is the intercommunication of God with man, revealing our own Divine nature.

Having had the privilege of starting Religious Science, I would wish, will and desire above all things else that the simplicity and purity of our teaching could never be violated. There is a purpose of simplicity, a consciousness of unity, a straight-line thinking in our philosophy that has never appeared before in the world outside of the teachings of men like Jesus and Emerson . . .

It would be my desire that simplicity and purity and directness, that straight thinking, should never depart from the techniques of our practitioners, or instructions of our teachers or understanding of our laymen. It is the most direct impartation of Divine Wisdom that has ever come to the world, because it incorporates the precepts of Jesus, and Emerson, and Buddha and all the rest of the wise. And I would that in our teaching there would never be any arrogance, for it always indicates spiritual immaturity to me. Others will arise who will know more than we do; they won't be better or worse, they will be different and know more than we do. Evolution is forward.

I would that we should not build, out of the body of our simplicity and grandeur and beauty, other creeds loaded with superstition, a fear of the unknown and a dread of the unseen. We have discovered a pearl of great price; we have discovered the rarest gem that has ever found setting in the intellect of the human race—complete simplicity, complete directness, a freedom from fear and superstition about the unknown and about God.

And we have rediscovered that which the great, the good and the wise have sung about and thought about—the imprisoned splendor within ourselves and within each other—and have direct contact with it. Whether we call it the Christ in us, or the Buddha, or Atman or just the Son of God the living Spirit, makes no difference. You and I are witness to the Divine fact and we have discovered an authority beyond our minds, even though our minds utilize it. Out of this we have prepared ourselves, I think, I hope, I pray and believe.

One cannot but feel from the human point in such meetings as these that it is entirely possible one might not be here next year. This is of complete indifference to me because I believe in life and I feel fine. Such an event is merely the climax of human events in anybody's life, and it is to be looked forward to, not with dread or fear or apprehension, but as the next great adventure and one that we should all be very happy and glad to experience.

But we must weigh and measure things somewhat from the human angle. No person or organization can make the provision for that which is paramount, for that which is of the most stupendous importance: that out of the ranks of all of us, innumerable people shall grow up who shall have caught a vision, who shall have seen a glory, who shall have experienced God.

The thing that interests me now is that every man shall find his savior within himself. If this is the only place he is going to discover God, you may be sure it is the only avenue through which any wayshower shall lead him to God. There is no other way. Jesus knew this, and when they sought to make Jesus, the man, the way, he said that it was expedient he go away that the spirit of Truth should awaken within his followers the knowledge and understanding of what he had been talking about—that he had come to reveal them to themselves.

As we think, speak, talk and commune with each other and with nature and God, there will never be an answer to us beyond the level of our approach. The level of our approach is the only avenue through which there could be an answer, else we would not be individuals. God cannot make a mechanical spontaneity, and that is why we are left alone to discover ourselves.

Those who bear witness in consciousness do not need to retire from life. The great man is he who, in the midst of the crowd, can keep with perfect simplicity the independence of his solitude. It is not in the mountain or the temple in Jerusalem; it is our own heart, our own mind, our own consciousness, our own being, where we live twenty-four hours a day, awake or asleep, that that eternal share of the Infinite comes to us, because every man is some part of the essence of God, not as a fragment, but as totality.

I think we have brought a blessing to the world, the possibility of something expressing through us that has never before been given to the world—a simplicity, a sincerity and, I trust, a love and understanding. But we too little practice it because the human mind is prone, even when it has discovered a greater good than it had before, to compare the degree of good it thinks it possesses with a lesser degree of good it thinks someone else has. And this is brought about only through the psychological projection of some unredeemed past of a person's own psyche.

You will never discover a person who is full of emotional judgment and condemnation of others, who is doing anything other than unconsciously releasing the tension of a burden—a burden so great to be borne that he does not even permit it to come to the light of day to be seen, for he could not face it. This has been scientifically proved, and that is why Jesus, with the profoundness of utmost simplicity, did not say: "Judge not lest God will judge you." He knew better. He said: "Judge not, that ye be not judged. For with what judgment ye judge, ye shall be judged." In other words, your judgment will judge you. "And with what measure ye mete, it will be measured to you again." God is not going to measure it back to you and say: "I will show you who is boss." You are the measurer-outer. As Troward said, we are dispensers of the Divine Gift and we are in partnership with the Infinite.

It would be wonderful indeed if a group of persons should arrive on earth who were for something and against nothing. This would be the summum bonum of human organization, wouldn't it? It is, in the life of the individual.

Find me one person who is for something and against nothing, who is redeemed enough not to condemn others out of the burden of his soul, and I will find another savior, another Jesus and an exalted human being.

Find me one person who no longer has any fear of the universe, or of God, or of man, or of anything else, and you will have brought to me someone in whose presence we may sit and fear shall vanish as clouds before the sunlight.

Find me someone who has redeemed his own soul, and he shall become my redeemer.

Find me someone who has given all that he has in love, without morbidity, and I will have found the lover of my soul. Is not this true? Why? Because he will have revealed to me the nature of God and proved to me the possibility of all human souls.

This is what Religious Science stands for. It is not a new dogmatism, it is not a new authority generated from a new alleged revelation of the God who never revealed anything to anybody, else He could not have revealed all things to all people. There is no special dispensation of Providence, but there is a specialized dispensation which the great and good and wise and just have known, even though they knew it intuitively.

Find me one person who can get his own littleness out of the way and he shall reveal to me the immeasurable magnitude of Universe in which I live.

Find me one person who knows how to talk to God, really, and I shall walk with him through the woods and everything that seems inanimate will respond—the leaves of the trees will clap their hands, the grass will grow soft under him.

Find me one person who communes with cause and effect, and in the evening, the evening star will sing to him and the darkness will turn to light. Through him, as the woman who touched the hem of the garment of Christ was healed, shall I be healed of all loneliness forever.

Find me someone who is no longer sad, whose memory has been redeemed from morbidity, and I shall hear laughter.

Find me someone whose song is really celestial, because it is the outburst of the cosmic urge to sing, and I shall hear the music of the spheres.

"All things are delivered unto me of my Father: and no man knoweth the Son, but the Father; neither knoweth any man the Father, save the Son, and he to whomsoever the Son will reveal him." And each of us is that Son. No use waiting for avatars. Jesus is not coming again—he is wiser than that. He has earned whatever he has. And to you and to me no single kernel of grain shall come unless we have planted it, no meal shall be made unless we have ground it, no bread baked unless we have kneaded it and put it in the oven of our own consciousness where the silent processes of an invisible and ineffable light precipitates itself into that which for us stands for the start of life.

But how we have put off that day! We say to each other that we don't know enough, we aren't good enough. The ignorance of our unknowing, the blindness of our unseeing, the condemnation of the ages weighing against our consciousness, known and unknown, conscious and unconscious, have created the greatest negation the world has ever known and heaped upon the greater possibility of the larger progress of humanity a burden so tremendous that even men's adoration of God has been saddened by fear. Like the man* who Newman said prayed: "O God, if there be a God, save my soul, if I have a soul." He did not know, so was afraid to take a chance.

Find me one person who no longer doubts, no longer wavers. But not

<hr>

*"O Lord, if there be a Lord, save my soul, if I have a soul" (Ernest Renan, *Prière d'un Sceptique*).

one who with a proclamation of superiority says: Look at me, I have arrived! I will not listen to that. Only that which reveals me to myself can be a message to me; only that which gives me back myself can save me; only that which leads me to the God within myself can reveal God. And only that person can do it to whom the vision has come through his own efforts, through the gift of God. Of course, the grace of God abounds by Divine givingness. God has forever hung Himself upon the cross of men's indifference; God has forever, but without suffering, given Himself but we have not received the gift.

Find me one person who has so completely divorced from himself all arrogance, and you will have discovered for me an open pathway to the kingdom of God here and now. Up until now the search has been in far-off corners of the earth and we have knelt upon a prayer rug and been wafted away, in our morbid and fearful imagination, over ethers of nothingness to places that have no existence, the temples of our unbelief, and we have come back empty. "What went ye out into the wilderness for to see . . . ?"

And now comes Religious Science. We are no more sincere than others; if we felt we were that would be a projection of an unconsciousness sense of guilt. Anyway, it would be stupid and there is no greater sin on earth than just plain stupidity.

What shall reveal the self to the self? The self shall raise the self by the self.

Find me somebody who has detached his emotional and psychological ego from the *real* self, without having to deny the place it plays in the scheme of things and without slaying any part of himself because the transcendence is there also, and I will have discovered the Ineffable in this individual and a direct pathway for the communion of my own soul.

Now what does this all mean? I am talking about you and myself. When I say "find a person" I don't mean go over to Rome, or London, or back to your own church. The search is not external. All of these people I have been talking about have no existence as such, other than as figments of my own imagination, until they are finally centered in our own soul. Then this Guest for whom we are looking will be the Self redeemed from the lesser self. This is a very interesting thing, for nature is foolproof, and when the fruit is ripe it will fall; when the kingdom of God is perceived it will be experienced simultaneously, instantaneously and in its entirety.

But these people all exist in us. They are different attributes, qualities of our own soul. They are different visions; not that we have multiple or dual personalities, but that every one of us on that inner side of life is, has been, and shall remain in eternal communion with the Ineffable where he may know that he is no longer with God, but one of God. If it were not for that which echoes eternally down the corridors of our own minds, some voice that ever sings in our own souls, some urge that continuously presses us forward, there would be no advance in our science of religion or in the humanities or anything else. But ". . . he left not himself without witness . . ."

These are simple things that call for discipline. Not as one normally thinks of discipline, but a different kind of discipline that one discovers. I often sit for several hours at a time, sometimes all day, thinking one simple thought, no matter what it is. It isn't a waste of time to find out what this thought means to me, or what it should mean in my life, or what it would mean everywhere. This is something no one can do for us but ourselves. We are "the way, the truth and the life."

We have come to Asilomar, spent this wonderful week together in love for each other and adoration for the God we believe in. Many wonderful things have happened that would seem miracles if we didn't know about them. And now we meet for this fond farewell after the spiritual bath of peace, the baptism of the spirit. Not through me, but you to me and I to you through each other—the revelation of the self to the self—we go back into the highways and byways of life with something so great that never again will anything be quite the same. A little more light shall come, a little greater glory added to the glory that we already possess, a deeper consciousness, a higher aspiration, a broader certainty of the mind.

You are Religious Science. I am not. I am only the one who put something together. I do not even take myself seriously, but I take what I am doing seriously. You are Religious Science—our ministers, our teachers, our practitioners, our laymen. You find me one thousand people in the world who know what Religious Science is and use it, and live it as it is, and I'll myself live to see a new world, a new heaven and a new earth here. There is a cosmic Power wrapped up in a cosmic Consciousness and Purposiveness that is equal to the vision which looses It.

What I am saying is this: There is a Law that backs up the vision, and the Law is immutable. "Heaven and earth shall pass away: but my words shall not pass away." There is a Power transcendent beyond our needs, our little wants. Demonstrating a dime is good if one needs it, or healing oneself of a pain is certainly good if one has it, but beyond that, at the real feast at the tabernacle of the Almighty, in the temple of the living God, in the banquet hall of heaven, there is something beyond anything that you and I have touched.

Find one thousand people who know that, and the world will no longer be famished. How important it is that each one of us in his simple way shall live from God to God, with God, in God, and to each other. That is why we are here, and we are taking back with us, I trust, a vision and an inspiration, something beyond a hope and a longing, that the living Spirit shall through us walk anew into Its own creation and a new glory come with a new dawn.

Now the Lord is in His holy temple. Let all the earth keep silent before Him as we drink deep from the perennial fountain of eternal Life, as we partake of the bread of heaven and as we open wide the gates of our consciousness that the King of Glory shall come in.

And may God bless and keep us, and for all the love you have given me may I bless you.[6]

A Fable

Time stretched in the arms of Eternity and yawned—longing for liberation from its bondage—it was tired of doing nothing.

Eternity embraced both Time and the Timeless—holding them fondly to itself lest it be without offspring;

But all three of them—Time, Eternity and the Timeless—were weary with the monotony of inaction;

And so they held a conference to see if they might not find some way to come to a solution of their desires.

Not knowing just how to proceed, since they had but little mind of their own, they decided to consult the Old Man of the Mountains—the Self-Existent One—who possessed the Apple of Wisdom.

So they journeyed into the Mountains where the Old Man lived and laid their problem before him.

The Old Man received them graciously and promised them to do whatever was in his power to help; together they held long conferences, but it was difficult for them to come to any conclusion.

Eternity was not particularly concerned, having been around for a long while, and being used to his own company and not lonesome—except for those periods when he wondered if he were not dreaming the eons away.

But Time and the Timeless were most impatient indeed—they just couldn't wait; for, you see, neither of them were beings in themselves; they both lived by a sort of reflected glory from Eternity—while Eternity depended on the Old Man of the Mountains for its life.

Now of course this was why they were having a conference.

The Old Man looked across space and down on Chaos and Old Night and said: My beloved children, I just want to make you happy; I can understand you do not wish to be waiting around for countless ages with nothing to do, so I have decided to grant you some powers which until now you have not enjoyed.

But first I must move upon the Face of the Deep and disturb Chaos and Old Night. Heaven knows they have been asleep long enough—I had almost forgotten them—they really are a strange pair, sort of lawless at that—almost, but not quite, beings—*things* they are, with no minds of their own. I suppose I will have to breathe some kind of law into them so when they get stirred up they will not destroy themselves; but I will put some kind of order in them so they can be playthings for Eternity; then he will not be bothering me with his ideas about creating things—he just can't seem to sit still and enjoy himself.

To which the Timeless answered by saying he felt almost as Eternity did; he couldn't see any sense at all in waiting and waiting and waiting and having nothing to do.

To which little Time peeped up with a very small voice indeed, saying he too had waited for something to happen—he almost wished he had a mind of his own and was not compelled to live on the Timeless.

The Timeless responded by saying that in many ways he was in a worse condition than Time, because he was so much bigger and more important—which of course he would have to be since he furnished the background for Time to play in—and Eternity, who felt himself to be the Father of both Time and the Timeless, said he would go along with the idea.

So it was agreed between Time and the Timeless that they would work together—Time as the child of the Timeless—and Time was given power to be unhindered, almost but not quite, because the Timeless never would wish to be in the position of being bound by Time, who was prone to get into all sorts of trouble and might get caught up in what he was doing, and then nothing but confusion would follow—which it almost did, but not quite.

And it was agreed that the Timeless would cooperate with Eternity, because all three of them—Time, Eternity and the Timeless—were one family, really, and would have to work together.

So Eternity agreed to free the Timeless from its bondage, and the Timeless agreed to free Time so it might act somewhat on its own.

Now all these discussions took place in the Mountains where the Old Man lived who possessed the Apple of Wisdom.

The Old Man said he was quite happy where he was and never did wish to limit himself to anything in particular; but he did agree that he would find a lot of pleasure in watching the actions of Eternity, Time and the Timeless.

But he cautioned Eternity and its offspring, Time and the Timeless, telling them they must never do anything that would destroy his peace, because the Old Man didn't wish to be bothered.

Eternity agreed to keep faith with the Old Man: he merely wanted to partake of his wisdom; he didn't expect to act entirely on his own.

The Old Man agreed to give Eternity as much freedom as was necessary for it to set Time in motion, and Eternity agreed to pass on some of the power the Old Man bestowed on him to the Timeless, that it might activate Time.

Time, Eternity and the Timeless were very impatient to get started—but the Old Man motioned them to wait while he meditated—and the Old Man sat in thoughtful silence for a long time, once in a while eating from the Apple of Wisdom, which was never consumed, and in his meditations every once in a while he would smile and nod to himself, as though he were very satisfied with what was taking place in his mind—and finally he said: My children, I have an idea to put before you:

Let us create Beings and a place where they can function and live in happiness and freedom, but bound to us with enduring ties that can never be loosed.

Time, Eternity and the Timeless laughed with delight and danced around the Old Man, clapping their hands with joy.

Eternity said: I will gladly give birth to such Beings for you and will guard them very carefully, holding them always in my embrace, just as I have Time and the Timeless—and bowing before the Old Man, he thanked him for his wisdom.

But the Timeless was not quite so certain, while Time was really quite impatient with the whole affair, which he always had been from the beginning.

But after much discussion, they decided to try the experiment and see what would happen. But just how to begin, Eternity, Time and the Timeless did not quite know—which they couldn't, because they themselves were always subject to the will of the Old Man.

And again the Old Man ate from the Apple of Wisdom, which never diminished, and after a long while he unfolded a plan to them which he thought would work.

The Old Man said: In creating such Beings as these I have in mind, it will be necessary for me to impart some of my own life to them—which was reasonable enough, since the Old Man didn't have anything to make them out of but himself.

And so he explained to Eternity, Time and the Timeless that these Beings he was about to create would have to be a little different from them, since they had no real life of their own, and no mind with which to create ideas and no power except it were borrowed from him—for after all, they were but reactions of the Old Man's thoughts and ideas, enjoying freedom only in certain limits.

But the Beings the Old Man was about to create—he explained to them—would have within themselves certain qualities which the Old Man possessed. But he would hide these qualities so deep in their beings that they would at first be quite unconscious of them, for they had a long journey ahead of them before they could ever return to the Old Man and consciously cooperate with him.

Now here was something indeed difficult—or it would be difficult for finite Beings—but the Old Man, eating again from the Apple of Wisdom, which never seemed to be consumed, continued his meditations and finally said: Lest the Beings I am about to create would immaturely try to act on their own, I must create some kind of a cloud between them and myself so they will not be able to see me exactly as I am, because I am going to endow them with my own being—they will always have a curiosity and an urge to return again to me, because they can never really be whole until they do this—but should they seize the power I am going to endow them with before they know how to use it, they might fall into all kinds of confusion—which they certainly did.

So the Old Man reaffirmed that while he was going to impart his own nature to these Beings he was about to create, he would sort of let them alone to discover themselves and gradually to come under the Eternal Laws of his being—but the time of this would not be known to them—but of course the Old Man knew, since he knew everything, because he possessed the Apple of Wisdom.

He said he would move upon Chaos and Old Night and breathe some kind of law into them which would reflect back to the Beings he was about to create the images of their own thinking, like a mirror; and since their own thinking would be pretty chaotic to start with—and for a long time to come—they would look at these images—which were really reflections of their own minds—and mistake them for realities. But always there would be thoughts and ideas of the Old Man moving down through the cloud he would create to almost separate himself from these beings—but not quite; there would always be thoughts and ideas of the Old Man showing something through the cloud; and because he was endowing these Beings with certain qualities of his own nature, they would always be looking up as though they expected to discover something that would make them more complete and happy.

And so, you see, above these Beings would be the cloud through which the thoughts of the Old Man would be reflected down toward them, and they would feel these thoughts and ideas—because they were also within them; and because the Old Man would put some of his being into them; they too would have a certain kind of creativity which would reflect itself on the lower side of the cloud and all around them—because all the earth then would act like a mirror.

Then the Old Man explained to Eternity, Time and the Timeless that there might be quite a period of confusion down there, but it was the only way he knew to create beings that finally could act on their own but still in cooperation with him.

And the long time of their confusion would be called to Period of Ignorance—and gradually as the confusion cleared away and they looked up through the cloud that almost but not quite separated the Old Man from them, they would become more and more like him, and this process of becoming more like him would be called their Enlightenment; and finally as this Enlightenment grew, the cloud would disappear entirely and they would no longer reflect confusion into the great mirror of life, and the mirror would reflect to them only the nature of the Old Man's Being.

The Old Man explained to Time, Eternity and the Timeless that in creating this cloud of unknowing and the mirror of false appearing he was creating a medium which in a sense would be the Beings he was creating for a period of time, because they would be looking mostly at their own creations and mistaking them for realities, in that way becoming subject to them.

This would be part of the illusion through which they would pass into the Period of Ignorance.

And the Old Man said he would breathe on Chaos and Old Night and endow them with certain qualities that Time, Eternity and the Timeless did not and never could possess because they had no initiative of their own.

So the Old Man breathed two principles into Chaos and Old Night and endowed them with a certain amount of creativity: one of the principles would be reflected back to them, and in their experiences and conditions that would be like their own thoughts and ideas—and for a long while they might suffer some results of their own ignorance because of this; and the time of this period would be known as "evolution," or unfoldment of the life he was going to breathe into them—from complete ignorance, as far as the Beings were concerned, to gradually awakening to a realization of their own natures.

In other words, the Old Man said: The speck of my own life with which I am going to endow these Beings will lie dormant, but it will always be stirring and stirring and causing these Beings gradually to awaken to a realization of who and what they are.

And during this period the two principles which he breathed into Chaos and Old Night would be reacting to them in accordance with their own thoughts, and these Beings unwittingly, in complete ignorance of their own natures, would be reflecting into this mirror that surrounds them the thoughts and imaginations which sometime would prove to be their own undoing—but only for a period of time.

And there would come up among them those who, because of a more penetrating gaze, had looked through the cloud and mist and, receiving more intelligence, would look again into the mirror that is around them and become conscious that it was a mirror only, and it would be called a Mirror of the Mind, and the forms it created would be called the Mirror of Matter—but neither one would be real in itself.

But these Beings would be subject to their own creations until their time of emancipation—and the Old Man explained, because he possessed the Apple of Wisdom and knew all things, that during this period, not because of the spark he was going to breathe into these Beings, which would cause them almost to look up, but because of the inertia of the images around them in the Mirror of Mind and Nature, considerable confusion would follow.

For the spark with which the Old Man would endow them would always be groping its way through the cloud, and its very Presence would endow these Beings with hope and faith and an inward assurance that they would never become extinct. But because of the confusion around them, they would always be trying to reconcile that which they inwardly felt to what they were experiencing, as a result of the action and reactions in the mirror.

And he said all sorts of different beliefs would arrive among these Beings and distribute their arguments as they tried to adjust themselves to an inward seeming that knew but little about these outward things which would appear to contradict these inward feelings. And these Beings, following an inward knowing with which he was going to endow them, would, without knowing why they did it, announce there was some power that could make them whole. But everywhere they looked, it would seem as though what they said would contradict this. And only those who continuously looked upward through the cloud would really see things as they were, while the rest would be looking at them as they appeared to be.

And great systems of belief would arise, and much discussion and argument and dispute would follow, and these Beings would feel themselves alone and isolated but always speak of the knowledge to be theirs; and as it grew in brilliance and they reached up through the clouds that seemed to obscure their confusion and difficulties, these things would gradually disappear, and with them their fears, uncertainties and doubts.

The Old Man explained that because the life with which he would endow these Beings would have to be some part of himself, they would be eternal, and something in them would always know this.

But here too great arguments would arise: the Beings' confusion would create all kinds of strange beliefs about their destiny, and many of them would be very weird indeed; but this ignorance too would clear away.

The Old Man explained to Time, Eternity and the Timeless that this whole action would take place within them, and that since Eternity was forever, and never could be exhausted or its energies used up, it would not be disturbed very much by the process; and since the Timeless, which itself lived on Eternity, was by Eternity furnished a background for Time, it too would not be greatly disturbed. But little Time would fall into a lot of confusion, because the Beings he was going to create would often mistake Time for Eternity and the Timeless and, being caught in Time, would be bound to its limitations, but only for a period.

And he explained to Time this was why he had told them in the beginning that Time must never really be caught nor the Timeless confined, else Eternity would be bound. He said, You see, Time and the Timeless will be the action and reaction in Eternity; and Eternity itself is merely a reaction to the mind of Beings.

Having carefully explained all these things to Eternity, Time and the Timeless, the Old Man said: Now, my children, it is time for you to return to your homes. But remember this: I have breathed law and order into Chaos and Old Night, and you will never be permitted to do anything that can violate my Beings.

But Eternity was permitted to play with the Timeless, and the Timeless was permitted to play with Time; but none of them would ever be permitted to get caught even in their own actions.

So Time, Eternity and the Timeless, having thanked the Old Man for his generosity, hand in hand left the mountain and journeyed back again, happy with themselves and content with the power the Old Man had bestowed upon them. And having reached the Valley where they lived, and being fatigued because of their long journey, they all felt the need of resting for a while; and so all three of them feel asleep, not quite realizing what the Old Man had done to them.

And sleeping, they dreamed. Time dreamed it was Lord of all creation; the Timeless that it was Lord over all; and Eternity that it was Father of all. The dream was pleasant enough; but like all dreams, it must come to an end, to be followed by an awakening.

And the waking from this dream is the story of man's evolution.[7]

Afterword

This poem of Ernest's opens *The Science of Mind* textbook and is the perfect thought with which to close this one.

> Peace be unto three, stranger, enter and be not afraid.
> I have left the gate open and thou art welcome to my home.
> There is room in my house for all.
> I have swept the hearth and lighted the fire.
> The room is warm and cheerful and you will find comfort and rest within.
> The table is laid and the fruits of Life are spread before thee.
> The wine is here also, it sparkles in the light.
> I have set a chair for you where the sunbeams dance through
>   the shade.
> Sit and rest and refresh your soul.
> Eat of the fruit and drink the wine.
> All, all is yours, and you are welcome.

Chronology

1887   Ernest Holmes is born on January 21 near Lincoln, Maine.

1905   Moves to Boston, works as a butcher's apprentice for some relatives, the Steeves family.

1908   Enrolls in the Leland Powers School of Public Expression in Boston; studies Christian Science.

1909   Reads Christian D. Larson's *The Ideal Made Real*, becomes fascinated by mental science.

1912   Visits his mother (Anna) and one of his eight brothers (Fenwicke), who have moved to Venice, California, and decides to stay.

1913   Goes to work as a purchasing agent and playground director for the City of Venice; assists Fenwicke in his position as minister of a local Congregational church.

1916   Speaks at a metaphysical library in Los Angeles on Thomas Troward's *Edinburgh Lectures*; later that year Ernest and Fenwicke begin publishing a magazine, *Uplift*; Ernest is ordained a Divine Science minister.

1918   Ernest publishes his first book, *Creative Mind*; another, *Creative Mind and Success*, shortly follows.

1919   Ernest and Fenwicke lecture in New York, Philadelphia, Boston and elsewhere; Ernest spends most of the next six years on the Chautauqua speaking circuit.

1924   Studies briefly with Emma Curtis Hopkins in Chicago.

1925   Back in the Los Angeles area for good, Ernest speaks to 600 people per week at the Ambassador Hotel; a year later he moves to the Ebell Theater; crowds soon overflow that.

1926   *The Science of Mind* textbook is published.

1927   Marries Hazel Foster; incorporates the Institute of Religious Science and School of Philosophy; begins publishing *Science of Mind* magazine.

1935   Organization reincorporates as Institute of Religious Science and Philosophy.

1938   Revised textbook appears.

1949   Begins weekly radio program, "This Thing Called Life."

1953   Institute becomes Church of Religious Science, then splits; one group forms what is now Religious Science International; remaining group renames itself United Church of Religious Science in 1967.

1956   Begins weekly television show, also called "This Thing Called Life"; only one episode of this still extant.

1957   Hazel Holmes passes away in May.

1959   Ernest and Fenwicke complete *The Voice Celestial;* groundbreaking is held for Founder's Church of Religious Science, next door to the organization's headquarters.

1960   Founder's Church is opened and dedicated on January 3; Ernest suffers a stroke in March, passes away April 7 at home at age 72; he is survived by brothers Fenwicke, Gerome and William.

Notes

INTRODUCTION

The Inner Light, p. 220.

FRONTISPIECE

Ideas of Power, p. 222.

PART I: THE LAW OF MIND

That Was Ernest, pp. 31–33.

I: THERE IS ONE LIFE

1. *The Voice Celestial*, pp. 3–4.
2. *This Thing Called You*, p. 3.
3. *The Science of Mind*, p. 146.
4. Ibid., p. 75.
5. Ibid., p. 267.
6. Ibid., p. 5.
7. *How to Change Your Life*, p. 131.
8. *Living the Science of Mind*, pp. 70–71.
9. *The Seminar Lectures*, p. 85.
10. *The Beverly Hills Lectures*, pp. 96–97.
11. *The Science of Mind*, pp. 25–34.
12. *This Thing Called Life*, p. 35.
13. *A New Design for Living*, p. 170.
14. *The Science of Mind*, p. 295.

15. *It's Up to You*, pp. 44–45.
15. *Can We Talk to God?*, pp. 75–79.
16. *The Anatomy of Healing Prayer*, p. 117.
17. *This Thing Called You*, p. 34.

III: WHAT WE ARE LOOKING FOR, WE ARE LOOKING AT AND WITH

1. *The Voice Celestial*, p. 18.
2. *The Science of Mind*, pp. 279–83.
3. *A New Design for Living*, pp. 181–82.
4. *The Science of Mind*, pp. 174–75.
5. Ibid., p. 154.
6. *Living the Science of Mind*, p. 43.
7. *The Science of Mind*, pp. 330–31.
8. Ibid., p. 156.
9. Ibid., p. 111.
10. Ibid., p. 216.
11. Ibid., p. 317.
12. Ibid., p. 319.
13. *Creative Mind and Success*, p. 76.
14. Ibid., pp. 20–21.
15. *Science of Mind* magazine, July 1957, p. 40.
16. *Practical Application of Science of Mind*, pp. 54–56.
17. *Ideas for Living*, pp. 47–49.
18. *The Science of Mind*, pp. 35–39.
19. *This Thing Called You*, p. 63.

III: WHAT MIND CAN CONCEIVE

1. *The Voice Celestial*, pp. 81–82.
2. *The Seminar Lectures*, p. 78.
3. *The Anatomy of Healing Prayer*, p. 156.
4. *The Science of Mind*, pp. 266–67.
5. Ibid., p. 306.
6. Ibid., p. 124.
7. *This Thing Called You*, p. 4.
8. *The Science of Mind*, p. 408.
9. Ibid., p. 30.

10. *This Thing Called Life*, pp. 2–3.
11. *Ideas for Living*, p. 82.
12. *The Science of Mind*, p. 208.
13. Ibid., p. 312.
14. Ibid., p. 186.
15. Ibid., p. 225.
16. *Can We Talk to God?*, p. 32.
17. *The Science of Mind*, p. 307.
18. Ibid., p. 204.
19. Ibid., p. 417.
20. Ibid., p. 188.
21. Ibid., p. 185.
22. Ibid., p. 393.
23. *Creative Mind and Success*, p. 52.
24. *This Thing Called Life*, pp. 25–27.
25. *The Science of Mind*, p. 321.
26. *Creative Mind and Success*, p. 63.
27. *The Science of Mind*, pp. 40–50.
28. *This Thing Called You*, p. 63.

IV: THE POWER RESPONDS TO ALL ALIKE

1. *The Voice Celestial*, pp. 188–90.
2. *The Science of Mind*, pp. 51–60.
3. Ibid., p. 115.
4. *The Basic Ideas of the Science of Mind*, pp. 50–53.
5. *Living the Science of Mind*, p. 359.
6. *The Science of Mind*, p. 348.
7. Ibid., p. 273.
8. *Creative Mind and Success*, p. 11.
9. *This Thing Called You*, p. 46.
10. *The Science of Mind*, p. 349.
11. *Living the Science of Mind*, p. 13.
12. *Creative Mind and Success*, p. 27.
13. *The Seminar Lectures*, pp. 94–95.
14. *The Science of Mind*, p. 75.
15. *A New Design for Living*, p. 131.
16. *This Thing Called You*, p. 122.

Notes

PART II: THE CENTRAL FLAME

The Inner Light, pp. 88–89.

V: THE MEETING PLACE OF SCIENCE AND RELIGION

1. *The Voice Celestial*, pp. 217–19.
2. *Science of Mind* magazine, June 1947, pp. 4–6.
3. *Living the Science of Mind*, p. 136.
4. *The Science of Mind*, p. 79.
5. *Science of Mind* magazine, June 1938, pp. 5–13.
6. *The Science of Mind*, p. 102.
7. *A New Design for Living*, pp. 60–61.
8. *Science of Mind* magazine, July 1931, pp. 5–16.
9. *Science of Mind* magazine, May 1947, pp. 33–36.
10. *This Thing Called You*, p. 89.

VI: CONVICTION, WARMTH, COLOR AND IMAGINATION

1. *The Voice Celestial*, pp. 181–82.
2. *The Science of Mind*, p. 478.
3. *Ideas of Power*, pp. 197–99.
4. *The Seminar Lectures*, p. 86.
5. *Living the Science of Mind*, p. 311.
6. *The Science of Mind*, p. 346.
7. Ibid., p. 224.
8. Ibid., pp. 35–36.
9. Ibid., p. 207.
10. Ibid., p. 202.
11. Ibid., p. 194.
12. *Living the Science of Mind*, p. 311.
13. *The Science of Mind*, p. 398.
14. *Living the Science of Mind*, p. 312.
15. *The Anatomy of Healing Prayer*, pp. 98–99.
16. Ibid., p. 66.
17. *Living the Science of Mind*, pp. 162–63.
18. *How to Use the Science of Mind*, pp. 139–41.
19. *The Science of Mind* [1926 edition], pp. 299–305.
20. *The Science of Mind*, pp. 222–23.

21. "Alcoholism," as excerpted in the UCRS Practitioner I curriculum, Lesson VIII, pp. 6–21.
22. *This Thing Called Life*, pp. 82–86
23. *A New Design for Living*, pp. 118–19.
24. *Creative Mind and Success*, p. 17.
25. Ibid., p. 38.
26. *This Thing Called You*, p. 93.

VII: THE BODY OF GOD

1. The *Voice Celestial*, pp. 306–307.
2. *What Religious Science Teaches*, pp. 71–72.
3. *The Science of Mind*, p. 99.
4. Ibid., pp. 209–16.
5. Ibid., p. 291.
6. Ibid., pp. 219–20.
7. *Ideas for Living*, p. 83.
8. *The Science of Mind*, p. 144.
9. Ibid., p. 100.
10. Ibid., p. 373.
11. Ibid., p. 83.
12. Ibid., p. 76.
13. *Ideas for Living*, pp. 85–88.
14. *Practical Application of Science of Mind*, p. 74.
15. Ibid., pp. 35–36.
16. *Extension Course in the Science of Mind*, "Clinical Section," Lesson XLV, pp. 7–9.
17. *This Thing Called Life*, pp. 102–105.
18. Ibid., pp. 132–35.
19. *It's Up to You*, p. 44.
20. *Basic Ideas of the Science of Mind*, pp. 82–83.
21. *The Science of Mind*, p. 257.

VIII: WHAT IS KNOWN AT ONE POINT IS KNOWN EVERYWHERE

1. *The Voice Celestial*, pp. 240–41.
2. *The Science of Mind*, p. 399.
3. *Living the Science of Mind*, p. 313.

4. *The Science of Mind,* p. 399.

5. Ibid., p. 413.

6. Ibid., p. 212.

7. Ibid., p. 318.

8. Ibid., p. 168.

9. Ibid., p. 220.

10. Ibid., p. 198.

11. Ibid., p. 217.

12. *The Seminar Lectures,* p. 79.

13. *How to Use the Science of Mind,* pp. 147–48.

14. *The Science of Mind,* p. 165.

15. *Can We Talk to God?,* p. 71.

16. *The Science of Mind,* pp. 319–20.

17. Ibid., p. 119.

18. *The Seminar Lectures,* p. 94.

19. *The Philosophy of Ernest Holmes,* pp. 4–24.

20. Ibid., pp. 25–40.

21. *Ideas of Power,* p. 3.

22. *This Thing Called You,* pp. 120–21.

PART III: THE VEIL IS THIN BETWEEN

Ernest Holmes, The Man, pp. 5–16.

IX: THE WORLD HAS SUFFERED ENOUGH

1. *The Voice Celestial,* pp. 122–23.

2. *The Science of Mind,* pp. 107–10.

3. Ibid., p. 127.

4. *The Anatomy of Healing Prayer,* p. 94.

5. *This Thing Called You,* p. 30.

6. *Creative Mind and Success,* p. 16.

7. Ibid., p. 53.

8. *The Science of Mind,* p. 160.

9. Ibid., p. 269.

10. Ibid., p. 37.

11. *Can We Talk to God?,* p. 9.

12. Ibid., p. 66.

13. *Living Without Fear*, pp. 62–63.
14. *Words That Heal Today*, pp. 93–94.
15. *Living the Science of Mind*, p. 69.
16. KFAC radio talk, aired November 11, 1936, published in *Science of Mind* magazine, November 1937, pp. 64–66.
17. *Science of Mind* magazine, July 1955, pp. 1–3.
18. *Science of Mind* magazine, May 1951, pp. 5–10.
19. *Science of Mind* magazine, July 1953, p. 18.
20. *The Science of Mind*, p. 449.
21. *This Thing Called You*, p. 121.

X: JESUS AND THE CHRIST

1. *The Voice Celestial*, pp. 272–73.
2. *Science of Mind* magazine, April 1952, pp. 7–13.
3. *Ideas for Living*, pp. 51–52.
4. *A New Design for Living*, p. 112.
5. *This Thing Called Life*, p. 120.
6. *The Science of Mind*, p. 161.
7. *This Thing Called You*, p. 32.
8. *The Bible in the Light of Religious Science*, p. 19.
9. *The Science of Mind*, p. 359.
10. *Words That Heal Today*, pp. 205–206.
11. *The Bible in the Light of Religious Science*, pp. 133–34.
12. *Words That Heal Today*, pp. 144–45.
13. Ibid., pp. 132–34.
14. *The Bible in the Light of Religious Science*, pp. 116–18.
15. *The Anatomy of Healing Prayer*, pp. 184–85.
16. Ibid., p. 156.
17. *Creative Mind*, pp. 71–72.
18. *This Thing Called You*, p. 53.

XI: UNTAPPED POWERS IN THE SELF

1. *The Voice Celestial*, pp. 280–82.
2. *Science of Mind* magazine, September 1947, pp. 10–14.
3. *This Thing Called You*, p. 35.
4. *Can We Talk to God?*, p. 13.

5. *The Science of Mind,* p. 446.
6. *The Seminar Lectures,* pp. 105–106.
7. Ibid., pp. 109–11.
8. *This Thing Called Life,* p. 37.
9. *The Science of Mind,* p. 327.
10. Ibid., p. 329.
11. *Light,* pp. 11–21.
12. *The Science of Mind,* p. 313.
13. Ibid., p. 113.
14. Ibid., p. 308.
15. Ibid., p. 103.
16. *Can We Talk to God?,* p. 39.
17. *Light,* pp. 90–92.
18. *The Anatomy of Healing Prayer,* pp. 55–56.
19. *Light,* pp. 23–24.
20. *This Thing Called You,* pp. 123–24.

XII: THE BANQUET HALL OF HEAVEN

1. *The Voice Celestial,* pp. 255–58.
2. *The Science of Mind,* p. 104.
3. Ibid., pp. 377–80.
4. Ibid., pp. 383–84.
5. Ibid., p. 385.
6. *The Sermon by the Sea,* complete.
7. *The Philosophy of Ernest Holmes,* pp. 160–72.

AFTERWORD

The Science of Mind, p. v.

Bibliography

Armor, Reginald C. *Ernest Holmes: The Man.* Los Angeles: Science of Mind Publications, 1977.

———. *That Was Ernest.* Marina del Rey, Calif.: DeVorss & Co., 1999.

Holmes, Ernest. *The Anatomy of Healing Prayer.* (George P. Bendall, ed.). Marina del Rey, Calif.: DeVorss & Co., 1991.

———. *Basic Ideas of the Science of Mind.* Los Angeles: Science of Mind Publications, 1957.

———. *Beverly Hills Lectures on Spiritual Science.* Marina del Rey, Calif.: DeVorss & Co. and Los Angeles: Science of Mind Publishing, 1997.

———. *Bible in the Light of Religious Science.* New York: Robert M. McBride & Co., 1929.

———. *Can We Talk to God?* Los Angeles: Science of Mind Communications, 1992 [Originally published as *The Ebell Lectures on Spiritual Science.* Los Angeles: DeVorss & Co., 1934.]

———. *Creative Mind.* New York: Dodd, Mead & Co., 1919.

———. *Creative Mind and Success.* New York: Dodd, Mead & Co., 1919.

———. *How to Change Your Life.* Los Angeles: Science of Mind Publications, 1982.

———. *How to Use the Science of Mind.* New York: G. P. Putnam's Sons, 1948.

———. (Willis Kinnear, ed.). *Ideas for Living.* Los Angeles: Science of Mind Publications,1972.

———. (George P. Bendall, ed.). *Ideas of Power.* Marina del Rey, Calif.: DeVorss & Co., 1992.

———. (Willis Kinnear, ed.). *It's Up to You.* Los Angeles: Science of Mind Publications, 1936.

———. et al. *Light.* Los Angeles: Science of Mind Publications, 1971.

———. *Living the Science of Mind.* Marina del Rey, Calif.: DeVorss & Co., 1984.

———. (Willis Kinnear, ed.) *Living Without Fear.* Los Angeles: Science of Mind Publications, 1962.

———. and Willis Kinnear. *A New Design for Living.* Englewood Cliffs, N.J.: Prentice-Hall, Inc., 1959.

————. (George P. Bendall, ed.). *The Philosophy of Ernest Holmes.* Marina del Rey, Calif.: De-Vorss & Co., 1996.

————. and Willis Kinnear. *Practical Application of Science of Mind.* Los Angeles: Science of Mind Publications, 1958.

————. *The Science of Mind.* New York: Dodd, Mead & Co., 1938.

————. *The Science of Mind* [original text]. New York: Robert M. McBride & Co., 1926.

Science of Mind magazine, issues as cited.

————. *The Seminar Lectures.* Los Angeles: Science of Mind Publications, 1955.

————. *The Sermon by the Sea.* Los Angeles: Science of Mind Publications, 1967.

————. *This Thing Called Life.* New York: Dodd, Mead & Co., 1943.

————. *This Thing Called You.* New York: Dodd, Mead & Co., 1948.

————. and Fenwicke L. Holmes. *The Voice Celestial.* Los Angeles: Science of Mind Publications, 1960.

————. *What Religious Science Teaches.* Los Angeles: Science of Mind Publications, 1974.

————. *Words That Heal Today.* New York: Dodd, Mead & Co., 1949.

Hornaday, William H. D., and Harlan Ware. *The Inner Light.* New York: Dodd, Mead & Co., 1964 [later republished as *Your Aladdin's Lamp*].

Lathem, Maude Allison, and Ernest Holmes. *Extension Course in the Science of Mind.* Los Angeles: Institute of Religious Science and Philosophy, 1939.

Index

Index

Index

About the Author

Ernest Shurtleff Holmes (1887–1960) was an avid student of the world's spiritual systems. He found in these a common denominator he called the Science of Mind, a practical philosophy for abundant living. Beginning as a self-educated lecturer, Ernest developed a large following of students and went on to formalize his work by founding *Science of Mind* magazine, an educational institute and the United Church of Religious Science. His writings have inspired the work of countless clergy, business leaders, physicians and psychologists, and have helped to shape the guiding principles of the modern human potential movement, both spiritual and secular. Born and raised in Maine, Ernest spent much of his adult life in California.

About the Editor

Jesse Jennings was introduced to the Science of Mind philosophy in 1976, at age twenty, started a study group in a friend's kitchen a few years later and was ordained a minister of the United Church of Religious Science in 1988. He is the founding minister of Creative Life Spiritual Center in suburban Houston, Texas, is past chair of the UCRS Board of Trustees and in 1997 was awarded an honorary Doctor of Divinity degree by that organization. His "Q&A" column has appeared monthly in *Science of Mind* magazine for twelve years, and he has published seven sets of "Daily Guides to Richer Living" with them, and numerous feature articles in a variety of publications. His late father was the novelist Gary Jennings.